SO
REASON
CAN
RULE

Also by Scott Buchanan

SO
REASON
CAN
RULE

Reflections
on Law and Politics

SCOTT BUCHANAN

With an Introduction by
EDWIN J. DELATTRE
President, St. John's College

Published in association with St. John's
College, Annapolis, Maryland, and Santa Fe,
New Mexico

FARRAR • STRAUS • GIROUX
New York

The poem "Accidentally on Purpose" on p. 266 is from *The
Poetry of Robert Frost,* edited by Edward Connery Lathem.
Copyright © 1960, 1962 by Robert Frost. Copyright © 1969 by
Holt, Rinehart and Winston. Reprinted by permission of Holt,
Rinehart and Winston, Publishers

Library of Congress Cataloging in Publication Data
Buchanan, Scott Milross, 1895–1968.
So reason can rule.
Contents: Rediscovering natural law, 1962—Learning under
law, 1957—What every man should know: law—[etc.]
1. Law and politics—Addresses, essays, lectures.
I. Title.
K487.P65B82   340'.11   82-1384
                    AACR2

To Miriam Damon Thomas Buchanan

(1894–1969)

PREFATORY NOTE

This book is the result of a long-held conviction by friends, colleagues, and students of Scott Buchanan that his written works deserve an audience far wider than they had during his lifetime. Most of the pieces in the volume were prepared for discussion with associates at the Center for the Study of Democratic Institutions (now the Hutchins Center). Some were published in Center periodicals and pamphlets. Others remained in the form of memoranda. The selection of the material is the work of a committee: Stephen Benedict, Jay Alexander Gold, L. Harvey Poe, F. Palmer Weber, and Harris L. Wofford. Subsequent volumes are planned that will draw on unpublished or unavailable writings from earlier periods in Scott Buchanan's life.

Some readers may puzzle at the absence of footnotes or other explanatory devices. There were none in the texts as written. The author disliked them, as he once wrote, "not for themselves, but for what they do to the text. They slim it down to the point where the text becomes itself a footnote to the bibliography and the reader is again persuaded that life will not be long enough to know what ought to be known." The committee has chosen to follow the same practice, aware that there are topical and other allusions in some of the pieces that will not be familiar to all readers.

The committee would like to acknowledge important contributions to various aspects of the project from W. H. Ferry, John D. Mack, David Padwa, Bernard Rapoport, Adolph W. Schmidt, Jr., Stanley K. Sheinbaum, John Van Doren, and Peter Weiss. Special thanks is due Douglas Buchanan, the author's son, for his cooperation and counsel, the Hutchins Center for permission to make full use of materials written by Scott Buchanan while a Fellow of the Center, Nancy Miller of Farrar, Straus and Giroux for unfailing guidance, and Edwin J. Delattre for his introduction and ready acceptance of the invitation to associate St. John's College with the project.

CONTENTS

INTRODUCTION

THE indebtedness of St. John's College to Scott Buchanan is profound. The essays included here show him to be a man in whom an intellectual tradition lived, and so they help to explain how he could have left so durable a mark on a college.

Scott Buchanan arrived at St. John's College in Annapolis, Maryland, with his friend Stringfellow Barr, in 1937. The two, who had first met at Oxford in 1919, as Rhodes Scholars, subsequently taught and worked together at the University of Virginia and recommended in 1935, in the Virginia Report, that the honors course at Virginia consist of a prescribed program of study in the liberal arts. Funds necessary for the program were never obtained, and in 1936 the pair accepted the invitation of Robert Maynard Hutchins to come to the University of Chicago. They were at Chicago when Francis Pickens Miller of Virginia informed them that St. John's College in Annapolis might be the place for their experiment in liberal education, and so it was.

Buchanan and Barr were convinced that the prevailing trends in education—favoring specialization and a wide selection of elective courses—could not provide adequate preparation for life as a citizen. They were further concerned that the intellectual foundations of contemporary thought and institutions were being neglected in education. Accordingly, they designed for St. John's a program of study, the New Program as it is called at the College, which addressed these issues. As Buchanan wrote in July 1937: "It is the purpose of the new program at St. John's College to recover the great liberal tradition of Europe and America, which for a period of two thousand years has kept watch over and guided all other Occidental traditions . . . The tangible and eminently available embodiments and tools of this great tradition are the classics and the liberal arts."

The program required all who studied in it to work in classical and modern languages, mathematics, and natural science, and in classics from the Old Testament to the Federalist Papers, to Russell and Whitehead's *Principia Mathematica.* Inquiry and dialogue—the seminar—were at the heart of the program, as they are today. The focus was and is very much on the art of conversation, and on the skills of reading and listening that are essential to it.

Scott Buchanan remained at St. John's as Dean of the College for ten years, departing in 1947. In the succeeding years, in a number of institutional settings, he continued his Socratic mission of raising tough and demanding questions, as in these essays on law and politics.

It is particularly striking to me how the spirit of conversation Buchanan helped to make so much a part of St. John's carries over into these essays. In "What Every Man Should Know: Law," Buchanan writes that the Fund for the Republic, with which he was associated for so many years, deals with difficult policy issues that it "has pledged itself to clarify and pass on to the great conversation, which is the substance of our political life."

But there is much more than this. Above all, there are the conversations in which Buchanan himself is engaged throughout these essays. I mean by this that Scott Buchanan is not alone in these pages. He is very clearly enjoying the companionship of others who have thought seriously about the ideas of law, politics, persuasion, reason, and force. It is a companionship that crosses generations: here Buchanan converses with Lincoln on the purposes of government, there with Thomas Aquinas on what a law is, now with Plato on the law as teacher, with Kant on the prescription of the categorical imperative for the legislator, and again with Gandhi on personal responsibility for all injustice. The list goes on—with Meiklejohn on political freedom; with Martin Buber, Henry Maine, James Bryce, Tocqueville, and Aeschylus on the discovery of law; with Calhoun on political parties; even with the long-forgotten poet who recorded the Icelandic Saga of Burnt Njal as an account of the emergence of common law.

There is an intimacy to these conversations, a shared sense of purpose and interest, a quiet gratitude for the common willingness to face up to questions that are hard and whose answers have powerful consequences for political constitutions and the life of the body politic. The authors are not invoked; rather, their experience and ideas are recaptured and shared. The essays thus show Buchanan to be a patient, thorough, and conversational reader.

Learning to read in this way is one of the ideals of the St. John's program, and these essays are a compelling lesson in the fulfillment of that ideal. Too few readers nowadays learn what it is like to read authors as working friends, as co-participants in the ongoing human effort to understand how best to order our lives together. Buchanan clearly knew, and this knowledge made him one of the more powerful heirs of our tradition, enabling him to pass it along in his turn.

The essays themselves testify to Buchanan's awareness of this continuity. In "The Public Thing," he observes that "it may be well for us to recognize that our memories are the sources of our imaginations." When he turns to the future, as he does in "The Corporation and the Republic," he acknowledges the insufficiency of past thought: "Clearly we have some new thinking to do if the intelligence that freedom requires is to be effective." Yet he immediately reminds us of the need to be in touch with the intellectual foundations of the polity: ". . . Loss of freedom in a society is due in part to failure to understand its own vital processes." Throughout the text, one vividly feels oneself to be in the presence of a participant in a dialogue spanning centuries past and yet to come.

It is, accordingly, most fitting that St. John's College be associated with the publication of these essays written after Scott Buchanan's tenure as Dean at Annapolis. The essays embody the qualities of mind, the habits of thought, the seriousness about ideas and actions to which the St. John's program is dedicated. And on occasion, the playfulness, the humor, that Nicholas of Cusa described as essential to the practice of philosophy peek through, as in Buchanan's discussion of disproportionate power and corporate uses of technology. "A fair field and no favors, said the elephant as he danced among the chickens," he writes.

St. John's is pleased to have this opportunity to express its abiding gratitude for the inspiration Scott Buchanan brought to it, this chance to share once again the companionship of a vibrant friend and valued colleague.

EDWIN J. DELATTRE
President, St. John's College
Annapolis, Maryland
Sante Fe, New Mexico

SO
REASON
CAN
RULE

1

IMAGO MUNDI

AS YOU well know there is only one commencement speech. It has been delivered many times and it has many superficial variations, but it always says the same thing. An old man of the tribe tells the young men that they are beautiful and strong, that the world is full of evils, and that they must go out into the world to fight its evils and to keep the vision of its highest good. These are the sentimental instruments of the great rite of initiation of the young into the tribe, but in spite of the sentiment it must be clear that the great object that is being celebrated is the world, and that the appropriation of this object by each generation is necessary if it is to live out its life.

The dogma that goes with this ritual is full of irony, full of questions for seminar discussion, and I wish that my part in your ritual could be less one-sided. Perhaps the briefest statement of the dogma comes from F. H. Bradley: "This is the best of all possible worlds, but everything in it is a necessary evil." But the irony is more subtle than that, and the questions are more complex. A better statement says that the world does not exist, it is merely an idea, but an idea that insists on being entertained, and, once entertained, forces the mind to believe that the world exists as the most real being. In a few minutes today, I want to try to contribute to your celebration by initiating you as liberal artists to the exploration of the idea of the world.

Dogmas, such as this one, are best stated as myths, and this dogma is usually presented in a myth of creation. Here is a new one for this occasion. When God created the angels, the brightest

A commencement speech, St. John's College, 1952.

3

angel, Lucifer, immediately suggested that God create a world
for him to govern. This disturbing suggestion delayed the work
of the six days by making it necessary to create a hell for all liberal
artists who are too bright, and it also made God think twice
before he created man. God finally resolved the problem by his
delicate decision to give man an intellect that would have to
reach for the idea of the world, but that would never comprehend
it. The consequence is that Satan is never quite sure that he got
what he asked for, and man has to learn over and over again that
he cannot attain self-government unless he thinks and acts like
an angel or a devil.

But perhaps we should begin with the simple, familiar illustrations and go on gradually to the bigger questions. Mark Van
Doren, in his book *Shakespeare,* adds a point to Aristotle's *Poetics.*
Aristotle says that poetry imitates human action, but by the use
of the Greek word for poetry, the art of poetry, he presupposed
that the poet makes something, something artificial, that can
imitate action. If we ask what that something is, Mark Van Doren,
in a tone of voice that leads one to suppose that he is saying something that everybody knows, says that the poet makes a world.
This was startling when I first heard it from the lecture platform
here at the College, but when I read it in the book I found it both
disturbing and illuminating. I began thinking about it, particularly when I read a poem, but also when I began looking at the
world in the framework of world government. As a reader of
poetry, I found there was a world in a poem, not only in the
great poems, but also in the little ones; but as an advocate of the
devil in the Foundation for World Government, I found that a
world was always something in a poem.

Out of Van Doren's suggestion and my own perverse philosophical habits, I have come to an analysis of this addendum to
Aristotle. The form in the poet's mind is an idea; it has unity, and
a structure; it is a system, rather like a living system, it lives and
moves. Furthermore, it is self-subsistent, a self-sufficient whole,
needing and depending on nothing outside itself. Still further,
having this kind of substantial existence and perfection, it is good,
an object of love, a kind of Galatea to the poet's Pygmalion. It
attracts and assimilates the poet so that his words become oracles,

and the reader is attracted until he can no longer prevent a kind of self-immolation; he lives and moves in this veritable world. So it must have been when God created the world, and saw that it was good.

But then I realized that I was suffering a reminiscence, a recollection of the divine animal in Plato's *Timaeus*, which in turn had demanded an explication, an upward and downward dialectic. Plato's poetic intuition of his world, with its skeleton of being, nonbeing, same, and other, had been a preamble to his long discursive construction of the sciences, mathematics, astronomy, physics, chemistry, biology, and medicine. So there had been many poetic preambles to the sciences in the minds of poets turned scientists, or scientists turned poets. Lucretius, seeing the drift of his atoms and watching his Roman spearman testing the ramparts of the universe by eternally throwing his spear across the boundaries of space; Gilbert, supplying Kepler with the magnetic parts of the celestial motor; Newton, trusting that God's sensorium would be an adequate coordinator of gravitational pushes and pulls; and above all, Dante and Kepler, whose cosmologies of intelligence and love kept the planets in their courses —these were makers and knowers of worlds. It would seem that the eye of the poet travels out from the central intuition along the rays of light that the sciences provide to their vanishing points on the boundaries of the cosmos. The result of this total vision, so many times repeated and so variously formulated, is the persistently recurring dogma that the microcosm of man's mind mirrors the macrocosm of the universe, that the human intellect is the place of the forms, most of all, the place of the form of the world. It is the business of a man to view with ever-increasing awe the starry heavens above and the moral law within.

This doctrine once formulated and propagated by its own overwhelming charm, has had a most profound influence on the theoretical and practical affairs of our civilization. It has impregnated every incipient science with a hunger for wholeness and totality. Every abstract proposition seeks, like a wandering orphan, for its place in some deductive or demonstrative series; and the independent self-evident axioms of ancient contemplation reduce themselves to postulates of systems that pretend to comprehend the universe, just as cities grow into metropolises and nations into mother countries in order to preside over empires.

But there are signs that Satan has played his part in these works of speculation and conquest. As the universe of discourse tries to extend its boundaries, it finds itself full of imitating and expanding systems, each pretending to complete worldhood, and the more it impresses the one on the many, the more it spawns new possible worlds, until discourse loses itself in an infinite anarchical many. The principle of imitation, which operated first in the poetic creation of a world as an imitation of the small by the great, operates here in reverse; the little systems imitate the great cosmos without internal restraint or external restriction. Sometimes the great universe keeps a semblance of order, as in the concentric spheres of the Aristotelian cosmology, or as in the medieval cascade of analogies that connect two systems of circles in heaven and hell with a spiral purgatory; more often the universe reminds us of the Tower of Babel.

The modern world has for several centuries been spinning around us a new set of concentric spheres. They are not only crystalline, they also have high reflecting powers; they do it with mirrors. There is the system of gravity that impresses and diverts all particles from their inertial ways; there is the system of heat that releases by discreet degrees the random motions of subparticles or molecules; there is the system of electromagnetism that keeps all atoms and subatoms vibrating on all-pervasive waves of energy; and we now look, dazzled by these flashing mirrors, to find the new sphere of nuclear energy, which could be, we think, the unifying source of all our visions. But it may be well to remember Satan's challenge to God, and recall that the temptation to new creation is still continuing.

We did not need to be told some years ago that the universe is expanding, nor just yesterday that the recreative process is still going on in interstellar space. We have been imitating the imitators in more intimate ways. We have built gadgets that can transform energy from one sphere to another, heat to mechanical equivalents, electricity to light, heat, and power, and tomorrow atomic energy perhaps to life. Under the aspect of the world, these gadgets have become a system of technology, which in its turn accelerates and expands the spheres of economics and politics, affairs of ours that have also become systems and systems of systems. If we listen to the biologists, the anthropologists, and the geographers, we learn that they have drawn loci for other reflecting spheres to control the light of the world. It would seem that by the principle of imitation and reflection we are living in a world that is bursting with a dozen possible worlds, each preventing the realization of the one world that our cosmic intellects require.

But if we draw a little closer and view the world with a somewhat more analytic eye, we shall see that this Satan-ridden machinery is not yet the tragedy that it seems. Worlds and systems of the kind we have been considering, like empires and governments, have come and gone in our intellectual history. The tragedies have all turned into comedies, as soon as worlds, systems, and ideologies have been placed in the intellectual firmament. They are not principles, nor are they facts, although they borrow something from both of these. They are hypotheses, and for all their heroic dimensions and their high and mighty poses, they are only possibilities, which with boldness, laughter, and ingenuity on our part can be put aside and replaced. None of them has the sufficient reason that is needed to give it actuality. The best of all possible worlds is yet to be found, if Satan is to be confounded and God is to be justified.

We listen to the poet because he offers us a possible view of the world, and both he and we are ready to be fooled by the imposters, because we have great need of a view of the world. In that sense, possible worlds are necessary if we are ever to find our actual world. But there are several demands that the possible world never fulfills, demands that a possible world cannot by itself fulfill. An actual world has to be all there is; as Plato showed in the *Sophist,* an actual world has to contain even nonbeing. It turns out on examination that a possible world is always too big and at the same time too little to be a real world. It is not merely, as Kant would say, that a possible world leaps beyond experience; it easily goes beyond all possible evidence, and just as this point begins to fabricate its own evidence, its own self-subsistence. We see this imitative creation on a grand scale at present with the help of the spectroscope, the Palomar telescope, and the cosmo-tron. Lucretius's spearman was a very modest fellow beside these modern mechanics who draw geodesics with a ray of light.

But it is also true that a possible world is too little to be real. The poet, turned scientist and philosopher, being finite, leaves a great deal out of his vision; at the beginning he does this by arbitrary intention and then continues to do so on principle. If he falls in love with his Galatea, we know that the course of his love will not be smooth and that he will awake from his trance, knowing that there are more things in heaven and earth than he has dreamed of. A possible world is radically abstract and only parades in the habits of a world historic character.

Perhaps I should stop here and let you go out into the world armed with the comic spirit of the critical philosophy. But this is where Kant stopped and, rather irresponsibly, let the world set sail in the eighteenth century, not dreaming in his philosophy of half the things that would happen in its voyage through the nineteenth and twentieth centuries. But he left word that the idea of the world was an irreplaceable idea of reason, which although it led to speculative monsters that must be avoided, still guided the searching mind in its worldly work, and furthermore defined a duty for the individual to act on maxims that are laws "universal"; that is to say, world laws. And as a sanction for this last bit of moral advice he said something that sounds like the detonation of the big bomb: you can choose the peace of the grave, or the world state.

So the world, as an idea of reason, is not merely a fool's fable, not merely one of many possible worlds. If we allow our minds their speculative indulgence, even to the limit of a Satanic multi-plication of such worlds, a heavy duty is laid upon the practical intellect to weigh these worlds, to choose the best of them . . . and to will it. Although Leibniz trusted God to supply the sufficient reason to make this choice, there is a strong presumption that some of God's powers were delegated to man, and that among these powers are those of just government derived from the consent of the governed. It seems that the Founding Fathers of this country accepted this responsibility, to consider all possible worlds, to choose the best, and to will it. "It has been frequently remarked that it seems to have been reserved to the people of this country, by their conduct and example, to decide the important question, whether societies of men are really capable or not of establishing good government from reflection and choice, or whether they are forever destined to depend for their constitutions on accident and force. If there be any truth in the remark, the crisis at which we have arrived may with propriety be regarded as the era in which that decision is to be made; and a wrong election on the part we shall act, may, in this view, deserve to be considered as the general misfortune of mankind." The idea of the world in its practical imperative form was pressing hard on the minds of the authors of the Federalist Papers when this statement was written. It is pressing still more heavily on all our minds today.

It would require a new Virgil, with his pious Aeneus, to weigh the burden that the idea of the world has put upon us, and to distribute the weight among us so that it can be carried. We have something like such an *Aeneid* in Arnold Toynbee's *A Study of History*, which I am persuaded was written for twentieth-century Americans. As you know, he focuses his enormous working knowledge of the world upon those stages in civilization that, remembering Greek tragedy, he names "times of troubles." The troubles arise chiefly from the accumulation of unsolved problems and from the pervasive ambiguities in the situation. Toynbee describes these times of trouble in some twenty past civilizations, and then heightens the irony in ours by describing it as the locus of simultaneous confluence of the five or six civilizations still extant and in process of breakdown. Toynbee lacks the liberal artist's disciplined appetite for the broad general and abstract conceptions that lead from poetry and science to the idea of the world. He therefore sees the welter of cosmologies and utopias as the pathological content of the schism in the individual soul that suffers progressive separation from its neighbors and the community. Incidentally he sees our science, technology, economics, and politics as systems of deadly radiation that emanate from the still vital centers of Western civilization to the rest of the world. In this he is, of course, guilty of the cosmological disease himself, seeing himself as the head physician in a pathological clinic with

the world as his patient; he would be the last to deny this
observation.

I would not like to dispute his pessimistic prognosis, but its
depth might be increased by a bolder and more objective consideration of the cosmic content of the pathological symptoms.
If Kant and Plato are right that it is a man's duty to view all time
and eternity, and this not merely in the historical mode, cosmology is a normal, even necessary, human preoccupation. In
times of stress, it may be that the cosmos runs a fever and shows
other monstrous symptoms, but medicine has always known that
many symptoms of disease are the appearances of the process
of natural healing or even of recovery itself. At any rate, the
liberal artist, who has to have the final judgment on medical
matters, may have something to add to pathology.

Toynbee would not deny that in the midst of death there is
birth, as the world goes, and with a new world there will be need
of a new world view. Wendell Willkie, some years ago, made
himself the herald of a new world, which he called One World.
Soon after, we find ourselves needing to accustom ourselves to
Two Worlds, the East and the West, as they are defined in
ideological terms. One has only to go to the Middle East, or
almost anywhere else, to find that the idea of two worlds has
indeed taken root, but the two worlds are not the same that
Americans and Russians see. This is the idea of the world playing
its old game of dividing and multiplying by the rule of two, with
Satan joining in by proposing the Third or Middle factor. From
the point of view of the divine world-animal, it is the delegation and redistribution of powers. Each situation is a problem in
measurement and redefinition. In this view, it is not surprising
that there are paroxysms of mutual negation, veto, and deadly
conflict; in some cases, pacts of mutual suicide. Toynbee would
say that there is danger of the vast process grinding human
communities and individuals down to dust so that the particles
can be fitted into one vast universal state. But the sense of
panmixia, or promiscuity and abandon, and the opposite reaction
of asceticism in the individual need not be signs of immediate
dissolution. They could be signs of the first new impact of the
idea of the world, and a waiting readiness on the part of the

recipients to accept the measurement and redefinition that it promises. One of the impressive functions of the cosmic idea is to preside over the birth of possible, new, and good worlds, and to incite new wills to make them actual. Willing abandon, promiscuity, and asceticism are sometimes signs of grace.

There are many signs at present that measurement and redefinition are taking place. The instruments of precision and the terms of definition often buckle and fracture under the heavy pressures to which they are subject, but the world principle creates others to take their place, and finds new occasions for their operation. It is said that American influence at present radiates on beams of science, technology, economics, and politics, and that it is the reverse, echoing beams from the rest of the world that frighten us. For instance, our confusion of science and technology leaves us as pragmatism, and Russia sends it back as dialectical materialism. Our confusion of economics and politics leaves us as corporation law and returns to us as the Soviet republic. The scramble that ensues to get positions of strength makes us aware that the rest of the world needs and wants these gadgets, but that they will find new utilities for them that we have not even imagined, and may not be able to understand until we have invented new possible worlds to fit them.

There are signs in this country that we have forgotten a great deal of the political science from which our own government was constructed. We seem to think that a good government, once established, waxes strong and continues established forever unless it is destroyed from without. It should therefore be defended both externally and internally to preserve its way of life. But if it has a political life, we must remember the lesson in the eighth book of Plato's *Republic*, in which the world view of government sees a political beginning, middle, and end; with good luck, an aristocratic-philosophical birth, a youth of timocratic or military rule, a good plutocratic middle age under oligarchs, and a second childhood of democracy and tyranny—perhaps a rebirth, if all these possible worlds have been fulfilled faithfully. But even in our obstinate American way of life we are learning, not only that governments are born in philosophy and blood, suffer concentrations of power, and then indulge in high standards of living, but that any government, if only to defend itself, has to limit and adjust itself to other governments; so that each state is potentially and increasingly actually a province of a world state that federally defines and conditions the operation of the local laws. We now know from hard experience that international law, which governs unilateral relations of individual states with their neighbors, presupposes a world law that philosophers have from time to time vainly proposed, sometimes to conquerors who have used the idea for their own worldly purposes. A deeper thing we have learned is that this world law, like the idea of the world, has to deal with all possible legal systems. The world contains all sorts of governments today, and the problem of jurisprudence is to find the transformation formula that will rationalize the political relativity now nagging us with its apparent whimsies of local times and places.

But one of Plato's political categories seems, in the last century, to have sprouted a new monster. It is customary in a seminar to translate oligarchy into plutocracy under an ancient formula that the concentration of political power in a few hands follows the transfer of property from the many to the few. This formula has a very modern radical sound, even when it is a mere footnote in the reading of a great book, and it is fitting that it draws this attention because it is at this point that the monster has grown—the modern welfare state, in which the world of trade and industry and the science of economics touch public political interest in vital ways. The changed nature of war, in which industry plays a greater part than mere armaments, and the meaning we have recently given to security, beyond the limits of mere defense—these are signs that the economic systems that permeate the world are more than invisible governments, and that they must be recognized as subject to political growth. But as we see this, it also becomes clear that there are many economies, some of them never before recognized as economies, such as the feudal estate, from which capitalism and socialism have come historically. But, again, these systems do not merely show a life history of a single kind of economy but rather a contemporary mosaic of economic systems, none of which has ever existed separately or purely, but always together, like governments, in essential cooperation and conflict with each other.

The science of economics came into existence as a byproduct of capitalism. Under the pressure of socialistic theory, it has had to defend itself against the charge of being the science of scarcity and imperialism. From unsuccessful attempts to plan national economies it has now been forced to survey world economy, just to keep its predictions of the local market from too great errors. It is now clear that the theory of economic imperialism, like the theory of international law, is merely the first hypothesis that leads to a cosmological development within which the relativity of economic systems will act as the epicyclical components of a great economic cycle, which is not, by the way, to be confused with the business cycle—or so we hope. The economic intercourse between feudal, capitalistic, and socialistic economies is apparently unavoidable as a political concern, although the proper study of corporations as the mediums of this intercourse might show that giant national corporations are not the only competent sovereigns.

All this might be the airiest exploration of possible worlds if it were not for the groundswell of science and technology that has been built up by two world wars and propagated like a tidal wave of revolution all over the world. It is now common knowledge in the farthest corners of the world that hunger, sickness, nakedness, and homelessness—all those symptoms of the economy of scarcity under which we have all lived—can by the proper multiplication and distribution of science and technology be abolished from the earth. This is not something that can be brought to pass tomorrow or in the next decade; nor is it merely the demagogic sentiment of a political orator. Science and technology themselves have gone far enough in their own estimates of themselves, under the inspiration of the idea of the world, to measure and redefine the possibilities. Through all the sound and fury of the United Nations, this is what the still small voices of the F.A.O. and E.C.O.S.O.C. are saying, and little, hungry, sick, naked, homeless people everywhere are listening. This knowledge is rapidly transforming itself into the general will of the world and expressing itself in many revolutions. In spite of the surface phenomena of acceleration in the economic system of this country, the real industrial revolution has gone underground, and is now sprouting everywhere; it is no wonder that the face of the world wears a troubled look. This possible world needs God's as well as man's will to make it actual. But the stirrings of men's wills are at present expressed only in emotions of fear. We are not sure what our gadgets, planted all over the world, will do to us; we need a technological cosmology to quiet our nerves and to guide the conduct of our public affairs. If this view of the present world is at all valid, there is a remarkable enticement to reconsider Kant's proposal of the moral ideal of the world, the categorical impera-tive, in its three forms. He proposed it just as his contemporary, Adam Smith, was drawing in the first outlines of the industrial revolution and trying to estimate its effect on the wealth and welfare of nations. Kant was trying to foresee the common reasonable legal forms under which nations and economies would assimilate the progressive developments in science and tech-nology. The necessary conditions for such laws were equal powers of legislation and equal rights for all human beings; the concep-tion of each person as an end in himself, not a means only; and finally, the conception of the whole natural world under men, as a kingdom of ends. Having stated these conditions as absolutely necessary moral principles, as if to confess his failure of imagina-tion, he called them merely ideals, things that we must will but cannot hope to fulfill. This is the way they have been presented in courses in the history of philosophy for almost two hundred years. At long last we have come to see that they are ideals that must be fulfilled if any part of the world that we know and love is to survive. We are now convinced that we must make another try, that it is our duty to hope. Laws must be made that are just for all men; economies must be made for all men, and not men for economies; and the means of science and technology must be made available for universal use. What we know we can do, we must do. The rotation of the spheres, beginning with the sphere of mechanics, then shifting to the sphere of heat, then to the sphere of electricity, has finally actuated a sphere of technology; and therefore the spheres of economics and government; and this has put a massive substance into the pure form of the categorical imperative.

But Kant's great questions still remain. What can I know, what can I hope for, what ought I to do? The idea of the world, coming to us through this imminently realized form of the categorical imperative, has us thoroughly frightened. It has particularly frightened us Americans, because the world has passed to us the primary responsibility for carrying out the duty, and we appear to have the primary means. But this is not the first time that the idea of the world has frightened human beings; the ideal has often turned into a menacing fate over which mere men seem to have no control. This is the phenomenon that is being diagnosed in Toynbee's pathology. He is describing the quasi-world of men as the receptacle for the idea, and to the lonely individual the world of men seems to have broken into fragments, and he looks around for another receptacle that can adequately take its place. Until he finds this, his consent is paralyzed. The individual in very un-Socratic manner thinks he knows nothing, and waits for fate to tell him what he can hope for and what he ought to do. I think there is a great general will in the world that will finally articulate and answer these questions, but it will take a long time for this idea of the world to express itself in individual minds.

I am going to take the liberty of acting temporarily as your class prophet. When I graduated from college, as I remember, we voted for Lewis Douglas as the man most likely to succeed, but we did not specify the category of his success. I shall try a more actuarial method, specifying categories and suggesting probable frequencies of your answers to the Kantian questions.

Some of you, probably the larger portion, will want to forget the infinity of possible worlds, even the best possible, and decide to cultivate your suburban gardens. As you know, you will have eminent philosophical authority for your decision, and realizing this, you may want to reread some of the great books to choose your style of garden—the Epicurean, or possibly a Stoic porch. I hope you will acquire the comic spirit because I am afraid you will not be left alone and undisturbed; your protecting hedge will have to be a stout sense of humor. A few others of you will smell adventure in a wide-open world, and your curiosity will lead you to explore all the possible worlds that you can get passports to. You may be frightened by the monsters that you meet, and also by those that you will help to create, but you will escape all of them, one after another, and find that each world through which you pass will be a university, a university of trial and error with the degree, bachelor of experience.

Some of you, who have come to St. John's looking for a philosophy of life, will by this time have fallen in love with an actual world of the recent or distant past. You will not realize that a past actual world, although it was once possible, is now an impossible world, and you will seek to defend it with your life. You may leave an island for some Sancho Panza to govern, and after many battles against evil find your Dulcinea and your final victory in heaven.

Still others, I presume a very few, will be bored with the cobwebs and dreams of the books of the past, with the State Department and the Un-American Activities Committees of the present, and will find your only escape in the future. You will think it your duty to smash this sorry scheme of things entirely into bits from which you will be willing to build the only really possible world, the city of the future. You may remember that Aristophanes wrote his *Birds* about you, and realize that you are probably already a citizen of a city not built with hands.

The rest of you, if there are any left, will, I take it, become citizens of the world. You must already know that it is a feverish, impatient world, not very tolerant of any full exercise of the liberal arts, especially those that contemplate alternative possibilities, not generous or sympathetic with those who find it necessary to measure and redefine their loyalties. You may find any simple loyalty you have suddenly canceling other loyalties that you wish to keep, and you may be charged with many treasons within the hour. You will find the words you use and the deeds you do marvelously ambiguous. All these things will be so because you have made the idea of the world the rule of your life, you have found a way of accepting the actual world, and of accepting the fate that it contains as the necessary condition for solving your problems. This may mean that you see the need for a world government or a universal church, as Toynbee suggests, but it more probably will mean that you will want to see that the laws that you live under are made truly universal and the God you serve less like an idol. It should lead you to see that the persons with whom you work are not merely useful but with you serve common ends, that the parts of nature that you exploit are made useful to your fellows as well, that the science and skill that you have is made available through education to everybody.

These simple-sounding truths were accepted by the Founding Fathers of this country; they have regularly been accepted in the Western world; and they are now being accepted by all of the rest of the world. They are all rules of world law. They with the possible worlds that they comprehend and permeate are making the world revolution that will probably continue through the rest of your lives.

Perhaps the most important thing that the contemporary cosmopolitan, the present citizen of the world, has to remember is that the world lives and moves, it revolves, and that revolution is its natural property. The sudden and explosive phenomena that we often call revolutions are epicyclical rotations or mere perturbations, often retrograde, mere symptoms of the deeper and larger work of the world, the rattling and wobbling of the wheels of the great chariot. If you are sensitive, imaginative, and responsive, these agitations will disturb your feelings and your wishes, but your reason will say with Galileo, Still it moves; and your will will consent.

It may be that some of you will find that your consent has become a deep settled habit and sentiment, and that you will want to join your generation in its acceptance of one of the most characteristic expressions of the idea of the world in a time of troubles; that is, the almost universal movement of peoples. Tolstoy describes one such episode in *War and Peace;* General Smuts and Wendell Willkie refer to the present episode as "the people on the march." These movements usually start from the internal pressures and the external conquests of great wars and first appear as scattered and displaced persons, the victims of the malice that is generated by social frustration. But the movement quickly outruns the cause, becomes voluntary and self-directed on the part of both the proletariat and the intelligentsia. It falls into the pattern of willed possible worlds of many kinds. Finally, it appears as the colonial spirit with the avowed pioneering purpose of resettling the world. As you know, I have recently been

temporarily participating in one stage of such a movement in
Israel, one that bids fair to become the model for many others.
Properly enough for the time, we in this country and in Europe
tend to see our part in the great movement as the development
of backward areas, and to see the prospective colonies as
appendages of one or another of the great empires. It is safe to
say that these less-than-world-views will suffer revision, if only
because imperialism is an outworn notion. The new view will see
the new settlements as colonies of the world. Those of you who
are attracted to the suburban garden, have a yen for adventure,
and an appetite for revolution, but do not want to leave the world
to indulge your private fancies may potentially belong to the new
pioneering stock. If this be your beloved fate, we shall welcome
you back to some class reunion to tell us what has been going on
in the world. The final paradox that I will not now try to explain
is that the light from the idea of the world is now shining on the
world's periphery; it is we at the presumed center who live in
darkness . . . and fear.

There are three words familiar in the Zionist tradition, *diaspora*
or wandering, *kibbutz* or in-gathering, and *aliyah* or going-up;
they indicate motions of the world. I could wish that they would
make the pattern of your individual lives.

2

LEARNING
UNDER LAW

TO a teacher who has been led by training and experience to a concern about the whole educational enterprise, the current popular and professional attempts to reconsider
it are alarming. These assessments fall so far short of the extent
and depth of the trouble as to raise the questions of the philosophers of history who warn us that we may have passed the point
of recovery in the career of our civilization. Long and expensive
research tells us that we need more money, more classrooms,
and more teachers; that the community must respect the teacher
and the intellectual; that we must cut out the frills and get back
to fundamentals; that we should consolidate schools and pay
more attention to the brighter students; that we must educate
leaders; that we should or should not imitate Russia. These
superficial criticisms and proposals rise from a deeper uncer-
tainty and concern about our society. They raise questions of
another order.

I should like to explore one of these questions here. Before we,
as a society moving into a new era, decide what our formal
educational system should be, we ought to find out what educational processes and products our society provides in the course
of its inevitable, natural, day-to-day life. This involves trying to
see our society and its several institutions as an educational
system; it involves the individual seeing his own life as an
educational enterprise. This is not the usual, nor perhaps even a

Presented for discussion to the staff of the Center for Democratic Studies
in 1957.

fair, way to look at and judge a society or the individual. But in
the absence of conditions for a controlled experiment, it may
provide a perspective from which we can see the root or source
of the educational energy that any deliberate formal system will
have to tap, or adapt itself to, if it is to live, survive, and
perform its functions. If a society has no built-in self-educative
process, it would seem unlikely that it could, by merely taking
thought, add or maintain any genuine educational establishment.
If we should find that our society has lost its organic educational
momentum beyond recall, this fact would be a portent of our
fate as a civilization. In spite of present evidence, such a sweeping negative finding is unlikely. If we are bold and shrewd in
our search, we may not only rediscover the original source of
our self-education but also haply uncover an educational process
that has been growing and generating new forms while we have
slept.

I should like to try to initiate such a search by constructing a
probing hypothesis. It begins with an insight that was held at
the center of the political thought of the Greek city-state, namely,
that self-government is a self-educative process. We do not have
to push this to the Platonic extreme of despair and say that there
is no hope for a polity unless kings or citizens are philosophers.
We can settle for the Aristotelian common sense that man is a
rational animal, therefore a political animal, and therefore a
learning animal. It was also common sense to the Greeks that the
laws are the teachers, and that the making, obeying, and remaking of laws is the essence of collective self-education. To put
it briefly, due process of law in any society is due process of
education. I realize that this is an implausible hypothesis for us
at present. We do not look at our laws and state in this perspective. Politics, in both its high and low meanings, is the enemy of
education. But this antipathy may be the symptom, perhaps the
cause, of our present blindness and paralysis.

With this hypothesis as a guiding principle, I should like to
examine our society for its capacities and facilities to learn. If I
were a sociologist or a psychologist, this examination would be
the exploration of a labyrinth composed of rapidly changing and
tangling ways of life. The labyrinth would also be haunted by

the guarding monsters of law, political science, and history. For
protection and guidance I would invite the authors of the Constitution and the Federalist Papers, Tocqueville, and Montesquieu,
adding what Montesquieu called the spirit of the laws to the
formalities of jurisprudence. With such help I would like to see
our free society formed by, or forming itself on, the laws by
which we reluctantly or enthusiastically live.

The Founding Fathers all learned through their tutors what
Montesquieu had said, that the principle of the republican form
of government is political virtue, and that the source of such
virtue is education. But, with the illustrious exceptions of Franklin
and Jefferson, none of them devoted his attention and energies to
the establishment of formal education. The evidence for their
adherence to the principle is in what they built into the constitutions and laws of the new nation. They did their best to give this
country the basic and comprehensive legal structure that would
make the day-to-day life and work of the citizen and the officials
self-educative.

It should be recalled at the start that the Founding Fathers did
not invent de novo much of the legal structure that they built. The
governments of the colonies came from England with the colonists
and their corporate sponsors. The seeds of law thus imported
suffered a sea change, and their transplanting in many cases
made all the difference. The new soil and free air of the frontier
worked miracles in the rejuvenation and in the forced growth of
new meanings and effects of the old laws. But by the time of
the writing of the state and federal constitutions, the imitation
of the spirit and machinery of British justice and liberty had
laid the basic pattern. As James Bryce has said, the authors of
the Constitution were chiefly exercised in fitting a keystone in
an almost completed structure, but this is not to underestimate
the originality of the result.

COMMON LAW

Before we look at the machinery and spirit of the written Constitution and the legislated statutes, we should consider the
massive and basic legal structure that was imported and taken

for granted: the common law made by the accumulation of cases in British courts. The peculiar genius of this body of law and the story of its development over several centuries of vital human experience and learning has often enough been described and celebrated. Lay judges sitting by the side of the road or under an oak tree to hear, judge, and advise on their neighbors' feuds and causes, then calling juries to extend and refine their intelligences; early opinions being cited as precedents for judging new cases; such opinions being tested and probed as much as the parties in conflict; the whole community remembering and anticipating judgment by peers as its members go about their daily business— we forget this fabric of our lives when, as we say, we avoid tangling with the law. Many of these lay judges became kings or the king's judges, many of the jurymen became legislators and magistrates, and the common law became the habits of the common man. It is the memory of this judicial transformation of needs, capacities, and conflicts into discovery, invention, rules, and habits that we imitate when we organize discussion classes in adult education and progressive schools. We have here a piece of the basic tradition of self-education in our society.

The facing of vital problems and the building of precedents by judges and juries flourished in the colonial and early national period of this country, so much so that Tocqueville writes at some length on the extensive and prominent part that lawyers play in public life. The majority of the members of Congress were lawyers, but leaders in states and towns were also members of the bar. They had been sensitized and alerted to the common good by their pleadings in court. Their basic professional training, then as now, was in reading and discussing books and cases under the several topics in the common law— property, contracts, torts, and crimes—as these had been sorted out and ordered. It is not so clear now as in Tocqueville's day that the lawyer has the same sense of the common good, or that the citizen thinks about his part in the common life in terms of these topics in the common law. The subject matter has become professional and special, and the common man has lost one of the instruments of his political and social intelligence. It is questionable whether sociology and psychology can take the place of this

instrument or whether the so-called social studies can go it alone
without the legal formalities.

As has often been said, the reception of common law in this
country was as fateful as the reception of Roman law in Europe.
Whatever the differences of Roman and common law may have
been, there are special affinities of certain topics in the common
law with another new discipline that has shaped our minds and
institutions, the discipline of the industrial revolution. When our
national existence was being shaped, we were an undeveloped
area, as we understand that phrase in connection with various
new nations at present. The colonists came with the farmer's
and the craftsman's skills, but very soon the curiosity and the
inventiveness of the frontier combined with the new science and
the mechanics of the old countries to refashion tools, to invent
machines, and to set up shops. The War of Independence was
fought partly to free such developments from the British imperial
restrictions. So by the time of the Founding Fathers, technology,
industry, and commerce had already set the pattern for the industrial development of the country. Since this pattern involved
new uses of property and new relations between men, the
common law notions of property and contract are in for continual
discussion and revision by both lawyer and citizen.

Without doubt, the industrial discipline, including those phases
of it that we call technological, financial, and commercial, has
been the most popular, the most fundamental, and the most
effectual of our informal educational enterprises. We began in
the colonies as farmers and craftsmen, and Thomas Jefferson still
saw us as such, but the combination of the manual arts and skills
with the machines and the mechanical arts began almost immediately. Yankee ingenuity and frontier resourcefulness wel-
comed machinery and organization. The instinct of workmanship
was open to mechanical development and was free to take on
organized efficiency as a virtue that magnified rather than restricted its capacities. Here, more than in the older countries, the
new discipline struck deep into the mentality of the people. The
American farmer and craftsman had inherited a mythical, ritualistic, and superstitious relation to animals, plants, and even
inanimate materials, but the machine steadily substituted matter-

of-fact and pragmatic understandings, even in the minds of those who still maintained the pious trusteeship and stewardship that the new Protestant orthodoxy imposed on the boss and his hired hands.

There was a great deal of learning in all this, and it took place in the pioneer's cabin, the frontier settlement, the New England village, the mill and the factory, and finally in the growing city. The learning resulted in the open, practical, relativistic, experimental mind, the mind that saw the benefits of tools and materials, the beauty of workmanship on a large scale, the infinite potentialities of the individual, and the multiplying effects of cooperation. The Transcendentalist and the captain of industry might quarrel about the promise of the mousetrap, whether for a greater market or an oversoul, but they both started from the practical reality and utility of the gadget.

It has been and still is customary to attribute the relatively prosperous and peaceful course of the industrial revolution in this country to the guiding theory and ideal of free enterprise as expounded by Adam Smith, and this economic interpretation of our history has been closely associated, if not identified and confused, with the political doctrine of Jefferson that that government is best that governs least. We tell ourselves, at least at election time, that we must keep business out of government and government out of business, if we are to keep our freedoms.

Quite aside from the historical complications and controversies between and around these theses, there is substantial and continuous bond between business and government in the common law of property and contracts. What an economist would call land and capital is called property in law; what an economist would call rent, interest, wages, and profits would fall under the law of contract; and the Founding Fathers are at much pains to repeat with emphasis their basic premise that the essential purpose of government is to secure the rights and powers of property and to protect and enforce the obligations of contracts. This is something both less and more than writing free enterprise into the constitutions and laws: less, in that it does not prohibit government regulation of business, but on the contrary promises regulation by due process of law; more, in that it guarantees whatever the rights, powers, and obligations of men in their economic activities turn out to be. There are alternative dangers in this legal underwriting of the rights of property and the freedom of contracts: the conservative danger that Charles Beard found in the constitutional convention and its documents, and the radical populist danger in the executive and legislative powers to shift the weights of wealth and welfare under Jackson and others; both dangers contained in what Franklin Roosevelt called the elastic constitution. The Founding Fathers could not have foreseen the developments and their risks in the American industrial revolution, but they discerned, reformulated, and reinforced effectively and precisely those principles of the common law, property, and contract that have given and kept such order as we have in the commercial and industrial world. In these principles they found the essential minimal parts of the invisible hand that have identified the industrial system with the wealth of the nation.

But these bonds of obligation to commerce and industry that the government has accepted for the sake of the general welfare are curious and subtle things. Although, in the colonial period, commerce and industry could have been conceived, under mercantile principles, to be branches of the government, and although there are suspicions of the continuation of these ideas in the policies that Alexander Hamilton promoted, the emphasis on property and contracts minimizes and breaks any such connection. Such government action on behalf of the general welfare as there was, as in the cases of the Homestead Act and the establishment of the railroads, distributes property to many individuals, who then manage to develop it by their own individual efforts or by contracts that they make with other individuals. The government does not insist on individual ownership, but it encourages individual appropriation and defends titles in courts, and by enforcing contracts, it defends any new uses of property that business and technology invent. Property in land, tools, and machines can be bought and sold freely; industry can be organized to exploit property by free contracts, and the government stands ready to justify and protect the rights and obligations so created.

It is these legal principles that put the floor of reasonable expectation under the structure of so-called free enterprise that has been built upon it. It must be this that free enterprisers refer to when they speak of the insurance of freedom in the Constitution, but they often overstate their case by claiming that the private conduct of business and industry is a natural and inalienable right that must not be interfered with by government. Of course, they add, government must put on the brakes when business goes to extremes, as in cutthroat competition, monopoly, conspiracy in restraint of trade, frauds, or false advertising. This ambiguity, almost amounting to schizophrenia, indicates that the provisions of the common law that have been subsumed in the Constitution have been and still are being stretched to contain the continually changing realities in the industrial system. The New Deal was one of the crucial moments when this was realized, and the statutory remedies were hustled in to meet the emergency.

The common law in England has had two apparently divergent reputations. Its generation in the courts by the cumulation of precedents had at various occasions made it into a bulwark of political and social conservatism, rigid and inflexible. Its defense by great jurists at times seemed to give it predominant restraining power over both king and parliament. At such times the common law seemed in principle incapable of adjusting itself to social change. It is this reputation that Charles Beard is invoking when he detects a bias to favor property in our constitutional documents.

On the other hand, the common law has a reputation of pragmatic elasticity and reasonable flexibility, which has been celebrated in doctrines of legal fictions and judicial legislation. Novel cases stretch the meanings of the precedents under which they fall; they sometimes, more often than not, involve conflicting precedents taken from centuries of recorded judgments. Invention and construction of concepts are needed to make the law fit the case. The novelty that such invention and construction introduces into the meanings of the legal terms may seem to violate the strict canons of judicial procedure, and a rule of reason or even of social expediency has to be invoked to justify it. When the novelty is admitted, it is often called a legal fiction; when it is incorporated in the judgment, it may be called judicial legislation; if it survives and becomes a precedent, it is from then on a permanent part of the body of law. This is the traditional way by which the law grows and adjusts itself to events and developments in society. It is reminiscent of the way customs survive by changing in an inarticulate society, but the legal formality brings it to a higher degree of rationality. In fact, it gives a nearer view of the process by which the legal process becomes the self-teaching and learning process. •

The American choice to live and learn with the common law has always interested the British observer. British jurists only reluctantly accept the doctrines of legal fictions and judicial legislation, but the American frankness and enthusiasm in accepting and practicing the doctrines have gotten British attention and even admiration. Part of the American ingenuity has been merely a readiness to accept necessary novelty. The settlement of a big empty continent, freedom from complicated customs, the ingenious filling of needs for new tools and machines have steadily eroded the traditional notions about property and have called for new kinds of mutual obligation under contracts. For one hundred and fifty years, separate colonies went their separate ways in meeting different conditions in different regions under different forms of colonial government. This made it difficult to write and to ratify a federal constitution; or perhaps better, the federal was the only kind of constitution that could have been ratified.

Private property and free contracts are like states' rights applied to individuals. The government encourages each individual to govern his own property and to make the agreements under which he lives his social life, and it leads him to trust his own decisions by protecting and guaranteeing them. It ensures to him a measure of self-government and imposes on him the responsibility of maintaining his own freedom. Our government multiplies the power of decision and distributes it to many individuals; to use Rousseau's dictum, it forces him to be free. The result is, of course, a fascinating and sometimes frightening web of ever-changing contracts and statutes, always passing away and coming to be, some falling behind and some jumping ahead of the needs of the whole society. This is the legal aspect of the cherished ideal of equal opportunity for rugged individuals. It accounts for the rootlessness and classlessness of our open society.

Ideally, this kind of freedom presumes the equality of all parties in social arrangements, and their voluntary, uncoerced participation in making and keeping promises, without fraud or deception. This means that the conveyance of property and the agreements for the use of property and for cooperation are made by deliberation and choice, not by accident and force. It is presumed that the points for the insertion of reason and will are widespread and frequent, and that proposals, bargaining, bickering, argument, and persuasion are everywhere and always welcome and effective. Tocqueville noted that the spirit accompanying these habits amounted to a unique genius for voluntary association; sociologists note that we are a socially mobile people; and we all say, with dogmatic defiance of immediate obstacles, that this is a free country, isn't it? This is no doubt the authentic voice of the American common law.

CORPORATION LAW

But there is another consequence of the close association of property and contract in the common law. Property is owned and contracts are kept. The courts, in fulfilling their duties to protect property and to enforce contracts, continually remind the citizen of the mutual obligations that his freedoms imply. When property consists of tools and machines, and when contracts require relatively permanent associations, properties are combined and contracts are generalized. A new power emerges, either by the accumulation of property and contracts around one individual or by the consent of many. In large and risky enterprises, competition and daring may amount to conquest, and the enforcement of contracts may imply imperium. In a developing nation, the government, speaking in a modulated mercantilist style, may wish to promote such enterprise for increasing the wealth of the nation. In consideration for this public advantage, the government, in the guise of a contract, grants a charter of immunity and privilege to a business or industrial company or to individuals who agree to organize such an enterprise. Thus, out of a matrix of the common law, and by a generative act of the government, a new legal entity, a corporation, is born. The generative act is simple, but it is great with consequences. It binds together many generalized contracts into one bundle of laws, which in effect becomes an estate, which is both a person who can make further contracts and a private government that can enforce already-made internal contracts.

The permanent structure of the corporation is composed of permanent general contracts, or bylaws, governing the making, discharging, and termination of other variable contracts, the whole facilitating the buying, hiring, sale, and other conveyance of property, and enhancing the use of property. Thus, a legal structure and power is conferred on business, and this might seem to make the corporation an arm of government. But the notion of free and inviolable contracts is retained, so that the government, far from using the corporation as its instrument or agent, is loathe to regulate it even on behalf of or in protection of the common good. Although a corporation's charter is granted by the legislature or by the executive, the government acts in the style of a court of common law merely to protect property, or to enforce contracts, as if the corporation were a natural person. Needless to say, this is not a stable, well-understood relationship. The government does regulate minimally to maintain competition and to moderate extremes of power. Latterly, the government enters into contracts with the corporation as a party or person, but it is a moot question now whether these contracts are ordinary, or treaties between sovereign governments through which the laws of the government increasingly become laws of the corporation; for example, note the security regulations that accompany contracts for munitions.

The contract-making that is enabled by the charter is of various kinds: contracts with investors, contracts for raw materials, contracts with wholesale and retail companies, contracts with legal firms, wage contracts, contracts with charitable organizations, contracts with consumers. Some of these can be understood as contracts with other corporations that are ostensibly peers or equals with the acting corporation, but many of them are with individuals or obviously weaker and unequal parties. The latter

kinds of contract increasingly strain the conception of free and
equal contract. Power implies influence, and influence connotes
coercion. In order to balance the inequality, the worker organizes
a union to negotiate collective bargains leading to wage contracts; retail associations spring up to bring pressure in contracts
with big corporations. Even the big corporations make agreements or cartels to divide the market and to administer prices,
to moderate if not restrain competition. This would seem to indicate that the contract that establishes a corporation is still a
legal fiction, still stretching the common law to cover somewhat
incorrigible content, whose rate of change and growth does not
abate. The businessman and the industrial manager tend to see
the corporation as a dubious device for accounting and conduct-
ing their affairs, but also as a trap set by the government, which
finds regulation more and more necessary. The corporation invents ways of helping the government in the difficult job of
regulation, or it gets a conscience with regard to its social
responsibilities, or it wonders if it shouldn't emphasize further
its status as private government and imitate the public government by becoming self-governing and accountable to its members.
Public governments all over the world increasingly appear to be
watchdogs and policemen waiting to take over and nationalize
corporations that are not able to discharge their public functions,
or that threaten to hurt rather than help the wealth of the nation.

Although the internal legal structure and both the internal and
external operation of the corporation seem to be wholly constituted and guided by the common law provisions for property
and contract, and although the substance of the corporation
seems to the businessman to be manufacturing, buying and selling, the charter and the seal are at least reminiscent of other
corporate forms that run back in European history through universities, guilds, monasteries, and municipalities to the Roman
family. All these held property and lived in the contracts they
made, but most of them had well-defined purposes for which the
chartered powers were granted and to which the use of property
and contracts was more or less sharply restricted. Most of these
purposes would be recognized as contributions to general human
welfare, not mere survival or advantage of the members of the

corporation. They run to such matters as health, education, morals, and religion; and they imitate professional services. The business corporation is chartered because it contributes to the common wealth of the nation, but its legally stated purpose is restricted to private profit only. Until recently, its board of directors could be sued if they indulged in charity, or made corporate contributions to charity, or to other corporations whose charters stated charitable rather than profitable purposes. The individual citizen was encouraged and protected in his pursuit of happiness both to seek profit in business and to indulge in charity, but the business corporation, a kind of fictive citizen, had to seek only profits. And the legal assignment of no purpose but profit seems to have struck deep into the internal habits of the corporations. The human relations inside the corporations have until recently been strictly business relations, for private profit only. The transactions are buying, selling, hiring, investing, and manufacturing. Courtesy, efficiency, and fair dealing to support these are welcome, but no nonsense is allowed about the firm being one big family, a team, a polity, or a society; and there used to be some distrust of executives and employees going in for this sort of thing in their free time on the grounds that it might lead to a conflict of interest. Business was business, and when business in cases of hardship, calamity, or national emergency temporarily lent itself to charity and welfare, the interval was closed with the other slogan, Business as usual.

Over the long course of history, it would seem that the granting of a charter created the presumption that the corporation and its activities were "touched with public interest"; that its objective purpose, if not its deliberate and conscious intention, was to contribute to the general welfare and the common good. But the extension of the charter privilege to the business corporation would seem to call the presumption into question, or at any rate to minimize its importance. Quite clearly, the common law insurance of property and contract is maintained to secure the individual in his private pursuits, and clearly this is good for a certain degree of peace and order in society. It is not so clear that the strengthening of this security in the law of corporations serves the society as well. The testimony of the organization man

himself seems to indicate that the private corporation is discovering that it is a team, a family, a polity, a society, and that
the welfare of its members, beyond the limits of business
success, and the welfare of the surrounding and supporting society
are its highest purpose. Corporation law no longer is restraining
corporations from offering goodwill in tangible forms for the
purpose of creating a climate favorable to business, although
the lawyers know that this involves a broad reading of the
chartered purposes of the corporations.

Corporation theory would seem to be a central and complicated
study in legal fictions, following the slow and cumulative developments in court cases, with very little help from statutory
legislation. The corporation for centuries has been called a fictive
person; it has for a shorter time been a fictive sovereign. The
source of the first fiction seems to be in common law; the source
of the latter in the legislative or executive charter. In certain
conjunctions of circumstances and operations, the corporation
seems to be a veritable monarchy floating freely in a republican
fluid. Various kinds of corporations, including the business corporation, have become governments or arms of governments.
But all these aspects and appearances are only fictive interpretations and analogies with familiar traditional polities; they aid
the courts in dealing with cases, and the lawyers in pleading
cases. The fictions have not been assimilated in the body of either
common or statutory law. They stimulate thought but do not
substantially legitimize practice.

It is difficult to identify the educative function of the corporation and to estimate its influence in our society. But some such
attempts are being made inside the corporations themselves at
present, and there is a growing body of serious study originating
not only in congressional committees but in academic and foundation projects. Many leads are being followed, borrowed mainly
from sociology and psychology, and to a lesser degree from
economics and political science. Andrew Hacker's work, "Politics
and the Corporation," is a good example of the last, but it deals
with learning as the process of forming opinion, rather than as
the making of political understanding. Perhaps a lead from
Montesquieu's dictum will supplement Hacker's technical view:

virtue is the principle of republican government, and education is its source. Virtue in this context means political virtue in the citizen, not merely patriotism but an intelligent, energetic concern for all parts of the common good; and education means not only acquisition of the moral and intellectual virtues in formal schools but the continued cultivation and increase of these in civic life.

Our question then becomes, What habits essential to a self-governed polity are initiated and preserved and enhanced by the citizen's membership in the business corporation? We have seen that the private holding of property and the enjoyment of its use through free contract-making under the common law has not only developed the technological, industrial, and commercial system; it has emancipated and remade the modern man's mind so that it moves rapidly, tolerantly, and efficiently in the new matter-of-fact world. In addition to work and skill, the pragmatic world has enlisted general literacy; and this has made possible the acquisition of reading, writing, and arithmetic by more people than ever before. What has the integration of property and contracts into the corporation added?

Inside the firm itself—that is, the manufacturing establishment —the organization of business has more and more studied and disciplined itself in the arts of management, the management of men. The control of machines in a workshop entails the control of men. There was a stage when the critical observer of this development predicted that the machines would manage the men, but the study and discipline of human nature has turned the tide; men have learned to manage themselves as well as the machines. And there have been at least two clear ways to look at this process of man adjusting to the exigencies of the machine: at worst, he seems to fit as a biochemical link in the production line; at best, his power and skill seem multiplied by the ratio that multiplies his handpower into horsepower, and into ever-increasing productivity. We need a new word for the educational result: handicraft has now been replaced by "machinocraft," the skills that make a man master of his functional relation to the machine.

The other dimension of management involves the relation of

man to man on the job, horizontally, as it were. This requires another relation—vertical—of workers to managers, shop stewards, or foremen, and of managers to executives. Management implies both technological adjustment and personnel adjustment. The corporation claims that it has initiated, trained, and established a new profession—management; and that this is its contribution to culture, not to say politics.

Whatever the effect of this so-called managerial revolution on society as a whole may be, whether superficial or deep, whether predominate or merely pervasive, the presence and power of the pattern in the firm itself is real and decisive. Its roots lie in the original companies of simple ownership, where the boss ruled the hired help. The professional manager has more subtle arts than bossing, but these arts are limbs on the old tree; in political terms, the shift has been from monarchy to oligarchy, and the managers are engineering or financial oligarchs. Some would have it believed that the stockholders are an elective constituency for the managers, and that they are highly functional because they hold the power of the purse. But this is so extremely inaccurate in terms of voting and nonvoting stock, and in terms of proxy voting, that the argument about it ends in almost proving that the relation between stockholder and company amounts to canceling all the attributes of private property except nominal ownership, a fiction that still directs the flow of dividends, if and when the management declares them. The stockholder is pleased to let good management administer property and contracts for him. The manager manages or manipulates the so-called private rights and powers of the stockholder. The stockholder holds a ballot, can initiate a suit against directors, and can sell his stock, but none of these powers is understood or used as an instrument of control. Tacitly, by common consent, the power to manage the business and to manipulate consent has been delegated to the management.

Around the firm there is an environment of contractual associations—some of them organized, as are the labor unions; some of them, like customers, not organized—to bring bargaining pressure or to demand accountability. The degree to which the contractual relations are mediums of control, and the degree to which the corporate charter creates an imperial power over such environments and confers a second-class membership on such associates, are not matters of clear definition either in law or in the minds of the managers. The bundle of rights and privileges implicit in the corporate environment has not been sorted and ordered explicitly; the common-law cases that arise touch only the single strands, not the fabric of the implicit organism. It is only when the individual attends to the corporate fabric in which he lives that he realizes the pervasive influence of the corporations in society as a whole.

It is now said that the process of deliberation that leads to the decisions of directors and managers could be carried on as well or better by computers. Highly elaborate data are prepared and submitted for consideration, and the combination of these emerges as the decision. The introduction of business machines is easy, because the human beings have been habituated and accustomed to using their minds as if they were machines. It is not only the processes of manufacture that are being automated; management is also automatic. This is obviously an extrapolation from current practice, and is no doubt exaggeration, but it is a suggestion, verifiable by other kinds of observation, of the character and quality of the educative function of the body of corporation law, and the practice that seems to flow from it.

CONSTITUTIONAL LAW

Perhaps at this point we ought to take a closer look at the processes by which law teaches those who make and obey it. The oldest and most popular jurisprudence has said that law is a rule or command of reason promulgated by an authority for the common good. A parody on this is: a law is a command by the more powerful to coerce the weaker. American jurisprudence is famous for a more pragmatic view, that laws are rules agreed to by the people to further their social purposes. No doubt, each of these implies a recognizable theory and a method of education. But there is another dictum, that laws are questions asked by God, history, nature, or society to be answered by men individually and collectively. This formulation penetrates to the heart of human freedom. It says that no law, not even divine law, cancels out human freedom; the answer can be yes or no, or something else. It also tacitly warns of the consequences of the answer. But primarily it forces the human being to think about ends, or purposes. Law therefore provides a kind of complete Socratic teaching and learning, so that under self-government men can teach themselves, if they will learn to make good, questioning laws.

Within this notion of law, corporation law has been and still is asking important questions. Its reticence about the purpose of the business corporation appears to be withholding an answer, until it is found in the persons who so organize their activities. It is asking a big question about greed and the general welfare, about the citizen's concern for the common good. So far, the answer has been incoherent and dark, like the system of free enterprise itself and the various attempts to tame it. It may be that the question has been unanswerable as a whole until now; it may be that the integration, now imminent, of the technological system into one manageable thing has been the missing part that now makes the question intelligible. If the industrial, economic, and technological development of the country has been the implicit answer of the profit-seeking corporation to the question concerning its purposes, this answer is now turning into another question; namely, what is that development for? Common law in property and contracts cannot give the answer to the questions that it has raised. We must look to the powers of the various constitutions in our federal system to see if they have raised, are now raising, or can raise the relevant questions for us to answer.

There is a curious ambiguity in the tradition of political thought in the West from Aristotle to the present. Aristotle says that "the state comes into existence, originating in the bare needs of life, and continuing in existence for the sake of the good life." This statement presumes that the state arose to meet the bare or minimum needs of human life, and that it normally goes on to discover ends and invent means for the sake of a maximum "best" of human life. It is not a complete state until it has done this. Historically, something like this seems to have been the goal of ancient political as well as educational life. The long European

experience in political life up to the seventeenth century seems
to have found this goal illusory, therefore dangerous and vicious.
For a century beginning with the British Revolution and continuing through the French and American Revolutions, there was
a great political debate that seems to have concluded that that
state is best that limits its aims to the "bare needs of life." The
state that wishes to survive will not invest its energies in, or allow
its responsibilities to extend to, the means and ends of the good
life. There was not complete unanimity in this conclusion, but
enough preponderance of opinion to last until our time.

It would seem that the American Constitution was written to
keep the controversy alive; that is, to allow readings that will
justify those who wish a minimal government and also those who
wish a maximal government, or even a government within which
both readings are combined to continue the theoretical and practical debate by checks and balances. The Constitution and the
laws that are made pursuant to it keep a dialogue of questions
and answers going. Government, for us, is a continuous dialectic
about the means and ends of common life.

To some, the system of checks and balances appears as an
array of baffles to stop any impulsive and irrational power drive,
a defense of conservatism. To others, it is just the opposite, an
incitement to agitation and the building of pressure and power
blocs to balance the checks. To some, it is just irritating or futile
red tape. But what these see as a "conspiracy" has resulted from
many considerations that lie deeper than any tactical advantage
or disadvantage. One, and perhaps the deepest, of these would be
the essential practical problem that goes with the fundamental
theoretical problem of democracy. It had been said and believed
that monarchy is the best form of government, because the
common good can become the general will of a people only
through a single person, half-prophet and half-hero, perhaps
chosen by God and accepted as king by the people, and
clothed with office and its facilities. Legislation is a kind of
soothsaying, not delegable to the many common men. When this
office had been so often misused and turned into tyranny, and
recourse had been had to the many common men, there had to be
an alternative political process appropriate to the function. The

many interests, convictions, opinions, and reasons of many men had to be given due process by persuasion and deliberation. Otherwise, no general will would be generated to approximate the common good. Persuasion and deliberation had to be formalized by devices, like *Robert's Rules of Order*, but also multiplied, disseminated, and learned by the population. For this purpose, degrees and measures of local government would have had to be invented and set up if they had not already existed. And these essentially political units had to retain or defend their degrees of independence. Therefore, between the degrees and units of local government, town, county, and state, there had to be checks and balances; and these amounted to any individual falling under double, triple, and quadruple sovereignties or jurisdictions. Even drafters of colonial constitutions had to take account of the checks and balances that these units entailed. Interest, opinion, and conviction underwent an ordeal by persuasion and deliberation concerning local matters, but where local matters presupposed larger matters, representatives were chosen to belong to higher units where their opinions, more or less informed by the lower local process, would in turn be put through a similar trial by persuasion and deliberation. The representative was clothed with the formality and immunity of office in order to clarify and protect the function. The deliberative body of the higher unit had to be restrained from interfering with the merely local powers of the lower unit. Here were more checks and balances, and the principle that later became states' rights; all powers not delegated to the higher authority were retained by the lower authority.

Geographical locality seems now to be too simple a principle of the division of political work, but there was plausibility in it in our early years, because of the agricultural base and a comparatively homogeneous population. We have not kept up with European reexamination of the proper divisions of a more complex society and economy, and their articulation within the political process. Our inattention to political craftsmanship has been overcompensated by sociological thought, with its all-pervasive doctrine of radical social pluralism, which glories in the coexistence of many self-styled independent social units under a new brand of philosophical anarchism. This amounts to the

diversion of vital thought from the political process, and hence
the unreality of much of our local and national politics.

But the geographical paradigm of political division and articulation, expanding as the country expanded, has been the base on
which the original constitutional and statutory structure was
built. Its quite remarkable functional success has borne out a
principle that the Founding Fathers learned from Montesquieu.
Montesquieu had noted that large countries had been successfully
governed only by imperial monarchies, and that only small countries or cities had had successful republican governments. In
countries that had the proper basis in political virtue and in
self-education, he had proposed that a republican government
could be successful over a large area and population if it articulated its many and possibly diverse parts according to the federal
principle. In essence, this principle calls for the independence of
the local units and its articulation by treaties between units that
become also substantive components of their own internal laws.
This, when carried out to its logical conclusion, means that
sovereignty is divided: first, there are separate sovereignties distributed among the geographical units, as in local governments;
and second, between the local and the national governments,
with definite distinctions and powers to fit the specific functions
of the lower units, and general functions that belong properly
to the higher units. The articulation of such a structure was, of
course, the task of the Philadelphia Constitutional Convention;
the Revolutionary War had already forced an attempt of this kind
in the Articles of Confederation, which helped to define the
problem. The resulting Constitution appears as a highly skilled
job of making the distinctions between federal, state, and local
functions. But it indicates that the authors were also aware that
a developing country would generate new functions that would
have to be sorted between local units and the federal levels. The
power and procedure of amendment was provided for.

The Founding Fathers also learned another principle from
Montesquieu, the division of powers. Montesquieu, with his
empirical roving eye, had noted that when the legislative and
executive powers are in the same official hands, there is a loss of
liberty due to the consolidation of power. Laws confer powers

of a general kind, which, if they are not interpreted by an intelligence that penetrates the concrete case and circumstance, become mechanical and tyrannical. Similarly, if the judges are merely the agents of the legislature or the executive, and not independent and locally informed intelligences, there is loss of liberty and justice. He therefore laid it down for any government, monarchical or republican, that liberty required that there be division and some degree of insulation among the legislative, executive, and judicial powers; and that these divisions should be pervasive throughout the governmental structure. Again, the Constitution is the embodiment of this principle. In fact, because of these two principles, the federal and the division of powers, the Constitution is recognized all over the world as a model demonstration in political science.

But the purpose of the demonstration goes further than these two principles of political science. "It has been frequently remarked that it seems to have been reserved to the people of this country, by their conduct and example, to decide the important question, whether societies are really capable or not of establishing good government from reflection and choice, or whether they are forever destined to depend for their political constitutions on accident and force." We shall not understand the system of checks and balances in the federal system and in the division of powers if we fail to see it as ordered to the end that Alexander Hamilton formulates in this statement. The system is elaborate and delicate for a high and difficult end. It should not be seen as a doctrinaire or ceremonial embroidery to give republican processes a hypocritical and merely formal majesty. As the source of republican government is education, so may republican government become the means of high human education. It took a very peculiar man to see, in the gathering crisis of his time, as far as we have seen in this direction. Fifty years after the writing and the ratification of the Constitution, Calhoun thought himself through the immediate problem before him and the country to what might have been the keystone of the arch, and his thought sharpens the divisions and the articulations of the whole governmental structure. That his interpretation and his proposals were not accepted should not justify us in neglecting the insight.

He was one of the first to see what we now see as power corrupting government by reflection and choice, and back of this corruption as its cause was not merely the industrial development but also, politically more relevant, the loose or broad reading of the Constitution. He saw the great dialectical process, by which opinion and interests were led and educated to express the general will and the common good, vitiated, interrupted, and destroyed by petty political machinery for getting a numerical majority to decide the issues of prosperity, peace, freedom, and justice. The political parties had already demonstrated that numerical majorities could be manufactured by accident and force, and by their more subtle manipulations. The more educational processes of persuasion and deliberation could be bypassed and canceled out by the machine and the steamroller, as they were later called. In many matters, decision by majority vote still functioned as a handy ad hoc device and did no harm; but where power, either economic or political, was involved, as it was in the extreme in the issues that were leading to the Civil War, the danger to the republican political process was mortal.

Calhoun might have played, and possibly did play, the game of numerical majority, the numbers game in politics, but he also saw implied in the Constitution the rules for another, better game that he proposed should be recognized and implemented. He called it the game of the concurrent majority. It called for a preliminary decision in the case of any issue—whether it was to be decided by the numerical majority, or whether it should be decided by something approaching unanimity, which at least would ensure that the minority interest and conviction would be included in the persuading and deciding process. It should be noted that minority opinions are sometimes minority opinions merely because they have been smashed or chiseled down to their minimal dimensions by nonpolitical processes. The procedure for constitutional amendment took account of this and called for special treatment, including the increase in the required majority to something approaching unanimity.

Not getting much attention from those party politicians who were operating the machines that produced numerical majorities, Calhoun made the proposal that is now popularly associated with

his name without the context of reasons he gave for it. He proposed that the minority nullify the decisions of a numerical
majority, if those decisions ignored vital convictions and interests.
Such nullification would indeed call for disobedience of the law,
but its aim would be reconsideration for concurrent majority
decision. He asked for the formal recognition of such a right and
the legitimizing of the procedure that would follow it.

The usual current criticism of Calhoun is that he was too intellectual, and this epithet, like "egghead," is used as if it meant
that he was not acquainted with political reality. He is also
associated with the secession of the South, as an early instigator
of that rebellion. His answer to such a charge would have been
that the secession of the South was the political catastrophe that
his proposal was framed to prevent. The spirit and principle of his
proposal are nearer the principle of unanimity as it is practiced
by the Quakers. On unimportant matters the Quaker business
meeting finds it easy to come to unanimous agreement, although
the preceding discussion may show that not all members are
equally convinced; but on important matters there is unanimous
agreement not to make a decision as long as any "choose to
object." There is here a concern about freedom of conscience and
thought, but there is also a determination that both conscience
and thought shall be informed and disciplined by common life
and mutual persuasion. It is this logic that Calhoun was following,
although he was not a Quaker. He wanted the government to
maintain the educational process that he thought the Constitution
protected, not only in its provisions for amendment but also by the
federal principle and the division of powers. He wanted to see
the formal recognition of the power of mutual veto between parts
of the government commensurate with the issues that had to be
weighed and decided by reflection and choice.

The reasoning that went into the determination of the elementary units and the superior parts of the body politic, and into
the formal relations between the units and between the units and
the superior parts, is fragile and precarious, as most reasoning
about liberty seems to be. Much of it was not new. Depart-
mentalization of government from local element to central
authority is common to all forms of government by law. Repre-

sentation, although it was not easy to invent, is a commonplace of all democracies above a certain size. But the authors of the Constitution emphasized and maximized the separateness and independence of the parts in a new and radical way. The Constitutional Convention probably would not have used the words *nullification, negation,* and *mutual veto* as Calhoun did, but Calhoun was following a logic inherent in their thought when he thus described the operations of the constitutional provisions. This is confirmed in the implied operations of the lower levels of government, as when the township even today objects to the encroachment of state laws on local prerogatives, or objects to any meddling by the selectmen in the affairs of the school committee. The division of powers is not merely the boundary line between jurisdictions; the doctrine of checks and balances created gaps between jurisdictions, gaps that could be closed only by the formal processes of mutual persuasion and resulting unanimous agreement, never by a one-way edict or command.

Part of the motivation for making such gaps comes from the fear that the Founding Fathers had of elaborate and precise tables of organization through which kings had governed empires by dividing and ruling the provinces and the colonies. In these, the precise articulations were mediums for the rapid and unchecked exercise of centralized power. The new American nation would need elaborate and precise definition of its parts and their functions, but the danger of tyranny in such an organization could be checked and liberty protected by valves and detours that would run interest and will through channels of persuasion and deliberation. The gaps with their valves and channels would then be the loci where intelligence and wisdom could be engaged, and in turn where the public mind would be exercised and lifted to the level of the common good. The gaps in the legal system would mark the stages in the political process where the laws should be seen as questions put to officers and citizens for their considered answers.

An example would be a bill providing for a federal income tax. Government expenses have exceeded the income from tariffs, and some new tax source is sought. A bill comes before the House of Representatives, and a similar bill before the Senate.

The House sends it to a committee for expert study or for hearings; it is brought back to the floor with revisions and is debated there with special emphasis on its "political incidence"—in lowest terms, whether the congressman who votes for it and thus touches the pocketbooks of his constituents can be reelected. The parallel bill in the Senate is sent to committee, where it is submitted to experts who will find out what the influence of the income tax will be on the economy of the country, and it comes back to the floor, where the possibility of the income tax being used as a power to destroy or aid business or to redistribute wealth is debated. The two bills are brought to votes in the respective chambers and are passed, but with significant differences in the rates and scales and in the methods of filing returns and making collections. There is a conference between committees of the two chambers, with new argument and substantial revisions, but final agreement. Then the bill goes to the President, who refers it to the relevant departments of the executive branch. There is a veto, and the bill is returned to the two houses and passed over the veto.

Now it is an act of Congress to be administered and enforced by the executive branch through its relevant bureaus, presumably by the officials who had advised the President to veto it. The difficulties that had occasioned the veto now have to be dealt with by interpretation of the act or the invention of executive machinery, and the reflection and choice of the executive branch and its parts are brought into effect. It is then channeled back down through the local agents of the executive department, who by trial and error work out the details that fit.

Finally, the taxpayer brings his judgment to bear on the fitness or unfitness of the law to his particular case, and the anomalies are referred to the courts, where the cases are pleaded before judges, with or without juries. Difficult cases may be appealed and may end up in the Supreme Court.

This hypothetical course for a federal measure has crossed many gaps where powers are specifically separated. It might have been stopped at any of several of the gaps; it *was* stopped, temporarily, even in this comparatively smooth passage. The stops are made to allow, encourage, and in some cases force an increment of reflection, a deepening of persuasion, and a public dialectic for informing and enlightening the citizen's as well as the official mind. It is possible that the issues and the causes thus generated will raise the level of discussion above the means and ends of the government to the level of constitutional amendment, and even beyond that, to the causes of civil war.

Actually, we are of two minds as we watch and participate in processes of this kind. We like to think that the essential process is persuasion and reasonable deliberation, and that the gaps controlled by specified checks and balances are filled with the kinds of reflection and choice that refine and weigh interest and opinion, and that the decisions are just and freely accepted. We are vaguely aware also that this process is a learning process by which we together and individually acquire and share knowledge of ourselves and the world.

But we also know that the gaps often appear to be vacuums into which chance, force, and organized interests are drawn before the reasonable process gains our attention. Tocqueville discerned a national habit already formed at his time. He saw the democratic concern for private interest and opinion struggling to understand itself as a political factor, and he thought he saw the American solution in the processes by which minority opinion and interest built itself into majority interest and opinion. The test of the validity of an opinion was its power to generate majority approval and commitment to it. The American citizen came to believe very quickly under the democratic system that the common good consisted in private opinion getting itself rightly understood. We have had other illustrious expressions for this national trait; for instance, Justice Holmes's dictum that the validity of an idea is tested by its power to survive in the marketplace of opinion. Tocqueville saw in this a powerful trend to conformity of thought and opinion. The pragmatists have often allowed the full test by practice to thin out into a social pragmatism that is almost identical with salesmanship and propaganda. An idea is true if it fits the prevailing set of ideas. This reduces persuasion and deliberation to the most superficial, quick processes by which a majority vote is achieved, and we have some familiar American expressions for this: logrolling, passing the bacon, the steamroller.

These expressions imply something besides the propagation of

ideas. They imply the accumulation and concentration of power of
all kinds—personal, economic, psychological. Politics truly becomes the marketplace only where everything is up for sale, and
let the best man and his interests win. Politics in this style, however, becomes the making of deals. The man who has made the
best deals finds it easy to make more deals, and the deals alto-
gether build an organization or machine. In a curious way, the
political parties seem to have imitated the corporations. The deal
is an informal, privately enforced contract; money and personal
favors are property; charm and prestige confer a kind of imitation
of chartered authority; there is an inherent tendency to monopoly
of politically effective opinion that generates power; membership
in the party is a vaguely defined status, fictively determined by
registration at the polls but actually defined by current operations
such as getting out the vote at elections, or distributing and receiving patronage in the form of appointive offices or privileges
from the bureaus. Actual party policies, either those that are
formulated as propaganda for party platforms and campaign
speeches, or those that determine deals, emanate from a very small
minority manipulating goods, interests, and principles. The political parties are para-political governments combining in complicated ways a feudal and a democratic style, the latter now
explicitly imitating the advertising methods of the big corporations.

It is these organizations that stand guard at all the gaps in the
constitutional processes of government. Wherever reflection and
choice are legitimately invited, some party agent or instrument
stands ready and alert to inject power and privilege. We might
get more efficient, perhaps not better, government if the political
parties openly organized themselves in the manner of the Communist Party in Russia, and accepted the full responsibility for
using the constitutional processes for its own ends.

But there is a more incisive view of these matters. It would
appear that the original constitutional provisions are not adequate
to many of the quasi-political developments of our society. The
industrial revolution introduced and continues to introduce technological systems and financial institutions that swell and burst
through the old political forms. The corporations take over and

set up their own para-political organizations. Professional men cultivate their activities, and when they become powerful enough, they seek legitimacy in associations. Similarly, political parties have developed to fill what looks to the ordinary practical man like a vacuum of power and authority in the constituted government. Their legitimacy is only partly recognized by the government, and the power that is left over, or overflows, ramifies and grows without definite restraint. The result is that a dynamic society has split splinters off the block of sovereignty, and the government proper is surrounded by pseudo-sovereignties.

Each of these independent centers of decision, as the pluralists like to call them, takes on a peculiar kind of life. It is partly parasitical, since it gets some authority by its charter or licensing power from the government, and its independence is such that it would not survive without its borrowed authority. But its operation also takes on a piratical style; it intercepts the flow of the government's grants of privilege and patronage and distributes the resulting goods and services to its own clientele. In return, it offers its expert advice and its facilities to the government bureaus. Each of these groups maintains offices in Washington and in the state capitals, and the national and state party organizations serve as clearinghouses for this voluminous traffic.

The Greeks must have understood this para-political phenomenon. There is eloquent evidence that they did in Aristophanes's comedy, *The Birds*. The birds decide that they can accomplish their political destiny only if they set up their own kingdom, the kingdom of heaven, as they call it. They decide that their special skills and capacities would enable them to do this by setting up a barricade in the sky, a barricade between men and gods. They could thus intercept weather, and trade in prayers, favors, and messages between heaven and earth. If they get into trouble in carrying out this plan, they can make terms with either gods or men against the third party and thus get a secure political status.

The comic elaboration and outcome of this plan need not concern us. But there is a speculative moral in it. The political parties have become relatively permanent artificial satellites in our political space. They have set up and manned barricades that screen whatever influences emanate from heavenly or natural wisdom and filter into human reflection and choice. They mix the ideal residue of the screening process with whatever they have in hand of interest and force and feed it into the electoral, legislative, and executive receptacles through campaigns, hearings, lobbies. They confuse thought with propaganda and deals with consent, and use their contributions to ensure reelection and perpetuate prestige, office, and power.

We like to distinguish our politics from European politics, and to point with pride to our avoidance of the extremes of many splinter parties or dictatorships. We explain the difference by our genius for getting on without doctrines, ideologies; in fact, without ideas. It is ironic that we should criticize their faithfulness to the rational techniques of government that are demonstrated in our constitution, and that we should congratulate ourselves on our default in this respect. The European parties distinguish between ideas and interests, proceed to seek wisdom in various directions and from various sources, and then bring them to bear on the republican process. The truths they find are embarrassingly many and sometimes hard to face and bring to the point of decision. It may be that, although the problems and the realities that they reflect are many and hard to solve, the Europeans are learning more by a perverse intellectuality than we are by our anti-intellectualism.

SUMMARY

This paper began with a question and a hypothesis. The question was whether our society has in itself, quite apart from its institutions of learning proper, a principle and operation of self-education. The hypothesis was that law is such a principle, that law is the teaching principle in the self-educating process. The hypothesis helps to make the question definite and perhaps answerable. Within the narrow limits of my understanding, I have tried to make the question more definite by limiting my consideration to three kinds of law, the common law of property and contracts, corporation law, and constitutional law. These species of law are not exhaustive categories. They may not even be cardinal, the hinges upon which the body of law swings. In this short account, the omissions and the ramifications that have not been followed are many and weighty. But for what it is worth a summary must be made.

It would seem that the lively presence of the common law in a colonial country developing into a nation through the stages of the industrial revolution has been most important and consequential. Private property and free contracts enabled, guided, criticized, and legalized the industrial development of the country. The law in regard to these matters raised, through court procedures, the questions of purpose and method that the citizens answered both in the courts and in their day-to-day practical habits. These answers, in their accumulation, have become the unwritten charter of what we call free enterprise.

The habits and understandings that have developed under this use and development of the common law are recognizable in the character and temperament of both the frontier and the great city. Spontaneous individualism and mutual aid, curiosity and inventiveness, matter-of-factness and experimentalism, pragmatic adventurousness and competition, equality and fair play, compromise and deals, self-reliance and compensation, a faith in the infinite potentialities of the individual and the unlimited progress of society—these are the moral and intellectual habits, the virtues and the vices, that make the American character. Their operation in the context of business and technology is ubiquitous and clearly recognized under the aegis of the common law of property and contracts. The only reference to this basic law in the Constitution is in its laconic commitment to protect property and enforce contracts.

But the application of the common law to the steady and massive transformations of the industrial revolution stretched and transformed its meanings. From tools to machines and factories, from crafts to manufactures and machinofactures, from land and money to credit—these transitions mixed property and contracts and recombined them into new associations of men and organizations of both men and machines. Bundles of technology and law became organisms with lives of their own, concentrations of power that the government had to recognize.

Charters were conferred on them so that their power might be legitimate, so that private enterprise might serve the common good, or at least not damage it. The business corporations, thus generated from private property and free contracts, chartered and sealed by the government, had two natures. One of these, derived from the power to make contracts, made the corporation a fictive legal person. The other, "touched with public interest," made the corporation a private government. This offspring of business and government had a long, independent, but protected youth; until recently it has not been required to respect and undertake its public obligations. Now it is showing signs of growing up and examining its accumulated powers and skills to fulfill its as-yet undefined purposes. It is trying to discover the invisible thread that has from its birth tied it to the public welfare.

The corporate form again, as often in the past, is asking the questions of its members that may lead them to discover the purpose of their organization and incorporation. As yet it has had little help from government proper beyond an intermittent disciplinary regulation. Its members know that they have the industrial burden to carry for the society, and that its past education has developed the skills and organization for doing this; it has even developed the traditional skills of oligarchic government so useful in the management of affairs and the manipulation of opinion. It is quite sure now that these are parts or intimations of the common good. It is by no means certain that it will learn its next lesson; it is in great need of the laws that could bring it from adolescence to adulthood.

One of the reasons that the corporation is in danger of regressing to permanent adolescence is that the Constitution itself has a split personality. It was drafted by an extraordinary group of near-geniuses, who were ambitious to give this country an extraordinary government. Their aim was to transcend the analogies of political science that had accumulated in European history: the analogy of the machine, of the organism, of the natural family. They wished to fashion the government in the image of the mind, of their own well-endowed and well-trained minds. Representation, division of powers, and the federal principle are faculties of the human mind writ large. The Founding

Fathers seemed to assume that these faculties, once established, would develop themselves by proper exercise. For fifty years their expectations appear to have been justified. Persons like Justice Marshall in the judiciary, persons like Jefferson in the presidency, persons like Calhoun and Webster in the legislature sought out, discovered, and expounded the implied powers of the Constitution; and by their practice of the powers they realized many purposes in the institutions that they built. It is in those years that this country became the teacher of jurisprudence and political science to the world, and the teaching is still going on.

But the Civil War was something of a tragic catastrophe. Politics had followed the rules and conducted the debates provided by the principles of the Constitution. Deep deliberation and heavy choices had been supported and carried out by the citizens and their agents in the government. The energies of freedom had developed power; power had concentrated, as power does when it is blind; much of the fast-growing country had become colonial, not to European empires, but to the empire in its own country. This led to what has been called by Charles Beard the second American Revolution, and this became a Civil War. Force, violence, and terrible accident took the place of reflection, deliberation, and choice. The great tragic figure in this national drama was Abraham Lincoln, and the mystery of his ordeal still broods over the Constitution and its spirit.

James Bryce says in effect that the Civil War broke the backbone of our politics. Federalism provided a theory and a mechanism for defining and presenting the great questions of our society for the reflection and choice of the nation, its people, and its magistrates; it failed to deal properly with the issues of the conflict that then became irrepressible, and the spirit of the federation died. This means that the delicate structure of the Constitution was put aside and new mechanisms were improvised to carry on public affairs. These mechanisms imitated the forms of common law that had adapted themselves to the energies and accidents of the industrial development of the country. Power and deals took the place of property and contracts, and the parties thus generated became the agents that used the constitutional forms for their own ends. Management of great and small affairs on both the national and local levels, and the manipulation of opinion by political rhetoric, became the style of a new profession, the "politician," and the electorate turned over its responsibility to the parties.

The constitutional structure had been devised to educate the public mind and to bring the citizen to the understanding and love of the common good. The education of the American community was to be through its politics, so that each man, because he was learning to govern himself, would become a better man than he could become by his own efforts. On the level of business and technology, the common law has aided him to accomplish this. On the level of organization, corporation law has discovered and developed new human capacities. But on the level of constitutional self-government, there is confusion and frustration and a consequent regression to primitive political forms and to the mores of the marketplace.

But the story is not finished yet, and the questions that history and our legal system are now asking us to answer cannot be ignored or dodged.

3

WHAT EVERY MAN SHOULD KNOW: LAW

ABOUT two years ago, Henry Luce came to a meeting of the Consultants to the Fund for the Republic with a letter that he begged to read to his colleagues. The topic of the meeting was the common defense and foreign policy, one of the tough packages of basic issues that the Fund has pledged itself to clarify and pass on to the great conversation that is the substance of our political life. The letter had come from a *Life* magazine correspondent in Hong Kong, and it was asking for clear formulation of the basic American proposition to answer the stentorian voice of Russia on the Asian front of the great battle for men's minds. The voices in the conference room of the Fund were not stentorian, and I remember my own weak defensive remark that Mr. Luce was asking us to improvise an ideology, or at best a royal lie.

It appears that Mr. Luce, disappointed and disgusted with our response, went back to his office, chose a member of the *Life* staff, and freed him from his editorial duties to write a book in answer to the request from Hong Kong. At any rate, Max Ways wrote a book entitled *Beyond Survival,* which formulates the reasons why the request cannot be met in the near future. The American Republic is in no state to answer the question because it has not yet made up its mind. Mr. Ways sums up his reasons in

Presented for discussion to the staff of the Center for Democratic Studies in 1960.

53

a resounding phrase: the body politic has lost its resonance. There
are, as always, many stentorian voices, and there are many atten-
tive listeners, but the medium for transmitting intelligible political
thought has been lost. There is irony in this message from *Time,
Life,* and *Fortune* in the age of communication, but Mr. Ways
surmounts the irony. In effect, he says that each of the pictures we
circulate carries 10,000 confused words; and the desideratum, the
missing link, is a public philosophy, a popular jurisprudence that
would give us some notion of the natural law that would order
our thought. Without such resonance, neither leaders nor responsible citizens will be recognized. Both thought and action will be
frustrated.

Mr. Ways cites John Foster Dulles as such an unrecognized
and frustrated leader. He was one of the men of our time who
by training and experience had not lost a hold on the public
philosophy of the previous generation. He could make moral and
legal judgments that would once have been effective in national
and world opinion. But in the new circumstances there was no
resonance, no response, and no rally. The public literally did not
know what he was talking about. Without resonance, his own
intelligence was shortened, and his acts had little dramatic echo.
He officially withdrew into himself; even his subtle negotiations
were reduced to brinkmanship. Even his traditional words—
justice, durable peace, and *free world*—were degraded. These
words were not merely his words; they are our words, the names
of our common good.

Even if we do not agree with Mr. Ways's estimate of the person,
we have to admit the irony and the mystery of this phenomenon.
We have all the technical aids we need for the maintenance of
political resonance, not only the giant presses for newspapers and
magazines such as *Life,* not only the electronic multipliers of free
speech and free press in movies, radio, and television, but also
the great organizers of advertising and propaganda supported
and operated by giant finance and plentiful skill. But there is a
deadness in the speech, in the writing, and in the pictures; and
every attempt to revive them results in the degradation of words
and the ironic ambiguity of pictures, and the many other
irrelevant noises of communication. The scene reminds us of the

remark that Ruskin is said to have made when he was asked to comment on the completion of the British-Indian cable: "What have we to say to India?"

For those who are not absorbed or hypnotized by mass communications there is a great loneliness, and in place of resonance of the political kind there is a wish and demand for ideology, even if the ideology is merely the inverted mirror image of foreign opiums of the people. Some of the lies that we manufacture for ourselves are deliberate imitative lies: the desperate crisis, the cold war, the battle for men's mind, totalitarianism and the omnipotence of the dictator, the conspiracies without and within, encirclements and containments, liberations and retaliations, free enterprise and godless peoples. But these royal lies are not really identifiable and manageable, not only because some of them are justifiable attempts to simplify and communicate the vital and complex issues of the time but also because they rush in to take the place of the lie in the soul, our radical ignorance. As always, some of this ignorance is due to intellectual and moral laziness, but far more of it is incorrigible even by the best and most active minds. We have made a technology and a civilization that we do not and will not soon understand. There never was a time when lifelong universal learning was more needed as the foundation and goal of our collective life.

PERSUASION

The notion of political resonance that I have borrowed from Max Ways contains an analogy, a vivid, versatile image of the political community bounded by city walls, within which the voice of town crier or of the political orator can be heard everywhere at once. As the city-state grew to the larger city without walls, the operating heart of the community was compacted and walled within a meeting hall or in a house of parliament where the life and death of the political voice depended upon the acoustical conditions. Too little resonance could stop the political process; too much resonance resulted in the confusion of tongues. Acoustical metaphors abound in the language of politics. Votes are voices, the speaker takes the floor, the officer speaks from the chair, the

committee holds a hearing, the clerk opens the court by intoning
oyez, the government silences the opposition, the candidate gets
on the beam, and the elected representative gets in tune with his
constituency.

The electronic extension and multiplication of sounds and
sights seem to have brought a literal-mindedness into political
speech and narrowed the range of appeal. The voices of the
people no longer sound like the voice of God. Politics looks more
and more like the technical control of human behavior by a
computer issuing its solutions to our problems through a loud-
speaker. The voice of Stentor allows the infinite expansion of the
political community, but we are not sure that he has anything to
say that we want to hear.

But perhaps I kill the metaphor. I should like to try to revive
the political theme by appealing to another image. I want to say
that the lifeblood of the body politic is persuasion. The body
politic has a structure of bones, flesh, organs, tissues, and cells,
but all these are built and kept alive by the circulation of a highly
organized bloodstream of interests and opinions that nourish and
purge the living system. The process is subtle and pervasive, a
building–up and a tearing–down that amounts to a true metab-
olism. Persuasion is this vital process in the body politic.

A great deal of the political genius of the Greeks, their wisdom
and skill in making and carrying on politics, came from the conjugation of one of their favorite words, the verb *to persuade*. It is
the favorite verb of Thucydides in the *Peloponnesian War* and of
Plato in the *Republic,* books written to remind all future men of
a time of trouble like our own. The Greek word in the active
voice means to persuade by any means, including coercion,
reasoning, and charm. In the middle voice it means to persuade
oneself, to believe, or to be of a persuasion. In the passive voice
it means to consent or obey, and the passive form has a transitive
meaning: we obey or consent to persons, commands, or laws. The
verbal noun means faith, faith in right opinion, faith in physical
science, faith in persons and institutions, the good faith of the
man of character, the faith that can submit itself to Socratic
criticism in order to arrive at its own understanding. The survival
of this word in fourth-century Athens in all its systematic mean-

ings is a kind of measure of the intelligence that went into the permanent contribution that the Greeks made to politics.

Our minds recoil from the extremes of its meanings. We are willing to accept certain combinations of force with reason that obviously go into persuasion, but we think that the proper meaning has been stretched by wit or malice when a cowboy or a gangster calls a six-shooter a persuader. But a holdup man or a cop is presumably a rational animal. When he draws his gun, he is presumably trying to influence truly human behavior. His purpose is intelligible to his victim, and he is hoping that it will be reasonably accepted. He therefore allows time for the victim to argue with and persuade himself. He hopes for willing obedience. In case the persuasion fails, his willingness to shoot is the measure of ratio of force to reason in his rhetoric. The Thucydidean account of the dialogue between the Athenian envoys and the Melian city council spells out in exhaustive detail the rational content of all such encounters, and provides the paradigm for all the situations where might makes right. This is one extreme of the persuasive art. No one will deny that it makes politics.

At the other extreme are Socrates on trial, Antigone before Creon, Jesus under Pilate. In these cases, reason is at a maximum and force is nil, unless words and charm are also forces that preside over all persuasion.

Between these extremes lies the field of political life. Below the holdup man is the beast. Above the martyr are the gods. The city exists between them, but it can tolerate neither. Within the city, the political animal wields power and gives reasons in the home, in the marketplace, in the legislative assembly, in the executive offices, in the law courts. These institutions can be distinguished by the kinds of rhetoric they cultivate. In fact, they have been made by, and in turn maintain, the kinds of persuasion that are practiced in them.

The family, if it can be called a polity, is the institution that generates and maintains the greatest variety, the most faithful practice, and the highest intensity of persuasion. Hopes, fears, passions, imaginations, reasons, follies, and wisdoms are all grist for the mills of mutual persuasion. The Greek verb, or the words of any other language, do not have enough inflections to discern and trace the vast range of persuasion, from the family quarrel to the family's many ecstasies. Every other institution seems to be a partial cut or violent break from this archetypal model. It is worth noting here that many of the persuasive processes become habitual, are frozen into custom, and have been inherited from generation to generation, so that any given family only has to learn to use them. Perhaps the deepest and most comprehensive of these social habits is persuasion itself.

The mutual persuasion of the marketplace is of two kinds, which, no matter how sharply distinguished, are prone to mixture. One of these is commercial in origin, concerned with the exchange of goods; the other is political. In the commercial transaction, two parties in effect offer parcels of power or force in the shape of exchangeable goods. Each wishes to acquire the goods of the other, and each withholds his goods as inducement or persuasion of the other to part with his goods. An argument ensues, in which relative measurement of value and possible equations of values in terms of price imply the conditions under which exchange will become consent. As in the simple case of persuasion, one persuader and one assenter, each makes a shrewd estimate of the power and intention of the other. If the conditions do not make an equation and there is no meeting of minds, no exchange or contract is made. Each party may try out his persuasive powers on other parties in pursuit of his individual ends. If there is a meeting of minds, each purpose is served and there is mutual benefit. In this case, there is the deceitful appearance of a common purpose. Actually, there is no common purpose. The lines of persuasion have crossed at a moment and a point, as it were, but each continues on its course.

The body politic is busy with many such transactions, and Adam Smith thought he saw a pattern in the cross-purposes that integrated the wealth of a nation. By now we seem to have learned that the resultant sum of the sales and the consequent wealth of the individual parties, the so-called Gross National Product, does not constitute a common wealth; nor do the many points of intersection of private purposes determine the general welfare. It is true that Adam Smith was a professor of rhetoric and that his argument was addressed to the sovereign, but we must not fail to see that bargaining is a form of persuasion in which the ratio of force to reason is very high. It is a form of mutual threat and the calling of bluffs. And this is true when the political forum gets mixed with the commercial marketplace, as in a political campaign. Justice Holmes has said that the truth of a political idea consists in its ability to make its way in the marketplace. This encourages both small and great dishonest politicians to indulge in bluff and threat, and to settle for deals, fixes, and compromises of cross-purposes. The public gets in on the deal, and finally the whole body politic is up for sale. Tocqueville described in a bitterly ironic phrase the working of majority rule in this country in the early days. He said that generating a majority consisted in getting "self-interest rightly understood." He was describing the confusion of the rhetoric of salesmanship with the rhetoric of the political forum. His words now describe the substance of the political platform that presents the sum of the fixes and deals that it conceals, the gross political product of cross-purposes.

But the body politic is not easily sold out. After all the politico-economic deals have been made, there always remain residual powers and reasons more or less diffused by persuasion throughout the community. In the simplest sale or contract the bargaining and negotiation are more or less rightly understood in terms of the character and honesty of the parties, the degrees of freedom and goodwill in the claims and promises, and the fears of consequences of deceit and fraud. In any bargain or contract there sits a third party, the reasonable community, approving, disapproving, and persuading. The rhetoric contains reason as well as force or power, and reason, in addition to sweetening and facilitating persuasion, aims at truth or that measure of truth that human minds can claim. When this is formalized and generalized, it becomes contract law under which the freedom of the parties is measured, the legitimacy of the promises tested, and the fulfillment of them ensured, if necessary by enforcement. Not many heavy or complicated contracts would be made if the public persuasion were absent.

If the business undertaken is heavy and complicated enough, the two or more parties will have an interest in a careful, sharp, general formulation of the conditions that will make the contract institutional and permanent. They will in effect invite the public to grant them a charter in which the organized persuasion of the community will be permanently present and in which they pledge their consent to recognize the public interest. The charter originally represents a determination to maintain an equilibrium of persuasion and consent. It implies the pledge to consent to and conform to all corporation laws, those that regulate as well as those that protect and enable the corporation activities. The notorious fact of grumbling and evasion on the part of corporations is a kind of inverted respect that private interests pay to the common good.

As the habit of persuasion becomes law, there is an increase in the ratio of reason to force. Part of this increase comes from the will of the parties to summate and maintain the results of past persuasions, to draw conclusions from past cases and to take them for granted in future negotiations. This increases the power but also increases the domain of reason. This in turn induces an increment of goodwill and good faith; that is, the willingness to be persuaded as well as to persuade. In laying the issues before the public, there is an implied invitation to criticism from outside, therefore of argument, and a wider field of persuasion is opened. In the debate, each reason offered invites opposing reasons, or even a reason that will compose differences. In Plato's account of persuasion, this exploration of reasons is called upward dialectic and results in the discovery of principles and rules to implement them.

LAW

It is the current fashion to see a radical plurality in our society, and to take pride in, or console ourselves with, the possibilities of individual freedom that appear between the many independent centers of power and decision. In the familiar motto *E pluribus unum,* we substitute *libertas* for *unum.* In its original, the formula stated the problem of federation, how to form out of many independent states a more perfect union. One civil war and almost all of our politics have been devoted to the solution of the problem.

It would now seem that we have retreated from the problem and are moving away from the solution. In place of many states, we now find and want to recognize associations, institutions, and corporations as independent political entities. When their powers grow and their independent decisions become anarchic, each generates an equal opposing power and reason. This pluralization may well turn out to be a strategic retreat that will eventually result in the broadening as well as the complicating of the mutual persuasion and dialectic. On the other hand, it could be the beginning of a rapid dispersal of power and the weakening of debate.

If we take the business corporation as the typical unit in the plurality, there is a theory of the corporate organization that seems to apply to all independent associations. The corporate managers see their organization as an organism in an environment. Part of the environment is favorable, part of it threatens. Adaptation to these conditions is necessary. The corporation therefore sets up organs of adaptation, a research department to recruit ideas and personnel from university laboratories, a labor-relations department to deal with the unions, a corporation counsel to find a way around government regulations or to build corporation law into internal policy, a sales force to deal with customers, public-relations experts to improve the environment for business, buyers to deal with suppliers of tools and materials, a finance department to deal with banks and shareholders, a cartel department to deal with dangerous competitors, a contract department to get government contracts. These organs of adaptation constitute the organizational structure of the corporation. A similar table of organization could be drawn up for the organizations of all kinds that imitate the management of the business corporation. Management, of which these devices are the details, has one overall function, which in this theory is called "satisficing." The word and the description are obvious references to the biological analogue of adaptation in which struggle for existence and survival of the fittest would be the associated terms. Applied to the whole society and all of its constituent parts, the theory might better be called corporate ecology. The theory is obviously an attempt to take account of the at least relational unity of the so-called pluralistic society, and the interpenetration of powers and decisions of its parts.

If human society is more than biological and more than economic, there must be more of reason in it than the persuasion of the jungle and of the marketplace provides. The typical persuasive artists of our time, the advertising men and the politicians, indicate the inadequacy of the ecology and the economy of the pluralistic society by groping for images, ideologies, charismatic persons, causes, and crusades to capture men's minds. These synthetic rhetorics prove to be pathetic and dangerous substitutes for the laws that we as free men have vowed to uphold and respect, but that we are failing to understand. We have agreed to recognize the laws as the means by which we shall persuade ourselves, but we ignore or neglect them in our fascination with their glamorous substitutes.

There are many kinds of law. We must not forget customary law, of which we have been persuaded by the long, mysterious rhetoric of experience and tradition; the case can be made that no other laws would be effective in the absence of this great unwritten corpus. Then there is common law, which is made out of customary law and reason by the actions of courts. There are statutes made by legislatures as the outcome of deliberation and debate among the people and their representatives. There is constitutional law, accumulated by habits of persuasion, drafted by conventions, and ratified by the people. But the experience with these so-called human laws, sometimes smooth but often rough, has forced men to probe deeper and higher to find reasons in natural law, divine law, and eternal law to found, support, correct, and improve the human legal effort. A crisis in human law is the occasion for discovery in jurisprudence.

The kinds of human law are resting points or shelves for the persuasive struggles to find reason in human affairs. Two men collide with one another on a low level of custom; each is to the best of his lights right. If they do not fight it out, they go to court and plead their causes before a judge who helps them add reasons to their interests. The judge brings their reasons under the reason that he educes from the customs, and renders a decision. Customary law has been raised to the level of common law, and the decision may contain a rule of law that will function as a precedent in future cases. When a new government, such as ours in 1789, sets up a constitution that undertakes to accept the common laws and enforce them, it also undertakes to correct, improve, and add new laws to them; and it does this by the direct method of legislation. A special institution is established to make laws, and it operates under rules that will ensure full deliberation or mutual persuasion and the maximum infusion of reason. The constitution provides immunities for the members of the legislative assembly against the external pressures of interests and powers that may impair the use of reason in the legislative process. Committees and hearings may deepen the deliberations.

Once the law is made, it is passed on to the executive institution to be administered. Here the rule of reason directs that the law shall be equally applied to all cases. To ensure this difficult task, the administrative agency is empowered to make supplementary rules to fit the law to the case, and to hold hearings to persuade and to be persuaded by the parties intended by the law. Here there is at least the possibility of another great extension of rational persuasion.

When such rational persuasions of the legislature and the executive fail, as they often do, whether because of the incompetence of the laws or because of the ignorance and obstinacy of men, a third institution stands ready to recover and repair the persuasive process. A court of law supplies the stage, the scenery, the dramatis personae, a chorus, and a playwright for a full dramatic exposition and summary reenactment of the persuasive processes that have made the case. The furniture of the courtroom opposes the adversaries, the plaintiff or prosecutor and the defendant. An attorney is assigned to each adversary, and they put facts and arguments in formal briefs. They call witnesses and present real evidence according to procedural rules enforced by the presiding judge. When there is a jury, the whole case is delivered to them by the attorneys and the judge in proper form. Indefinite time is allowed for the deliberation of the jury so that persuasion and consent may come to a unanimous decision. Failing unanimity, a new trial is ordered. Even if there is unanimity, there may be an appeal to higher courts up to the

Supreme Court. It should be added that the laws, as well as persons, are being scrutinized and judged in the various judicial institutions.

It is often said that the division of government into three institutions, each independent in its operations from the others, is a safeguard of the liberties of the citizens. But this is a dark saying unless it is realized that these departments, separately and together, ensure that the reasonable part of persuasion is clarified, generalized, and purified by them. This is no place to give an analysis of the dialectical processes by which the rhetoric of persuasion becomes the logic of the law. The classical definitions of law say that law is rule of reason for the common good. It is somewhat of a mystery how apparently infinitely complicated persuasions result in rules of law.

An ordinary conversation may become heated and consequential because it has its roots in interests and power. There is a phase that becomes speculative and detached so that inferences, evidence, assumptions, and definitions may be reconsidered. In the discourse of the marketplace there is an interval when goods are weighed and prices calculated; and likewise in the legislative assembly, the executive office, and the court there are procedures of review and reformulation for proposed measures and transactions, with special attention to formal reasoning. The law must be looked at in almost a contemplative mode, as one would look at a piece of pure mathematics or a hypothesis in science, to see if it is consistent with itself or with other laws, if it has general comprehension and incisiveness, perhaps to see if it is faithful to its intention and just and workable in a wide range of circumstances. A legislator does this in one way, an administrator in another, and a judge in still another. If such considerations are successful, the law itself appears to be independent of the pressures and persuasion from which it has arisen and it takes on a life of its own. The workaday lawyer does not often approve of this appearance, and perhaps fortunately his business does not often allow it to happen. But scholars often see historic or foreign systems of law in this character. The law can be such an object of contemplation for the common man, as many religious cults have found it. Law at this summit of dialectic is luminous and majestic.

Some of the Greek tragedies are celebrations of this moment in law. The Aeschylean trilogy, the *Oresteia,* summarizes and epitomizes an indefinitely long period of violent dialectical persuasion during which the crimes within one family were dealt with by feud and vendetta. An eye for an eye, a tooth for a tooth, went to the limit of a life for a life. The guilt of generations was distilled and concentrated in the mind of one man, Orestes. Aeschylus used the dramatic form of tragedy to lift this man to a heroic type and focused the situation in a court improvised and presided over by Apollo. The Furies prosecuted; Athena was assigned to the defense. The pleadings of the case resulted in the discovery of a new law and a new legal institution. Extreme injuries done to and by individuals under a rule of vengeance became crimes against the state, to be indicted, prosecuted, and judged by the community through its courts. These plays were repeatedly performed in Athens to celebrate the discovery of law and to teach the citizens jurisprudence. It was one of the teachings by which Athens became the school of Hellas.

Aeschylus allowed the intervention of the gods in order to explain and celebrate the apotheosis of law. The case of Oedipus in the style of Sophocles is perhaps simpler and clearer. Oedipus the King is disturbed by a plague in the city of Thebes. He decides to discover the cause and to take whatever measures are necessary to cleanse the city. It is believed that the cause of the plague is a crime. As he investigates and indicts, it appears that he himself is under suspicion. Undeterred, he traces the evidence until it proves him guilty of the crimes of regicide, patricide, and incest. As judge he condemns and sentences himself to exile. Here there is no divine intervention at the end; the law itself judges on the evidence, and it is justice and freedom for the consenting man. In this play, the king plays all the roles of the courtroom. He is prosecutor, defendant, judge, jury, and witness for and against himself; he persuades, is persuaded, and persuades himself, thus personifying the logic of self-government.

Aristotle says that the purpose or end of tragedy is purgation and recognition, the purgation of the passions and the recognition of reason. More often than not, the tragic pattern is an imitation of the law court, in which the fevers of persuasion are purged and the recognition of law in its essential character is accomplished. Other legal institutions contribute their respective kinds of clarifications.

CONSENT

Dialectical and dramatic clarifications are necessary parts of the political process, because mere pressure and power do not move the whole human being. Persuasion enlists human beings for the common pursuit of an end. Individuals or groups can be brought into service to ends by force, fear, or flattery; they can be bought; but the cross-purposes involved in these transactions will cancel themselves out. It is only by reason that the purposes can be articulated and consolidated into common purposes. When the reasoning is made clear, not much force or power is needed to make persuasion effective. Reason, even the minimum that is assumed in the threat of the gunman, is the key to persuasion. The more reason in the persuasion, the less force is needed. Effective persuasion requires the proper proportion of reason and force.

At the summit of persuasive dialectic, there is a reversal of the aim and direction of persuasion. The mutual persuasion between individuals and their representative organs has resulted in agreements in laws. Now the laws are charged with the rational essences of the interests and arguments of their makers. Although they appear in merely verbal and rational styles, they contain the concentrated persuasive powers of the community. As if they were persons, they exercise a high persuasive power through the institutions and offices that they have created. The power is penetrative because it is precisely measured and fitted to the instruments through which it reaches the citizen. As in the cases of taxes and of regulation of corporations, the laws appropriate powers to accomplish the common purpose. Finally, as insurance, they carry sanctions, fines, and penalties. All this is meant when we refer to the state monopolizing force, although we often forget that the secret of this legal power is the rationality of the laws.

But there is another, too easily forgotten aspect of this coercive power. The validity of the law rests in the common good, the justice, peace, freedom, and order of the community. The laws, as the classical definition says, are made for the common good, for its establishment and for its distribution. It is to the common good and its operation that we consent when we establish and maintain self-government. We are persuaded ultimately by the common good in the laws. They command and we willingly obey. It is we who have asked to be coerced when we fail to conform, and to be punished when we disobey. The laws are the instruments by which we persuade ourselves, and in this general will we are free.

This aspect of the laws is best seen when we conceive them as questions that we ask ourselves. In a given situation, what ought we to do, what do we really want, what is our real will under these or those conditions? The right question is half the answer. The laws help us to make up our minds, our individual as well as our common minds. In the extreme case we may not be persuaded. We can say no.

By now it must be clear that I have been outlining a utopia, a cloud-cuckooland, made out of the conjugation of a Greek verb, *to persuade*. I believe it is the vision that our Founding Fathers saw when they wrote the Constitution. It was an ideal to be fulfilled as far as human beings were able with the help of law. We have failed miserably in many respects, but we still persist in the vision. As Hamilton said, it still remains for us to prove to mankind that government can survive by deliberation and choice rather than by accident and force. And this means that we are committed to the arts of persuasion.

The loss of resonance that Max Ways reports measures our failure in the arts of persuasion. He is asking for leaders and responsible citizens, but he knows they cannot exist without a public philosophy. I suggest that the public philosophy is the philosophy of law which is not being taught or studied in our law schools, in our universities, or in our schools. Neither is it being practiced in our institutions. We are legal illiterates and incompetents.

I can think of no more important task than research and teaching that would give us in this country, for the first time, a glimpse of jurisprudence, a popular jurisprudence that would create a general confidence throughout our population in the real existence of law, the rule of law, and the due process of law. Such learning and teaching of law would rediscover for us our individual and our common purposes, and revive in us the spirit of reasonable persuasion.

It would be a surprise to our supposed enemies and friends in the rest of the world to learn from their advisers that Americans are strong and free men because they are governed not by men with ideologies and sales talk, but by laws that they themselves make.

4

ELEVEN PROPOSITIONS ABOUT JUSTICE, CONSENT, AND GUILT

I. Each human being is responsible for evil anywhere in the universe.

II. Each citizen is responsible for injustice anywhere in the community.

III. All men by nature will that justice be done.

IV. Governments are established by men as the means of discharging their responsibilities for justice and injustice.

V. Full consent is given only to justice, and partial consents, understood as the resultants of the compositions of assents and dissents, are given to the officers and procedures of law only to the degree that they effectively discharge or promise to discharge the citizen's responsibility for justice.

VI. Democracy, as self-government or government by the consent of the governed, is not one of many forms of government. It is a principle of all government: governments derive their just powers from the consent of the governed.

VII. The breakdown or withholding of consent is due to the failure of government to provide and articulate adequate means for discharging the responsibilities of citizens, or to educate citizens in the function of the laws.

Presented for discussion to the staff of the Center for Democratic Studies on January 5, 1962.

VIII. When such failures become chronic, they result in the
accumulation of guilt in the people, guilt for their individual and collective failure to discharge their responsibilities
for justice.

IX. When such failures become incorrig:ble by political means,
the people turn to nonpolitical institutions and procedures
of purification and purgation, such as the Greek mysteries
and tragedies, the sacraments, psychoanalysis, and revolution.

X. The present occasion shows need of both political and nonpolitical purgations in order to recover consent. Evidence
of the underlying guilt is to be seen in the growing impotence of parliamentary government, in the increase in
power politics, and in the easy acceptance of nonpolitical
pluralisms.

XI. The community must undertake, or at least tolerate, a program of purgatorial politics. Taking its cue from the extension of suffrage in the last century, it must extend political
status and powers to the institutions of labor and technology, to corporations both for profit and for charity, and
to large extra- or supranational institutions that will lead to
world law.

I WOULD like to preface my discussion and the general
discussion of these eleven propositions with some remarks about the form of this presentation and the probable best
kind of discussion that it may generate. The form may seem to
show a dogmatic intention on my part, dogmatic in the bad sense
that I am throwing heavily loaded propositions at the members
of the staff and asking them to accept or reject them, or else. Or
it may seem that I am gently inviting the consideration of the
propositions as hypotheses to be verified or refuted by the adduc-
tion of empirical evidence or acts of belief. As far as I understand
it, my intention is of still another kind. I am proposing the consideration of these propositions, after the style of the Declaration
of Independence, as truths that we hold to be self-evident. I
might invite the members of the staff to consider the meaning of

the propositions without reference to their truth or falsity; instead, I am asking that their truth be granted so that we may consider their meaning or meanings.

It may be noted that the eleven propositions fall into four groups. The first three are very abstract and general. They may be considered as propositions in the metaphysic of ethics or morals. Because they are concerned with justice, I should like to call them metapolitical. Propositions IV, V, and VI concern the foundation of government in justice and consent. Propositions VII, VIII, and IX consider one kind of cause for the failure of government and one kind of consequence. Propositions X and XI attempt to make applications of the preceding propositions by way of diagnosis and therapy for the present concrete situation.

Proposition III is the central and key proposition. Proposition VI states the basic principle of democracy. The order and connection of the propositions are not deductive, but they are compendent; they hang together so that common terms allow the passage of the mind from one proposition to another in the exploration of meanings. Together the propositions make a gloss on the second paragraph of the Declaration of Independence.

I shall now proceed to comment on each of the propositions merely for the purpose of establishing likely starting points for the general discussion.

I. Each human being is responsible for evil anywhere in the universe.

Although this proposition has deep roots in Western and Oriental thought, it had three eminent authors in the nineteenth and twentieth centuries: Tolstoy, Dostoevsky, and Gandhi. When I quoted it in a lecture to a college student body some years ago, the president of the college came to me after the lecture and asked me if I did not think that it was a dangerous statement to make to the young. He was thinking of its power to lead the young idealist to attempt impossible tasks and romantic feats that could lead only to tragic consequences. He found it full of hubris. As a follower of William James, he was of course right; it is not a pragmatic proposition. But there are deeper doubts. Is one responsible for evils that one does not know, for evils that one has not knowingly caused, for evils that one cannot right?

For one reason or another, in the course of history these questions have been deeply probed. Perhaps the most impressive series of probes, impressive because of their spontaneity and thoroughness, were the Greek tragedies and comedies. The tragic blindness that accompanies hubristic rationality, the ignorance that follows knowledge like a nemesis, guides and traps the questioning irony of the hero, who is the typical lover of the good. The dramatists fix and elaborate one situation after another, typically and pre-eminently in the stories of Orestes and Oedipus, in which the virtuous and rational man seeks his highest good unwaveringly until he discovers in the resulting sea of troubles the unknown, unintended, irresolvable evils for which he must recognize and acknowledge his responsibility. The Greek tragedy never ends in the absolution of the hero from this responsibility. In fact, his recognition of the inescapable constitutes his salvation, such as it is, and if he survives he carries it as his burden of wisdom.

The comedies study the same problem, but they also take into account the accidental and the chance circumstances that tempt the hero into sophistry and self-deception. Then comedy punctures the illusion and the imposture, forcing the hero to face and acknowledge his folly and his error; he also recognizes his responsibility for the fortuitous as well as for the gratuitous evils, albeit with laughter.

The heavy lesson to be drawn from the Greek studies of responsibility does not seem certain, but it does seem inescapable. As the ancient period draws to a close, there is a sense of doom, the encirclement by fate, the burden of responsibility for unknown evils that men uncover by their attempts to deal with known evils. The doctrine may be a cruel and dangerous one to teach young people, or indeed any people, but the Greeks seem to be uncommonly and grandly mature by comparison with ourselves.

The doctrine is, of course, a part of the great view of the universe as a system of goods and evils. We cannot help but love and will the goods, but in so doing we enmesh ourselves in a web of evils. We learn, if at all, by suffering. If we do not choose to learn, we may escape evil. This is the doctrine of the modern trimmer.

The Christian revelation also penetrated to the so-called problem of evil and responsibility. In effect, it accepted the tragic lesson and the fatal encirclement. But it erected a tower beyond tragedy. There would be only one escape from the cosmic tragic fall of man in original sin: after confession and repentance, the free gift of God's grace would bring absolution and salvation. The noblest souls of the ancients are assigned in this scheme to limbo, a sad paradise on the boundaries of hell. The recipients of grace go to heaven, from which evil has been drained. Then there is a middle realm where the others can work out their salvation with the help of grace. The tower and the rest of the drastic scheme measure the depth of the problem. We shall postpone till later the political consequences.

It is not surprising that Tolstoy, Dostoevsky, and Gandhi restate the doctrine of responsibility for evil in its stark form. They were watching the modern drama come to an end without much benefit of grace, and from a kind of middle world they remind us that both our religion and our politics have tried to shrink our responsibilities into a false and complacent holding position. We have said that responsibilities are limited by our knowledge, our good intentions, and our relative impotence. They perhaps remind us that even the foundations of these will crumble if we do not reassert for ourselves the old wisdom.

II. Each citizen is responsible for injustice anywhere in the community.

Augustine, quoting the Bible, said that God has disposed all things in number, weight, and measure; and in saying this he is pointing out that the universe, as well as man's mind, has reason. It is a kind of charter for the pursuit of science and technology, but it also gives the basis for the pursuit of justice. Justice is the disposal of goods and evils according to reason. Justice throughout the universe is a good topic for theological and metaphysical exploration, but we would do well to indulge here only in its more familiar usage, restricting it to the human community.

Man with his incorrigible rationality will be concerned with the disposal of goods and evils in his community; and the number, weight, and measure of these goods and evils will give number, weight, and measure to his responsibilities for them. These goods and evils will often be beyond his knowledge, intention, and power, but he will not find it possible to limit his responsibility by these terms. He will find it necessary to learn, to enlighten his will, and to increase and redirect his power. Even, as the myth runs, if he pays attention only to his individual goods and evils, food, shelter, and clothing, he will have to care for their distribution, giving each man his due, treating equals equally and unequals unequally, respecting the intrinsic goods in each thing and men as ends-in-themselves. If he forgets these things, he will be reminded of them by encountering the clear and present evils that threaten them.

III. All men by nature will that justice be done.

This proposition is written in imitation of the first sentence in Aristotle's *Metaphysics*, "All men by nature desire to know." It has the same relation to morals and politics that Aristotle's statement has to physics and metaphysics. (If my intention were to argue from premises to conclusions in the demonstrative fashion, this would be the major premise and would have been Proposition I rather than III.) It is because men by nature will justice that they are responsible for evil and injustice. By ignorance and confusion in the face of life's complexity, and by the consequent perversion of the natural will by particular and passing desires, the responsibility for justice may be forgotten or denied temporarily, but in the long run natural will will reassert itself and acknowledge justice as its proper object. All men may also by nature be hungry, greedy, amorous, and power-seeking, but all these passions are touched by the love of justice and the hatred of injustice. Therefore, politics is not only possible, but necessary.

IV. Governments are established by men as the means of discharging their responsibilities for justice and injustice.

In proposing this proposition I am not hoping to beg the many questions with which it is associated in this company. There may be parts of the individual's responsibilities for justice that can be discharged by individual acts or by voluntary associations or by nongovernmental institutions. There may even be wisdom or prudence or necessity in limiting government and prohibiting it from monopolizing the means to justice. As I have said many times before, it seems quite clear to me that government is not and cannot be omnipotent; totalitarian government is an illusion of the school of power and managerial politics. Therefore, at its maximum, government would always leave a residue of strictly individual freedom. The question of minimal or maximal government seems to me a pragmatic question, to be solved by taking the relative needs and remedies into account.

This proposition does intend to say that there will always be some responsibilities for justice that only laws can discharge, that these laws provide the offices and procedures for so doing, and that government consists in making, executing, and adjudicating these laws.

> V. *Full consent is given only to justice, and partial consents, understood as the resultants of the composition of assents and dissents, are given to the officers and procedures of law only to the degree that they effectively discharge or promise to discharge the citizen's responsibility for justice.*

I am understanding here that consent is the will that something be done or not be done. I am continuing the presumption in earlier propositions that there is a steady and settled will that justice be done; so there is a steady, settled consent that justice be done. Consents to laws—customary, constitutional, statutory, administrative—are given as consequences of the full consent to justice and therefore as hypothetical and instrumental, with a variety of combinations of assents and dissents to fit their effectiveness and workability under various conditions.

I should like to think that participation is synonymous with consent, but in current usage participation means the arrangements and the mechanisms by which consent is expressed. The great variety of these still raises questions. For instance, participation in litigation and the acceptance of the court's judgment is a very old way to express consent, long antedating the inventions of the eighteenth century: political parties, the ballot, elections, representation; in short, parliamentary government. In fact, parliamentary government worked well only in the context of many other mechanisms of expressing consent. Consent is a highly complicated and versatile process. The mechanisms for its expression change and adjust or fail to adjust themselves to the basic processes, and when one or more mechanisms become ineffective, chances are that some other mechanisms are operating or ought to be found. The failure to find or make others is no reason to abandon government, or to despair of consent and turn to the nonpolitical forms of decision-making.

> VI. *Democracy, as self-government or government by the consent of the governed, is not one of many forms of government. It is a principle of all government: governments derive their just powers from the consent of the governed.*

I believe that this part of the Declaration of Independence is the announcement of a discovery in political science. It is saying that, although democracy in the sense of self-government has hitherto been conceived as one among many forms or a part of mixed forms, to be chosen or rejected as it fits temporary circumstances or needs, arbitrary will or ulterior purpose, or to throw off tyranny, it is now found to have been, and to be for the future, an essential principle of government. No government can exist or operate without it.

The author of the declaration, no doubt, saw freedom as the paramount end of government and found consent in the style of the social contract theory of government as a necessary means to that end. My preceding propositions have proposed justice as the end of government, and have tried to show that consent is a necessary means to that end. Freedom and justice are mutually implied in the common good, which is the comprehensive end of government.

> *VII. The breakdown or frustration of consent is due to the failure of government to provide and articulate adequate means for discharging the responsibilities of citizens, or to educate the citizens in the functions of laws.*

This does not necessarily means that any given set of officers or procedures are alone the causes of breakdown. It may be that the citizens have failed to give themselves good officers and laws.

Government is always imperfect; it never completely succeeds in implementing the citizen's responsibility for justice. It may make too many or too few laws; it may make false laws. It may fail to execute or to adjudicate properly the good laws it has. It may ignore the need for laws as it develops in the life of the community. With a sufficient accumulation of mistakes, the result will be the frustration of the will to justice and the alienation of consent, and what I have previously called misonomy, the hatred and fear of law and government.

Our own revolution was caused by our hatred and fear of the laws of a mistaken British government; some of the details were listed in the declaration. We have never recovered from the habit of hatred and fear of all government that that occasion engendered. These habits lead us to give bad reasons for our constitutional system of checks and balances; they supply us with specious reasons for favoring one party rather than the other; they lead our academic thinking in the social sciences to theories of power and managership. They lead us to forget political liberty and to prefer individual liberty, and to allow both to eclipse justice, upon which both are founded.

> *VIII. When such failures become chronic, they result in the accumulation of guilt in the people, guilt for their failure to discharge their responsibilities to justice.*

When failures to achieve justice are frequently repeated, the corresponding habits tend to reinforce each other. The habitual failure to support schools leads to the habitual acceptance of bad education, which in turn eases our acceptance of the immobility

of the masses and our trust in the elite. Our failure to control
economic competition leads us to the admiration of large organizations and the doctrine that corporations are intrinsically and
necessarily oligarchic. The citizen learns to accept rationalizations
of his failures, to punish himself, to belittle his powers, and to take
pride in his humility. All these are signs of the accumulation of
guilt.

> IX. *When such failures become incorrigible by political
> means, the people will turn to nonpolitical institutions
> and procedures of purification and purgation, such as
> the Greek mysteries and tragedies, the sacraments, psy-
> choanalysis, and revolution.*

When it becomes clear that the government cannot do what needs
to be done for the people, which cannot be done at all or as well
by individual effort, or when there is no political ensurance that
the people can do what they ought to do, then the people will
turn to other means of salvation from their guilt. They may temporarily turn to voluntary associations that they hope will be effective in collective, but nongovernmental, efforts. Where these are
numerous and ubiquitous, it may take a long time to discover
their illusory character. Some associations may transform themselves from voluntary to governmental function and status; for instance, welfare societies becoming governmental bureaus, as in
the New Deal. Those that do not prove practically effective become clubs, lodges, and fraternal organizations, their merely
social forms imitating the Greek Eleusinian and Orphic mysteries.
They become esoteric, secret, and ritualistic. American togetherness shows signs at present of this development—note the John
Birch Society and the Great Books seminars. In Greece, this led
to the public performances of tragedy and comedy, great public
rites of purgation. Plato condemned tragedy and comedy on the
grounds that they were subversive of public virtue and law, and
Aristotle discovered their para-political purgative functions; the
temporal sequence of these judgments shows the deepening concern of the Greeks with corporate guilt as their polities lost effectiveness. The Greek tragedies always dealt with the themes of

justice, its reality and its dialectical puzzles. The ordinary man represented collectively in the chorus was always lost in the maze of customs and laws, while he sympathized with the hero in seeking a solution. Solutions came in two forms, either as a theophany, the revelation of a god, or from the recognition of a new determination of justice in the ruin or suffering of the hero.

The church supplied a theophany for the ruined and suffering polities of the ancient world. It gathered up and clarified all the purgative rituals and dramatic forms and constructed from them a sacramental system that could save the individual from the accumulated guilt of his worldly life. The church was the tower beyond tragedy and beyond politics. As an institution, the church was recognized as a perennial need of the human being, no matter what his earthly polity might be. There would always be a residue of guilt, no matter how effective the state might be in providing the means of justice. However sophisticated the sacraments might be, the doctrine was simple: evil, even accumulated evil in the sense of guilt, can be overcome by the good of divine grace or charity. The sacraments can be preventive, as well as ameliorative and remedial with respect to chronic guilt.

But the church undertook to treat only individual guilt and the salvation of individual souls; the guilt might have been generated by participation in the corporate polity, but the sin was understood as solitary. There were exceptions, about which I am not well informed, when Mass was said on the cathedral steps for a whole community, but confession was private and absolution specific. It was therefore almost inevitable that the dissenters who set up the economies and polities of the modern nation-states would seek other and more collective means of purgation. Their first attack was on the sacramental system, and their slogan was the common confession and the public celebration of the common faith of the congregation. They substituted labor and good charitable works for the individual sacraments. Hard work and public enthusiasm were signs of salvation, of purgation, purification, and justification.

But these surrogates for the sacraments, at long last, have proved illusory. It was probably these that Marx had in mind when he called religion the opium of the people. Religion became a matter of emotion rather than thought and practice. It has been easy for the psychoanalyst and the propagandist to take over the individual and collective therapy that is needed. There has always been a great deal of both of these in the pageantry and pomp of the election campaigns that have purged and renovated the body politic since the birth of the Whig Party and parliament in the seventeenth century.

The demagogues and dictators of our time have found out what it takes to recover politics today. It takes a psychopathological mass diagnosis of guilt, a spectacular ceremony of purgation, and a mass initiation into the new order of the ages; in short, a revolution. We do not know whether this is the death or the rebirth of democracy.

X. *The present occasion shows need of both political and nonpolitical purgations in order to recover consent. Evidence of the underlying guilt is to be seen in the growing impotence of parliamentary government, in the increase of power politics, and in the easy acceptance of nonpolitical pluralisms.*

The genesis and accumulation of political guilt seem to follow a pattern: first, a major failure to achieve a just solution to a problem, a failure to make a determination of justice in concrete; then, attempts to patch up the failure by the application of pressure and power; finally, a retreat from the problem and the substitution of false problems and issues. These stages are well illustrated in the failure of congressional government to solve the irrepressible conflict of the Civil War, the application of pressure and power of the industrializing North to the broken processes of government, and finally the recourse to the pursuit of social justice by parapolitical means.

There are, of course, more flamboyant symptoms of guilt, such as those two exponential curves that plot the rise in sentimental religiosity as evidenced in increased church membership against the parallel increase in crime and delinquency. There is the beatnik reaction known as rebellion without cause. There is the strange confusion of chrism and charisma in the cult of leadership, and the contagion of the political rally and the revival meeting.

> XI. *The community must undertake, or at least tolerate, a program of purgatorial politics. Taking its cue from the extension of suffrage in the last century, it must extend political status and powers to the institutions of labor and technology, to corporations both for profit and for charity, and to the large extra- or supranational institutions that will lead to world law.*

This program will not be supported or tolerated by those who believe that politics is the art of the possible. It will involve tragedy and martyrdom, those self-purifying political acts that are again becoming familiar all over the world.

5

THE CORPORATION
AND THE REPUBLIC

A S WE look for the shapes of our liberties as reflected in
the Declaration of Independence, the Constitution,
and the Federalist Papers, we are struck by their thin outlines
and the great spaces that are left empty. Years ago, Lord Bryce
noted these omissions with admiration and attributed them to
the wisdom and skill of the authors, to their shrewd avoidance
of controversy, to chance, and to a kind providence that inhibited
the Founding Fathers. As we now try to face our contemporary
problems, we can add the hindsight of more history and congratulate our forebears on having been born in the eighteenth
century, when clear and distinct ideas had not yet met the
realities of the nineteenth and twentieth centuries.

The eighteenth century knew the corruptions of tyranny and
power, but it did not clearly imagine party politics, pressure
groups, and congressional committees. It proposed federation as
the cure for big government and its inherent imperialism, but it
did not anticipate big business and big labor. The Constitution
is silent when it comes to corporations, with which the age of
reason was very familiar. And more is the wonder, since it was in
this age that the social contract, its theory and its practice, had
transfigured many private corporations into state governments,
whose constitutions were the models for the federal Constitution.
It is even more wonderful that Adam Smith thought the business
corporation had no significant future. It is said that the eighteenth-

Originally published in April 1958 as a pamphlet issued in connection with
The Fund for the Republic's discussion of the Free Society.

century philosophers had more faith in posterity, that is, in the nineteenth and twentieth centuries, than they had in God. It seems that now we must learn to put their and our trust in the corporation in which we live, and move, and have our being.

Our new awareness of the corporation is evidenced daily in the news we read, and in weekly commentaries and business reports. As we look to these mirrors of our lives, we must realize that it is not only the business corporation, the private corporation for profit, in which we have invested our lives and fortunes. The business corporation has old and familiar companions. It is immediately connected, as donor, to the charitable corporations in which we worship, learn, and exercise our private charities— the church, the school, the "voluntary organization." The business corporation often becomes the public utility, serving our common life and submitting to rules that ensure that service. These familiar organizations of the economic world operate under charters that are granted by the public corporations that we recognize as mature governments: city, state, and national. All of these, save the business corporation, have long histories, and together they divide and unite the jurisdictions in our free society.

Clearly we have some new thinking to do if the intelligence that freedom requires is to be effective. I should like to propose a principle and a hypothesis for some of the new thinking to pursue.

The *principle* is that the loss of freedom in a society is due in part to a failure to understand its own vital processes. Habits of feeling, action, and even thought are established and accumulated unawares. Until they are recognized and understood, they cause frustration and disorder similar to those complexes that cause hysteria in individuals.

The *hypothesis* is not a new one, but the reframing of it seems to cut across many lines of cliché and orthodoxy, and for that reason it encounters resistance. It is that the corporation, taken in its generic sense to include the separate kinds mentioned above, has for a long time been generating and nurturing a set of habits of feeling, action, and thought that are only now becoming recognizable and articulate; and, as they are at present expressed, they appear to be incompatible with our understandings of the principles of the Bill of Rights by which we think we have been living our common life.

This formulation bristles with questions that need further definitions and answers. It may therefore call for an attempt to understand the principles in the Bill of Rights as they bear on the twentieth century.

An initial explication of the hypothesis will seem amateurish in the sense that established proverbs, precepts, and rules that govern the treatment accorded to corporations may seem to be torn from their context and transferred to the comparatively unprofessional contexts and methods of philosophy and history. For instance, it was often said in the last generation that the business corporation—to take one form of corporation for the moment—is a government, private and invisible perhaps, but also touched with public interest. The warning is often given that this is a metaphorical statement, not therefore to be taken literally. It will come very close to the central purpose of this memorandum to take this statement literally, to explore what it means, and to draw the fire of professional criticism, and, perhaps, professional attention.

If corporation is a genus, it has many species and varieties; in fact, it has an elaborate and complicated evolutionary tree. Without tracing the long and detailed history or exhausting the specific differences between the presently extant forms of the family tree —both tasks being impossible in the present state of our knowledge—we can identify the varieties of the form and the threads of heredity and kinship that bind the varieties together. Sir Henry Maine in his half-forgotten classic, *Ancient Law*, seems to have made the best judgment, guess and myth though it may be, about the origin of the corporation in the Roman republic. He judges that it arose on those frequent occasions of crisis when the father of the family died, and the family with its sons, daughters, adopted children, and slaves had to be reorganized in order to perpetuate the property and the civil functions of the members of the family. It was perhaps in this context that the fictional "legal person" first raised its fearsome head. Some such historical image must have been in Justice Marshall's mind when he wrote his opinion in the Dartmouth College Case:

A corporation is an artificial being, invisible, intangible, and existing only in the contemplation of the law. Being the mere creature of the law, it possesses only those properties which the charter of its creation confers on it, either expressly, or as incidental to its very existence. These are such as are supposed best calculated to effect the object for which it was created. Among the most important are immortality, and, if the expression be allowed, individuality; properties by which a perpetual succession of many persons are considered the same, and may act as a single individual. They enable a corporation to manage its own affairs, and to hold property without the perplexing intricacies, the hazardous and endless necessity, of perpetual conveyances for the purpose of transmitting it from hand to hand. It is chiefly for the purpose of clothing bodies of men, in succession, with these qualities and these capacities, that corporations were invented and are in use . . .

It may be well, in stretching one's mind to comprehend under one conceptual unity the Roman family, Dartmouth College, and the modern business corporation, to recall Maine's thesis that the connecting theme in the history of the law is the passage from status to contract; that is, from natural to artificial association. It may be time to stretch our minds to another concept—the adopted or artificial son in a Roman family, a Dartmouth student, and a worker in the Chevrolet plant as members of their respective corporations.

Between the corporate families in the Roman republic and the big corporations of the American republic there have been many intermediate forms, some leaving fossils that are now being dug up. F. W. Maitland in his introduction to Gierke's *Political Theory of the Middle Ages* lists the forms in a section of the evolutionary tree:

> Let us imagine—we are not likely to see—a book with some such title as English Fellowship Law, which in the first place describes the structure of the groups in which men of the English race have stood from the days when the vengeful kindred was pursuing the blood feud to the days when the one-man-company is issuing debentures, when parliamentary assemblies stand three deep above Canadian and Australian soil and "Trusts and Corporations" is the name of a question that vexes the great Republic of the West. Within these bounds lie churches, and even the medieval church, one and catholic, religious houses, mendicant

orders, nonconforming bodies, a presbyterian system, universities old and new, the village community which germanists revealed to us, the manor in its growth and decay, the township, the New England town, the counties and hundreds, the chartered boroughs, the guild in all its manifold varieties, the inns of court, the merchant adventurers, the militant companies of English condottieri who returning home help to make the word "company" popular among us, the trading companies that became colonies, the companies that make war, the friendly societies, the trade union, the clubs, the group that meets at Lloyd's Coffee House, the group that becomes the Stock Exchange even to the one-man company, the Standard Oil Trust and the South Australian statutes for communistic villages.

The English historian would have a wealth of group life to survey richer than that which has come under Dr. Gierke's eye, though he would not have to tell of the peculiarly interesting civic group which hardly knows whether it is a municipal corporation or a sovereign republic. And then we imagine our historian turning to enquire how Englishmen have conceived their groups; by what thoughts they have striven to distinguish and to reconcile the manyness of the members and the oneness of the body. The borough of the later middle ages he might well regard with Dr. Gierke as the central node in the long story. Into it and out from it run most of the great threads of the development, economic and theoretical. The borough stretches one hand to the village community and the other to the freely formed companies of all sorts and kinds.

This catalogue of ships with its startling categories and epithets is only a middle section of the long history, but it should be associated with an earlier section in which the threat of ecclesiastical splits caused lawyers and philosophers to precipitate a dialectical and speculative consideration of the proper government of the church as the Mystical Body (corporation) of Christ. The exploration of the possibility of the church becoming a Christian republic planted the seeds of republican political theory throughout Europe, the harvest of which is still being reaped outside the church in far-away places. Maitland also divined the future in which the giant business corporation elbowed its way to the top, where it shares with the nation-state the honor, power, and glory of having no superior.

It seems an absurd generalization, but still a good guess, that there is no human purpose or treasure that the corporation has not carried, or can carry. This does not mean that society has ever trusted its whole burden to the corporation in its many forms, nor that it ought to, but it does mean that it could happen; there is nothing in the nature or principle of the corporation that would limit its capacity to serve human purposes. It also suggests the many historic instances when a small business corporation became a colony and then a nation-state—James Bryce cited the United States and India as the familiar examples. Not only is there great variety in the possible forms, but any individual is capable of continuous development through all these forms, with chance circumstances and small acts of choice building the series of contracts that are periodically sealed with charters of approval by reigning sovereigns of church or state. There is a great deal in this story that parallels the Darwinian story of biological evolution, but the fact that human reason and will have always been the prime movers in the evolution would seem to argue that the individual organisms in the series are *persons* in more than an artificial legal sense, and that the survival of ancient forms in the present species is due to more than accidental causes, or merely natural selection.

As corporate forms, the church and the nation-state are so familiar, so massive, and so pervasive that we take them for granted and forget that their chronic troubles are and always have been struggles for corporate existence, or coexistence. The nation-state is conceded to be the model of the corporation-without-superior; there might be a controversy about the church, whether in its unity its superior was only God, or whether in its disunity it gets its many charters from many states. But these two corporate forms, the church and the nation-state, have been the sources from which chartered authority for the other forms has been derived. Corporations without superior would seem to have a uniquely procreative capacity; they give birth to lesser corporations and serve as their superiors, and in these cases the offspring can choose their parents by petition. Four natural persons sitting in a room at a stated place can call a meeting, outline their purposes, elect officers, record minutes, and petition the secretary of state; this is the act of conception. The secretary of state consults substantial citizens; this is gestation. He then grants a charter and records it; this is parturition and baptism. There is a new person with a habitation and a name, who can perform acts: to wit, make contracts with other persons, natural or artificial, with an official seal. Delaware is said to be the most prolific of the states of the American Union, and the street in Wilmington where the charters are filed is said to be the most densely populated area in the world. The birthrate of corporations in this country in the last fifty years is said to be the highest in all history.

But the main trunk of this evolutionary tree—formerly the church and now the state—does not breed true, and the species do not follow even the laws of formal logic. One can only speak of varieties, grouped in flexible classes. Churches, for instance, are now subvarieties of the general class styled private and charitable, along with universities, colleges, schools, hospitals, orphan asylums, foundations, and some welfare associations. Tax laws have recently been throwing all these into doubtful classes. In a complementary class are the so-called business corporations, legally classified as corporations for profit. These are the most numerous, the most lively, and the most familiar—so familiar, in fact, that in the popular mind they are synonymous with the generic corporation and the capitalistic enterprise that is, or was, their purpose. Latterly, these corporations have been acquiring vicariously "the conscience of the King," have been showing charitable tendencies and a concern for educating themselves and their members. (They are also worrying the tax collectors.)

Historically considered, the boroughs or municipalities are the nodes into which all forms merged and out of which they emerged, but the surviving members of this variety are tending to return to the protection if not the apron strings of their mothers, the nation-states, or the states in the American republic. They are the unruly, corrupt, and sometimes underprivileged arms of the larger units of government. James Bryce in 1888 called these American municipal corporations "the schools of corrupt politics," which trained the then-small class of professional politicians to which the citizens delegated their powers. This suggests the weak political habits that all citizens now acquire by the parting and parceling out of their lives and persons to the many corporations to which they belong. The corporation is the perpetual adult school of our society, as cities like Athens have been in the past.

Perhaps the most instructive variety at present is the public utility corporation. This was apparently invented to cure the ills and counter the threats of corporations whose functions were by nature monopolistic. Many public utilities started as private corporations for profit, but if they dealt in water, gas, electricity, or sewage, their technical systems had to be united or consolidated. This threatened competition, which is the life of profit, and the supposed protection of the citizen, so their charters became heavily impregnated with public regulatory prescriptions. By a thin distinction they are not public, but they operate under a cover of public law. By the extension of legal logic and association, public utility corporations have suggested corporate inventions, such as the Tennessee Valley Authority and the New York Port Authority, which serve public purposes—the welfare of the people of a region, and the order of the port—but they do this under quasi-private charters and in a style of business management.

The public utility corporations and these "authorities" imply, or at least suggest, what seems to be the major, perhaps fateful, development in corporation theory and practice; namely, the identification of business management and governmental administration with a consequent confusion of public and private purposes. Private corporation practices touched with public interest and competitive teamwork in government bureaus are now hard to distinguish on any level of operation: directors, managers, and membership. This could be the deeper reality that lies back of the slogan, Corporations are governments, and the origin of the frustrations in our civil life.

The three-hundredth or four-hundredth anniversary of the invention of the private corporation for profit should be celebrated by emblazoning on a medal the likeness of a sailing vessel. Although sailing vessels were often built and operated by the sovereigns of corporations-without-superior—whence comes the

designation, ships of state—they soon caught the eye and enthusiasm of the private investor, and what could not be done by
the individual was done by the company. The companies were
chartered because "the objects for which a corporation is created
are universally such as the government wishes to promote." These
were risky enterprises in terms of credit and bankruptcy and of
wind and wave.

The masters of the ships were rugged fellows, able to persuade
investors and to command obedience of seamen. They could
become privateers, convert their ships from merchantmen to
men-of-war and vice versa, and exchange their roles with pirates
if need be. Their character and their authority were derived
almost wholly from their knowledge of the nature and technology
of the sea, and their jurisdiction extended from the home port to
the limits of their voyages. When the steam engine took the place
of sails, the authority and discipline of the shipmaster was transmitted back through the prime mover to the factory master, who
also persuaded investors, navigated a land ship, and was a captain
of industry.

The picture and symbol can be rapidly brought up to date by
substituting the airplane for the sea vessel, with its leviathan
body, wings instead of sails, its gas or jet engines generating its
own wind. The substitution emphasizes two important points:
the adaptability of the corporation to science and technology,
and the easy convertibility from private to public purpose or from
peace to war. To be the mediator between nature, science, and
technology, on the one hand, and private and public purpose on
the other—this is the basic function that the modern private
corporation for profit has demonstrated it can perform.

For any organized study of the corporation, the multiplicity,
the high birth- and deathrates, and the current diversity of forms
pose a numerical problem. The best guess from tax information
places the number of business corporations alone in this country
between half a million and a million. How many private charitable
corporations, public utilities, and public or governmental bodies
there are depends upon definitions and distinctions of units. How
many quasi-corporate entities there are, not legally incorporated

but imitating corporate organization and operations, and so treated by the courts, is not an easy matter of public knowledge. It is not certain that this kind of numerical knowledge is important. A more significant basic knowledge can be had by a kind of parody on pollster methods. Take a group of moderately well-informed people and ask them how many corporations they belong to as members. In a trial run with a class of teachers of current issues, with no agreement on a sharp definition of membership, but with considerable conviction, the average person claimed membership in 150 corporations of all kinds. But the network of contractual and treatylike relations that enmeshes the corporations and the individual members makes membership and the habits it generates hard to interpret. Any case in corporation law and the questions it raises for the mind not trained to keep to legal channels illustrate the maze.

The Marxist would speak here of the stage of finance capitalism at which we have arrived, and he would point out the mergers, the holding companies, the federations, the cartels, and the government contracts that tie together the mixed economies of the world. If these are economies, what is the shape of the market or markets? If these are governments, what are the shapes and structures of the authority, purpose, and responsibility that the corporations distribute?

The Marxist used to speak vividly, if not too accurately, about the concentration of capital and the expropriation of the worker. If the dialectic is still working, he ought now to point out the next stage or moment when the labor union applies for corporate membership in the big corporation whose directors grant annual tenure and salaries, pensions, and the power of veto on the policy of the corporation instead of the right to strike. As a result, the corporation is a government by and with the consent of the workers as well as the stockholders. As Adolf Berle puts it in *The 20th Century Capitalist Revolution,* creeping socialism has become galloping capitalism, and, we might add, corporate communism, free-world variety.

In the seventeenth century the Earl of Shaftesbury was engaged with Titus Oates and King Charles II, with the Popish

Plot and the reformers, with the establishment of the powers of
Parliament and the foundation of the Whig Party. He had John
Locke as secretary writing charters for trading companies and
sailing ships, charters for colonial commonwealths, and treatises
on government. These activities occasioned a great sorting of
corporate categories in the light of the new theory of the social
contract. Out of this came many written constitutions and bills of
rights. Viewed from this distance, the main theme of these think-
ings and writings seems to be the separation of governmental
powers and the distribution of many of them to individuals and
groups generated in the ferment of voluntary association. More
than we realize, our liberties are implicit in the separation and
quasi-autonomy of self-governing corporations.

We may then be coming close to a diagnosis of our present
discontents if we note that the political, economic, and social
phenomena of the twentieth century are marked by the mixing
and confusion of corporate forms and functions. This may be
partly due to the closing of the world, each part of which is in
effective contact with every other part, all parts of which are
penetrated and heavily influenced by our Western civilization,
with its corporate structure and style of operation; the result may
be the congestion of corporations. There is no longer an un-
incorporated frontier; corporations everywhere meet and either
conflict or coalesce, and consequently lose their identity and
independence. Such a mixing and confusion of corporate forms
may be comparable to the breakdown of the villages and the drift
to the great cities that have marked the nineteenth and twentieth
centuries in Europe and America.

It is more likely that both these drifts, from villages to cities
and from the separate corporations to mergers and affiliations, are
due to the great integration of technologies that we are witnessing.
From the stage when the hand and the tool of the craftsman were
moved by the bodily energy of the individual, to the stage when
many metal fingers were attached to one machine of wheels and
levers and moved by steam power, and on to the stage when
hundreds of such machines were combined in a factory, we are
now rapidly moving to a stage when the factories are energized
by one electric grid. The prime movers, factories, machines, and

tools organize human beings horizontally as workers and vertically as managers. Although they are together called the means of production, and therefore should be subordinate to ends and human direction, they are all too often master automatons. With thinking machines and automation they can be autonomous autocrats, and a few more steps in the integrative process will bring into view the possibility of one master autocrat, with a further question whether leviathan is human or subatomic.

The development of the modern corporation has been parallel with the building of this monster. In some subtle way, perhaps describable by a Samuel Butler, the corporation has been the collective builder, not only of the machines and the factories but also of the craft guild, the factory company, and the giant corporation itself. By contracts, licenses, and franchises that attach to chartered bodies for the buying of raw materials, the selling of products, and the hiring and organizing of workers and managers we all, one way or another, contract ourselves into the technological system. We belong to the corporations as we earn or enjoy our living. We have become socialized in the building process, and we are not sure whether we are masters or slaves of the resulting organization. If the corporate structure is a person, as it is made of persons, it may assert mastery of the technology. At present it is fair to say that the person has not yet made up its mind whether to master or to succumb to the apparent technical necessities. It would seem that we are already past the point where centralization and decentralization, pluralism and totalitarianism, are things we need worry about. Nothing short of genuine political invention can inform the artificial corporate mind.

The twentieth-century phenomena mentioned above can be described in corporate terms as corporate linkages or affiliations. The Church created schools in our civilization, and the filial relation has lasted longer than many such. But the schools have labored long to be free by setting up boards of directors or trustees for themselves. The personnel of the boards and the financial support they represent have generated strong bonds of affiliation to the business corporation, and when this has not worked the state has taken over. The schools are the orphan charities of the private profit and the public governmental corporations. Universities, addicted as they are to idle curiosity in their laboratories, as Veblen would say, have supplied the basic science for the factories. Reluctantly, and sometimes from bad conscience, the business corporations have increasingly tried to pay a debt of gratitude by donations to the universities. Two world wars have channeled tax funds into government contracts and veiled the laboratories in secrecy for reasons of security that have also dictated the choice of personnel in the laboratories. This affiliation and contagion of corporate forms has raised the question of academic freedom and autonomy in a new and acute way.

Heretofore, corporations-for-profit could be sued by stockholders if they made donations to charitable corporations. In the last twenty years states have passed new laws that permit such donations, and these laws, together with tax exemptions, have resulted in the formation by both business corporations and colleges of weak federal associations for collective bargaining leading to donations. There are law firms that specialize in merging colleges with businesses into one mixed corporate form, with resulting headaches in the tax division of the U. S. Treasury Department.

Business firms have long known the profitability of pure research and have increasingly established not only laboratories but research villages for universities to envy. They have recently recognized the low estate of liberal education as evidenced in its graduates, and they are now either sending their employees back to the universities or setting up their own liberal arts colleges beside their own laboratories.

I shall not enter the web of filiations between business and government. We are far beyond the issue of regulation or control that Woodrow Wilson explored in the public interest. We do not know which regulates or controls which, when it comes to government and business. The newspapers and the reports of commissions such as that on the freedom of the press reveal an all-enveloping web.

All this—the private corporations, charitable and for profit, the public utilities and the "authorities" that are budding from them here and abroad, the public corporations from incorporated towns and municipalities to the super-states and federations, the myriad associations that imitate the explicit charters in both internal organization and external operation—all these artificial social organisms in which we live and move and have our being are before us for a gigantic attempt to understand them, if the Republic in its full function is to survive. The corporate idea has been a leading principle in arriving at such an understanding on at least two previous occasions in Western history: at the time of the transformation of the Roman republic into an empire, and at the time when the government of the church was threatened by the Great Schism. On both occasions, the idea of the corporation was not only the hypothesis guiding diagnosis; it was also the idea that, by being stretched to receive new light and invention, was renewed and led to a new epoch. The Earl of Shaftesbury and John Locke probably led a similar great dialectical and practical reconsideration. Our own time and our discontents would seem to need like treatment.

There is much material ready for further treatment: the work of Beatrice and Sidney Webb on the English poor laws, the local governments, and the trade unions, not to mention their controversial study of the Soviet Union; the study and thought and pleading that went into Justice Brandeis's cases and opinions; the many reports of Congressional committees, particularly the work on the concentration of economic power; and finally, but not least, the work started by Berle and Means in *The Modern Corporation and Private Property*. Perhaps one should add the studies that have been done by *Fortune* and the Harvard School of Business Administration. These studies have been made for various purposes—the Fabian Society, the Progressive movement of the first decade of the century, the New Deal, and for the comfort of the business executive. They all have a split mind about the corporation, preventing the comprehension that may become possible from a study of the *generic* corporation, for here the distinction between the corporation as an economic institution and the corporation as a political institution can be transcended.

This schism between economics and politics must be healed if we are to consider the current problems of mixed economies, integrated political economies, and even the foreshadowing of the economy of abundance, as these are presented in such a study as Gunnar Myrdal's *An International Economy*. To the eighteenth-century mind, which sought to ensure its liberties by separating governmental powers and trusting them to rational debate, the addition of economic powers, money, industry, and welfare to the fragile political forms of the republic is letting the bull loose in the china shop. Russian Communism has done just this. But we might get a clearer view of this, as well as of our own politics, if we tried to see some reasonable distribution of these powers to the various corporate forms that are at present performing similar services for us. Russia has invented three separate but coordinated giant corporations and entrusted the whole social burden to them. Other socialist countries have invented other forms to meet their needs. It is not to be supposed that we are lacking in inventive imagination.

This brings us to the problematic area where one can see only shadowy lines of research and study, lines that at present pass through knots of paradoxes. What about the lines of authority, responsibility, loyalty, and consent that pass from the Defense Department to the General Electric Company or General Motors, from them to the IUE and the UAW, and from them to the citizen worker? These lines are the traces of contracts made by corporate bodies, and their junctures are conflicts of laws that reach constitutional foundations, economic conflicts that are loaded with weights of welfare and security, and moral dilemmas to paralyze citizens. We have watched congressional committees test these lines at various points and trespass on fundamental law in their attempts to find new statutes. Then there are the tax courts that cast doubt on all charitable corporations because tax evaders have invented corporate labyrinths for the charity that begins at home.

These are the deeper, almost invisible processes that work behind corporate veils, and the individual sees a conspirator in every neighbor and suspects himself when he looks in the mirror because he does not know the underground network that he joins when he buys, contracts, or gets a job. It is no wonder that we project this habitual suspicion on the giant public corporations with which we fight cold and hot wars.

It was from a like suspicion and an accompanying fear of civil war that Thomas Hobbes in seventeenth-century England made two prophetic observations on the new style corporations that were then exploring and organizing the new world. He said they were "worms in the body politic," and that they were "chips off the block of sovereignty." By the first he meant that they were private associations that were taking on a kind of spontaneous autonomy in their parasitical way of life; by the second he meant that they were no longer mercantile arms of the state, but had taken some of the power of the government into their own management. He was foreseeing what we have come to recognize as the corporate veils and legal fictions under which corporations carry on their vital private governments. Our courts have become familiar with certain procedures in corporation law which they call "piercing the corporate veils." The purpose of this procedure is to discover and designate the individual responsibility for obscure and puzzling corporate behavior that may be touched with public interest.

Now that we have realized many of the possibilities that Hobbes only suspected, it might be well if we looked through the corporate veils to the political realities that have been developed in private corporate operation and have filled the empty spaces and thickened the lines of our public constitutional liberties. The analogy between public and private governments suggests the application of two principles of federal government as criteria for judging the legitimacy and health of corporate bodies. The Constitution says that the federal government assures to each constituent state a republican form of government. It may be recalled that this was the alternative chosen in place of the direct exercise of police power as a check on undue growth or irresponsible use of state and factional powers against the federal government. In effect, this constitutional provision implies that the justice and freedom not only of the individual state but also of the whole community will be secured, if the orderly processes of republican government are ensured to the constituent parts. It would be important to find out whether republican forms of government are ensured to and upheld by our respective corporations.

The other principle is the now much misused principle of states' rights, that the states retain all rights not explicitly delegated to the federal government. The principle might better be stated and understood as the principle of federation; namely, that there should be explicit formal recognition of the separate powers, rights, and duties of the parts of government. It is the chief genius of our government that this principle has been honored in the original allocation of powers and that it has been extended beyond its original meaning in the discovery and recognition of the implied powers. On the other hand, we have not been able to see the principle working under the veils of corporation law, where there is potentially another branch of the public government.

The charters of private corporations are remarkably reticent concerning the rules required for their internal government; each corporation improvises its bylaws and its table of organization beyond the minimal requirement that there be a president, a vice-president, a treasurer, and a secretary. When charitable corporations grow in size and function they tend to differentiate their organs and function more or less in the pattern of their predecessor and mother, the church. They provide for executive, legislative, and even judicial divisions. The business corporation shows, on the other hand, the pattern of an amoeba increasing to the size of a whale, but with no sharp differentiation of organs—either this or a series of fissions and fusions into colonies, such as the parts of General Motors, each with strong oligarchic controls within and weak federal connections with each other. It may be that there is still the implication of oligarchy in a plutocracy, and an incompatibility with democracy, but it would be interesting to see if replacing the Sherman antitrust law by the ensurance of a republican form of government to all private corporations would not take the strain off the heavily pressed executive and hasten the present tendency of the business corporation to accept more community responsibilities.

The analogue of the states' rights or federal principle would redraft the categories of corporations according to their distinctive functions, ensure them separation of powers and independence of one another, and restrict, or strictly define, the contracts and treaties (cartels) they are empowered to make. Agencies like the Federal Trade Commission might even be expanded and given permanent powers to revise corporation law.

These suggestions are proposed not as cures for diseases, but rather as procedures of explorative and diagnostic therapy. Before they are applied, there should be a preliminary study of the notion of membership. This would involve the further exegesis of the text from 1 Corinthians often quoted by the church in its study of corporation theory: "Now ye are the Body of Christ, and members of members." Civil liberties, as formulated in the amendments to the Constitution, are mainly concerned with the notion of membership. Many of our present frustrations in this field are due to the fact that our memberships have been confused, therefore also our loyalties, our duties, and our consents to our many tangled governments.

There is ample evidence in our Bill of Rights to show that the political principles it enunciates are derived from antecedent historic situations and metaphysical as well as religious doctrines. Some of the erosions of their meaning show in the opinions of the Supreme Court following the two world wars. There have also been attempts on the part of historians, philosophers, and theologians to recall and repair what has been forgotten. But something is still missing in this research; it is not reaching the nerve of present political thought, either on the professional level or in the citizen's conviction. The elegant eighteenth-century words and propositions do not mean what they have always seemed to mean, and the bottom has fallen out of our political courage. This memorandum is suggesting the missing term: the corporation seen as a body politic, within which the terms of the Bill of Rights need redefinition. What are the rights of a member of a corporation, or of many corporations, those pyramiding structures in which members of members can be discerned?

Both the Stoic Emperor Marcus Aurelius and the Stoic slave

Epictetus thought of themselves as citizens of the cosmopolis, the universe as a polity. The Christian likewise thought of himself as a member of the kingdom of heaven. But both Stoic and Christian entertained these thoughts as reasons justifying their withdrawal from many of the institutions of their times. There were frustration, futility, and chaos in the pluralism over which the Roman empire brooded. For many, Roman citizenship was a solution, a kind of center of gravity around which a multiplicity of other roles could be organized, but as the empire lost its internal freedom and order, a deeper strategic retreat from the community was needed to save personal integrity. It was then that the universe was discovered as the great community that was governed by natural law. This was the notion that was revived in the eighteenth century and accepted as the self-evident basis for self-government. The trust in this vision made it possible to draft constitutions with thin lines and many open spaces, few laws chartering many freedoms. The sentiments of one community including all men as members were expressed in many state papers.

But, as we have noticed at the start, these empty spaces have been filled in by older surviving institutions and many new inventions, most noticeably at present by corporations of all kinds. Something like what happened in Rome is happening to us, living as we do in super-states. We are withdrawing and detaching ourselves from many of our institutions, but we are not yet retreating to the wider community the Romans discovered. Rather, we are developing a passion for indiscriminate togetherness and trying to find the one subcommunity into which we can put our hearts and souls. Some of these subcommunities are trying to meet our needs, particularly the big business corporation that claims to be one big family, perhaps a revival of the Roman family from which the corporation originally grew. The current discussion of this development reveals a deeper worry inside the new artificial family. In many respects it is not a family, in spite of the fact that it provides many social securities; it is a public institution, and as such its life is shared with government, education, religion, and many other affairs, not all of which share its essential purposes. So we have what pluralisms usually exhibit: each separate part of the social pattern tries to take on the functions of all the others. The corporate linkages and affiliations become a labyrinth within which the individual loses himself.

The great community imagined by the Stoic, the Christian, and the eighteenth-century philosopher-citizen is a community in whose membership the individual can identify himself as a whole man. The communities and subcommunities of which we are now members are communities to which we distribute ourselves in parts, in which we dismember ourselves, and then shrink to one of these congested parts. We become identified with aspects of ourselves, masks that we put on and take off as our roles change from day to day, sometimes from moment to moment. Inside we are hollow men, zero members of "the lonely crowd," shadowy participants in the American way of life.

The notion of privacy is a further consequence of this division of the individual soul. Only a part of the man is received into these bodies politic; the rest is not received and is private. The First Amendment to the Constitution may be suffering a confusion on this point. If no law can be made that abridges *freedom of speech,* it may mean that speech is not a property of the individual as citizen but a private power at the individual's disposal, merely a privilege. This is probably not the correct interpretation in the context. It may mean quite the contrary—that the legal person or the citizen has the duty in a democracy to exercise his freedom of speech in playing his part in self-government, and that Congress should protect this right as the source of its own power to legislate.

Freedom of religion would seem to be a case where that aspect of the individual that is not assimilated to the body politic is reserved for his membership in a church, where his religious freedom should be exercised. Again, religion is not merely something that Congress should not abridge but something that it must protect if wisdom is to be available to the legislators and the electorate.

If our society has a corporate, or quasi-corporate structure, that is, if it is made up exhaustively on a certain level of corporations, then *freedom of association,* freedom to join and resign from corporations, may be as important as education, or may be essentially educational. One of the original aims of the free public educational system for the young was to prepare the individual for maximal diversity of skills and functions, and this implied the wide range of social mobility that is the mark of free Western civilization. There are signs now that both our educational system and our society are favoring specialization of skills and functions and the narrowing and hardening of the channels of social movement. The free, spontaneous circulation of the individual may well be something that the government wishes to encourage and promote as its own lifeblood.

These points would seem to argue that our civil liberties are degraded when they are understood as privileges merely; civil liberties of members of corporations are touched with public interest.

Montesquieu said that freedom, political freedom, is the assurance that you can do what you ought to do, and that you will not be forced to do what you ought not to do. To us in the twentieth century this assurance connotes economic power, and it seems to be the condition that underlies all our other powers of freedom. As Charles Beard has said, the Constitution and particularly the Bill of Rights need economic underwriting. This could mean direct governmental appropriations to meet the cost of public information, elections, and legal counsel for the poor, but he probably meant indirect legislative action to control large concentrations of money and credit and the redistribution of wealth. Autonomy and self-government for the corporations that manage and control wealth would seem to be implied, on the principle that, although unjust power corrupts, just or legitimate power ennobles; and justice is ensured in our society by the continuous and all-pervasive practices of republican principles.

But all devices of this kind seem weak before the massive power of money and technology that now is identified with the processes of free speech and assembly. Mass communication has become more and more massive, and less and less communicative, partly because public communications now have to pass through the physical facilities of giant, unwieldy bodies politic, incorporated newspaper chains and broadcasting systems, whose public functions are not yet sufficiently distinguished from their private business interests. As we understand and practice *freedom of the press*, it should not be supported or controlled by either the private corporation for profit or the public corporation of government, but these are the only two organizations that have the economic power to operate the means. This would seem to be the critical problem in the general field of economic underwriting for the Constitution.

The main weight of the considerations in this short essay has been put on the questions whether the political nature of the corporation has been recognized and whether it would not be good for our whole political life if the recognition were formalized in the body of corporation law. These questions are hidden in the phrase *private or invisible governments*. The answers to these questions have been in the negative for more than a generation. The evidence has not been clear enough, and when parts of it have been clear, they have pointed in too many different directions, often indicating restriction and regulation of corporation activities rather than giving them measures of self-government. But the evidence is rapidly accumulating and demanding understanding not only by lawyers and economists, as in the past, but also by sociologists, anthropologists, political scientists, and journalists. New evidence raises new questions, and finally directors, managers, trustees, administrators, and various categories of members are asking themselves questions about the corporations that they work with.

Many of the new questions concern the kind of human beings that are being formed by the corporations they belong to. These are difficult questions to answer, but they should be asked, and they can be answered if they are kept in order. This essay leads to one of these new questions: how do the political habits formed by members of corporations fit with the habits that republican forms of government have developed in their citizens heretofore? The answers to this question are not definite or final; such as they are, they can best be summarized by a sharp observer of a few years ago, Mark Twain: "It is by the goodness of God that in our country we have these unspeakably precious things: freedom of speech, freedom of conscience, and the prudence never to practise either." It may be that the corporation is the school of political prudence in which we learn not to practice what the political republic has always preached.

6

THE PUBLIC THING
(Res Publica)

The legitimate object of government is to do for the community of people whatever they need to have done, but cannot do at all, or cannot so well do, for themselves, in their separate and individual capacities. If all the people can individually do as well for themselves, government ought not to interfere. The desirable things which the individuals of the people cannot do, or cannot well do for themselves, fall into two classes: those which have relations to wrongs, and those which have not. Each of these branch off into an infinite variety of subdivisions.

The first—that in relations to wrongs—embraces all crimes, misdemeanors, and nonperformance of contracts. The other embraces all which, in its nature, and without wrong, requires combined action, as public roads and highways, public schools, charities, pauperism, orphanage, estates of the deceased, and the machinery of government itself.

From this it appears that if all men were just, there still would be some, though not so much, need of government.

Abraham Lincoln
"Fragment on Government"
July 1, 1854

This paper contains the following main propositions:

1. Common law is, in principle and in spirit, private law. It enables, protects, and sanctions the individual in his private pursuit of happiness.
2. Public laws are rules of reason directed to the common good and made by the common deliberation of all. The premises of public law are:
   (a) The legitimate object of government is to do for the people what needs to be done, but cannot be done at all, or as well, by individual effort.
   (b) Man is a political animal.
   (c) Each individual is responsible for injustice anywhere in the community.
   (d) Political liberty consists in the ensurance that one can do what one ought to will. This ensurance is provided by laws.
3. The citizen is enabled to perform his elementary political functions by the Bill of Rights, particularly by the freedoms of speech, press, assembly, petition, and religion ensured by the First Amendment.
4. These functions are cultivated and institutionalized in the many voluntary associations, most importantly in business and charitable corporations.
5. Through the offices and procedures established by the Constitution, the common deliberations of the people are consummated in the making, administration, and adjudication of laws.

Presented for discussion to the staff of the Center for the Study of Democratic Institutions on June 22, 1964.

6. By the contagion of the habits of wheeling, dealing, and management, learned under the common law, the public government has reduced itself to technical administration.
7. It is proposed that the corporations that are "touched with public interest" be constitutionalized by granting them charters that will ensure them of the powers of self-government by which they can discharge their public duties.
8. The frustrations of our political freedoms seem now to be concentrated in two unsolved problems, planning and the city. We are struggling to find the legal instruments by which we may be enabled to do what we ought to through them.

PUBLIC affairs are political affairs, yet they are being choked and suffocated by the petty practices of private affairs, not only in this country but in most parts of the world. This is a pathetic irony since public affairs are people's affairs, and little people everywhere have glimpsed the possibility of being citizens in a better and greater public thing or republic than has ever been imagined before. When we Americans tell ourselves that we are living in a new world, different from any that has been before, we are often puzzled and panicked to find that the mere extension of our institutions and the extrapolation of our ideas are not adequate solutions to the problems that we have set for ourselves. This should not be the case, because we have had many opportunities recently to realize that if we do not think and act better than we have in the past, we shall not be able to maintain and continue past achievements. I want to look into the causes of our puzzlement and our panic in the hope that we may break through these into a world that will be able to fulfill itself in what we hope is a long future.

Perhaps there should be a warning that we shall not discover the new world by jumping out of our skins or out of our minds. We shall not be original or creative by divesting ourselves of our old habits, no matter how bad they may be, or by ignoring our tradition, no matter how fixed it may seem. We may have to break our habits and our traditions in order to transform them, but we shall not be able to do even this if we try to ignore them. He who is ignorant of his past is condemned to repeat it. The ancients called their imaginations memory; it may be well for us to recognize that our memories are the sources of our imaginations.

Fortunately, we have some memories or histories that are closely connected with our puzzles and panics in public affairs. One such is our Constitution; many able, concerned people are calling its many dimensions, one by one, to our attention. Others view it as a whole and bow very low in veneration of it; still others, who also view it as a whole, condemn it as unworkable from the beginning until now. But it will have to be admitted that the Constitution, whether venerated or condemned, has been the vehicle of our tradition and the informer of our habits.

When the written Constitution was framed, the several states were already governing themselves under written constitutions that had been hammered out over a rather long period of colonial life under British rule. The Revolution and the Articles of Confederation had not attempted to overturn or reconstruct the legal system; rather, they managed to break through frustrations that the system had encountered and found ways to fulfill its spirit. The federal Constitution is silent about most of the laws that it subsumes and silently confirms. But this constitutional silence is perhaps most impressive when it confirms the legal system of the courts of common law, which was taken for granted, "received," from England, as Roman law had once been received by European states. The fateful weight of this inheritance from England is matched only by the massive consent to its reception evidenced in the constitutional silence. As James Bryce says, the written constitution is merely the keystone of a massive arch of law. We are still struggling to discern and make explicit the functional relations it has to the parts of the structure about which it is silent.

COMMON LAW AND PRIVATE LAW

Of course, the common law is not silent about itself. In a thousand and one courts every day it speaks for itself and carries on a noisy business. It not only speaks, it acts, and its acts make history. It informs our minds and directs our deeds. It has had a major part in the formation of the American character.

The systems of constitutional and statutory law may or may not have clear origins in legendary or historic social contracts, but the common law claims no date or act for its origin. It always has a history, but that history is of indeterminate length, tracing itself back through cases and precedents, as far as you please, or as far as judges, advocates, or parties allow it to go. The history is always a part of the judicial process, and that process seems to maintain a continuity and identity, although it meanders or tacks in this or that direction as it responds to developments in the affairs of the community. There have been periods in which this or that trend in a society has precipitated a series of connected cases, and the working of the courts has revealed legal doctrines and principles, and in the long run, legal institutions. The accumulation of all these things makes the tradition of common law. It appears now, when we have come to know more about such matters, that this process has taken place in all communities all over the world, although the term *common law* is associated most with the Anglo-Saxon tradition.

The basic elements of the process seem to be simple. A man gets a reputation in a community for wisdom and fairness in his observation of and participation in the common life of his community. When his neighbors get into trouble and dispute, they come to him and lay their situation and their arguments—their case—before him and listen to his opinion. Both he and they learn the benefits of his maintaining a detachment and a reasonableness that they then imitate in accepting his judgment. When a series of such occasions shows connections, similarities, and differences, the judgments themselves begin to reveal general rules, principles that distinguish and compare situations. When these accumulate, they are recognized as a body of law, a kind of reminder to the disputants of the justice that they hardly knew they were seeking.

The academic expounders of common-law doctrines are impressed with this process as the basic and universal legal process, and they come to think of it as the foundation upon which all other laws and politics are built. In fact, all other laws and

politics are relatively impermanent. The common law is the
terrain on which civilizations are built and destroyed. Institutions come and go; likewise, constitutions and statutes. These
ephemeral constructions are like the snow that falls on the land
and apparently transforms it completely, but when the sun comes
out, the snow melts and the natural landscape returns. The
common law may be refreshed and fertilized by the more
deliberate rational constructions of government, but it persists
as the true base of community life. No change in human affairs is
confirmed unless it has registered and established itself in the
common-law tradition.

This is the high doctrine of the school of common law in our
tradition. Oliver Wendell Holmes, in his book *Common Law*,
works within this doctrine, and has done much to make it the
prevailing doctrine of American law. Since the American experience was formed by the reception and presence of British common
law from the earliest colonial days onward, it should not be surprising to discover that the legal doctrine has counterpart theories
in our political thought.

For the purposes of writing, discussing, and teaching, common
law is divided into four topics: crime, property, contracts, and
torts. As Holmes discusses them, the divisions seem to have a
common genesis. Human individuals seem to have a propensity
to interpret various actions on the part of others, even inanimate
others, as wrongs committed against them, and to right these
wrongs by punishment. Such wrongs are differentiated and
classified, and correlated with proper acts of retaliations. The
differentiation and correlation involve the use of reason about
persons, their situations, and their powers. These reasons, with
the help of the courts, become laws. In Holmes's account of the
judicial process there is a suggestion of the Socratic method. Men
come to the judge to lay their troubles before him. Their troubles
have two dimensions. First, they are in conflict with each other—
in conflict over property, promises, or injuries—and their passions
and opinions about these matters may have led to violence. They
describe in practical terms the concrete situation in which they
find themselves. But they also give reasons for what they have
done and wish to do; they are at least dimly aware that they do

not fully understand, and that they seek illumination. This might lead to the simple imposition of reason in the form of legal or even philosophical doctrine to escape the threatening violence. But Holmes is insistent in his claim that this is not what takes place. The court, the judge, lawyers, and the jury pay attention to the situation and the facts, and listen to the reasons as they are given. The court then acts as a midwife, helping the clients to give full birth to the reasons. If the court adds reasoning from past cases, it is only to make fully explicit the logic of the situation. Only then can judgment be rendered on the case. The case is the thing, and it is only the reasons that arise from it that make common law.

As we read Holmes now, after all these years that he has governed the style of legal thinking in this country, and note his untiring attention to concrete detail and his relentless vigilance against the invasion of philosophical considerations into his empirical view, we cannot help but be struck by the busy, pervasive, and penetrating action of the common law in the humdrum day-to-day affairs of the individual. Common law is very common, and private law and the Holmesian view of it do not follow the Socratic flair very far. In other words, they do not lead to a search for the definition of justice nor to its implementation in an ideal republic. Rather, they lead to the shrewd reasonings that serve the individual in his pursuit of private ends, much as quick wit serves the bargainers in the marketplace. According to Holmes, criminal law originates in the strong urge to retaliate for wrongs done, and the individual calls on his fellows in the community to aid him in catching and punishing the criminal. The final form of criminal law, in which the community takes on the role of the individual as the injured party, is highly instructive concerning the limits of private law. But before this final stage is reached, criminal law is involved in endless crises in which it is administered through feuds, vendettas, vigilantes, posses, and lynchings, and even after the final stage is reached, it is constantly in danger of falling back into the ways of private enterprise. Criminal law may well be the exception to prove the rule that common law is private law; it will be discussed later.

Property law has often been the subject of philosophical, even metaphysical, development. Holmes dismisses all this and reduces it to the progressive resolution of quarrels about the acquisition, possession, use, and transfer of things. Likewise, contracts, which are often closely associated with property, become law by court judgments that reinforce the individual's insistence that other individuals keep their promises. The law of torts helps the individual to get restoration or compensation for damages or wrongs done to him by others. Thus the courts of common law can be invoked to justify the free exercise of the individual's will to avenge; to acquire, possess, and use things; to influence and agree with other individuals; and to prevent interference with others. The common law seems to encourage, protect, and sanction the individual in his private pursuit of happiness. More radically stated, the common law allows the individual to make his own laws and to live by them, as long as the laws and the individuals do not destroy one another. Such rules and such habits confirm the familiar doctrine of freedom that says that each man has the right to carry out his individual will as long as it does not interfere with the similar rights of others.

This doctrine of freedom, of course, did not originate in the theory and practice of common law. It has many other roots. But its standardization has given it a peculiar authority in both public and private conduct. The power of freedom of choice has become a very precious heritage, as we say, to be protected and perpetuated. If one choice contributes to freedom in general, then many choices multiply and increase freedom; and the summum bonum must consist in the maximum number of choices being ensured to individuals. This view has recently become the rationale of the current doctrine that freedom depends upon the perpetuation of pluralism in our society. It has also been satirized in the story of the intolerable burden of freedom of the worker whose job is the sorting of potatoes. It is obviously true that the retreat from large choices and their consequent responsibilities can lead to the chaos of willful whimsicality. There is said to be a great boredom in the suburbs, whose inhabitants have fled the city in order to escape its problems.

But there is another, opposite development in the quest for individual freedom. The notion that freedom comes from the free choice of ends and the mastery of the means to these ends is the premise on which technology, industry, commerce, and power politics are based. In the pure competitive society in which this freedom flourishes, the individual can, by the ingenuity, shrewdness, and determination that are fostered by common law, become a captain of industry. By manipulation of the conditions of choice and consent he can build large voluntary organizations that compete in the system of free enterprise. A fair field and no favors, said the elephant as he danced among the chickens.

In the foregoing references to Holmes's discussion of the common law I am not attributing to him an attempt to portray the system of common law as a self-subsistent regime. I am using parts of his work to make what is, for me, an enlightening intellectual experiment. His insistence that the processes of common law have arisen from the individual's sense of wrong and the attempts in the courts of common law to set them right by rational procedures is the beginning of my argument. Setting aside the great exception of crime, the argument goes on to identify the domains of property, contracts, and torts as private law—the determination of private rights and duties between individuals. These rights and duties for the most part arise through what the individual elects freely. This is clearly the case in contracts where the individuals make promises and accept the obligations to fulfill them. It is less clear in the case of property, but becomes clearer if we consider the modes of its appropriation and use: by labor, by purchase, or even by conquest. If torts include the suffering as well as the doing of injury, they are cases of doing-it-yourself. The remedies for the infringements of these common laws are requested or initiated by the parties to the civil suit who have created their respective statuses for themselves. The court merely confirms the terms of the case, the statuses of the parties, and the remedies. This part of the common law can therefore be identified with private law, I claim, but I am not attributing the doctrine to Holmes nor, indeed, to the current opinions of the legal profession.

I may be guilty here of accepting or constructing a romantic legend, borrowing part of it from the Icelandic Saga of Burnt Njal. Njal was a member of an Icelandic neighborhood. He sat

by the side of the road and heard the cases of his feuding neighbors, who were somewhat in the position of our contemporary
nation-states. They had found that blood feuds did not settle
disputes, and they were willing to give and listen to reasons. Njal
and his clients accumulated reasons that became laws about
property, contracts, and torts. The courts became known as
things. Since Njal had no formal authority and no superior, in the
course of time he came under general suspicion and the quarrel-
ing parties entered a conspiracy against him. The laws gave way
to a super-feud in which Njal's former clients became his enemies.
They surrounded his house and burned it over his head. He was
later found in the ruins, preserved rather than consumed by the
fire because he had taken refuge under a great ox skin. He had
been mummified by the desiccating fire, a martyr to his judgments and the resulting laws, which his neighbors finally recognized as just. They had been illumined by the fire, and they set
about establishing an *althing*, a primitive parliament in which
they all would take part as legislators. This is one romantic
account of the discovery of the public realm in the failure of the
common law, and the discovery at the same time of the implications of the common law for all law, private and public.

For me the legend, or myth, does not supply the missing history of common law; it rather serves to make sharp a distinction
between private law and public law, a distinction that I wish to
pursue. The legend allows us to see that the property, contracts,
and torts of the common law could exist and be seen as the only
law of the land. It also shows how such private common law
would not be sufficient to order a community. There would have
to be public law also. Such public law might well develop from
the failures of the common law, and might also generalize and
use the notions in common law for developing new public institutions, perhaps through a social contract, for instance. Such a
distinction is hard to see and maintain precisely because the history of modern governments, particularly in Anglo-Saxon communities, always pictures the common law operating partly in
the public sphere. This is particularly true in the case of crime,
but there are other titles similarly entangled. The main attempt
of this paper will be to use this hypothetical distinction, ad-

mittedly borrowed from a legend, to trace the tangle and clarify the confusion in which our institutions are caught, and to see if the public realm, purged of the spirit and habits of private law, might not be able to develop its now-smothered potentialities.

There have been crucial occasions when the rules and procedures of common law have been been borrowed, or have migrated and been accepted, for extension and use in the public realm. The advantages have been attended with risks when this has happened.

The preeminent example of the migration of private to public law through the formalities of the common law is the growth of criminal law. It seems that some acts and their consequences cannot be left to the ordinary transactions by which individuals deal with one another, even when these transactions are judged and confirmed by the courts. Such acts, usually acts of violence, have a tendency to perpetuate and multiply themselves ad infinitum. The so-called natural law of the vendetta called for an act of punishment that equaled or exceeded the violence of the original crime, and in the eyes of the community became another crime to be avenged in like manner. The *Oresteia* of Aeschylus is a dramatic study of this process, and parallels in most respects the Saga of Burnt Njal. The vindication of the rights of individuals in private law threatens the peace and even the existence of the community upon which the rights of all individuals depend. The breach of the peace and the threat to the community breaks through the customary and pragmatic reasoning of private law and brings the community as such into the action. As Aeschylus portrays the process, the spirits of vengeance are personified as the Furies, and they arouse Athena, the patron goddess of the city, and Apollo, the god of reason, who together transform the private processes of crime and punishment into the public law and public courts of the city. A similar transformation of private law into public law is imagined to have happened in our tradition, when the plaintiff or injured party was eliminated and replaced by the public prosecutor or finally the attorney-general, and the primitive judge strengthened by the addition of the jury. In effect, the private persons, even including the defendant who is represented by counsel, become public persons, members of the public court, and crime itself is defined by statute law. I do not know the technical details of this historical transformation; they are buried in the accumulations of inventions and precedents of the common law process. If there were a history of this development, it might provide a clearer view of the typical process by which the common law prepares private law for its transformation and initiation into the realm of public law. In general it seems that the basic features in this process are the breakdown in the effectiveness of private law, the gradual invention of new procedures, and finally, the establishment of public law in the statutes, procedures, and institutions of public government.

In the revolutionary period of the eighteenth century, when public monarchical governments were being transformed into more or less republican regimes, and the loss of traditional authorities required some rationalization of a new constitutional authority, there were the familiar attempts to raise the law of contracts to the level of constitutional law in the social-contract theories. There was no attempt, as the history of criminal law might suggest, to bring the ordinary contracts between individuals into closer relation with the public government; but rather, the notion of consent in the ordinary contract was generalized to show that the constitutional government rested and had always rested on some implicit contract between the governing and the governed. However strained and mythical the reference to an original social contract may have been, there is much in modern governments and in the practice of politics in the modern era that rests on the social-contract understanding. Can this be understood as a sudden eruption of common law—private law— into the realm of public law?

By analogy with this, socialism can be understood as the projection of the notion of private property into the public realm. One can describe this process as an imitation of the process by which crime was transformed. Property under the industrial process began to be touched with public interest in such a way that the community was threatened. Attempts to keep it within the bounds of common property law were continually and progressively unsuccessful, until a demand arose that the basic means of production be expropriated from private ownership and, by a doubtful analogy, placed in public ownership. Again, this does not mean that all private ownership be abolished, but only that kind of private property that in its operation breaks through the common-law rules.

Along with this migration of common-law concepts almost inevitably goes a large part of the concept of private contracts. Contracts had been used to build the corporations, which had by a legal fiction become the "private owners" of the means of production. But these bundles of contracts were, by charters from the government, granted the power as individuals to make further contracts. Operating under these arrangements, they were found to be touched with public interest; that is, with powers to affect either favorably or unfavorably the survival and peace of the community. They had to be regulated by something more than the rules of common law: to wit, statutes and government agencies or bureaus. In fact, this necessity has been seen twice: once in the original mercantilist system under the monarchs, and again under the new mercantilist regime of corporate industry. One might call this phenomenon the second social-contract movement, which is at present strong in practice, though weak in theory. Both practice and theory are now in their time of troubles, as is evidenced in the daily newspaper and the more strenuous struggles of learned journals and books dealing with corporation theory and law.

Just to show that the spectrum of common law is completely involved, the development of private and public insurance to cover accident and injury can be observed to be touching the law of torts with public interest. Under modern technological conditions, injury to property and persons is with increasing difficulty attributable to personal fault; blame is hard to place. Personal injury coalesces with natural and social injury and becomes, through the insurance idea, the burden of the community. That burden is accepted by governments as part of their responsibility for the security of the citizen. Much of the welfare state is kept busy calculating and predicting the needs for pensions and insurance that had until recently been understood as private risks. The so-called economic bill of rights is an announcement of a consensus that private wrongs are touched with public interest. Private wrongs become public woes; insurance becomes social security.

But there are subtler influences of the spirit of the common law on the rest of the polity, both in practice and in theory. The common man has acquired many habits under the rule of common law, since time immemorial. By the spontaneous reflex of the vendetta, refined and rationalized in the penal code; by the quarrels over possession of land and tools formalized in the property codes; by the shrewd habits of making, keeping, and breaking promises and agreements formalized in the law of contracts; and by the ways and means of compensating for wrongs, injuries, and negligences, measured and judged in the law of torts, the common man, newly introduced into the public world under democratic governments, gets his first understanding of politics as the negotiation and resolution of conflicts: conflicts of freedoms, of rights, and of interests. The so-called political arena is the place where private matters are made public. Power politics takes the place of the duel, the marketplace, and the joust. The publicity of the arena makes the original conflicts tougher and more savage, and to moderate and civilize them the little politician turns to private deals and fixes. At the same time, he ceremonializes the public dimensions of the quarrels and deals by organizing political parties and election campaigns, and arranging other great theatrical performances in which he can strut, gesture, and "represent" his constituency. So the public government undertakes the function of common-law litigation, but dramatizes it as public business.

This confusion of private and public law can be described in another way. Consents to public law, both in and out of the legislatures, are bought and sold in the wheeling and dealing of the marketplace. Each law that is passed carries implicit riders—deeds and contracts, deals and fixes—that have been necessary to get a majority to go along with measure. To parody the familiar Holmesian dictum; a law is passed when it has survived the niggling of the marketplace of ideas—and things.

It takes only a few second thoughts to see that the common law has provided the essential legal supports for the so-called system of free individual enterprise and the technological and economic developments of the industrial revolution. The law of crimes and torts has more or less protected the operations of the market, the factory, and the bank, which transact business according to the rules of property and contract. The bundles of freedoms that have grown and prospered under the common law have blossomed into concentrations of powers that have had to be recognized and chartered as institutions bearing public burdens and responsibilities. These institutions are now also recognized as oligarchic bureaus, collectives that try to behave vis-à-vis each other as competitors, but actually are bound together like all buyers and sellers by cartels, little contracts, and little charters. These are products of the common law, although they were not so intended; they are in fact quasi-public governments operating under the guise of private governments, visible governments thrown into the public arena by "invisible hands." In many cases, they are stronger and better governed than the conventional public governments that have allowed them to develop, and they use the public governments for their own purposes. In some cases, the private governments are jealous of the powers of public governments, treating them like their competitors. In still other cases, the private governments pay little attention to public governments, finding public laws only trivial nuisances to be circumvented.

It is not then surprising that much political rhetoric and some political science arises from the infusion of the spirit of the common law into the public realm. The freedoms of the market-place become quasi-civil liberties and defend themselves from government interference. That government is best that governs least. The platform of a political party should be constructed from the countervailing forces in the community by compromise and barter. Government regulation curtails freedom; socialism destroys freedom. These are the voices of common men trained in the habits of the common law, but latterly forced into a strange realm of public law by the successes of their own enterprises.

Finally, the weight of the immemorial tradition of the common law, the dominance of its doctrines, and the expansion of its jurisdiction through the industrial revolution have continually confirmed and developed the doctrines of individual liberty. In

the still earlier pioneering period of this country, the frontiers-
man repeated the oldest lessons in freedom. He discovered that
the natural impediments to his will—the mountains, the forests,
the rivers, and the plains—could be turned to his advantage if
he settled them, possessed and used them; in short, if he could
secure them as his property. If he found his fellow pioneers impediments, he found freedom in negotiating and keeping
promises. When tools became machines and partnerships became
organizations, he found his effective freedom extended under the
laws of property and contracts. The courts of common law were
sufficient to resolve conflicts between neighbors without appeal
to public government and public law. Thus under both pioneer
and industrial conditions, common law established the bourgeois,
commercial, and industrial classes: first under absolute monarchs,
then under constitutional monarchs, until they finally overthrew
or defunctionalized them. Individuals supported by property and
secured in their individual ways by contracts increased the powers
and freedoms of the people. The new republics therefore incorporated the common law as an unwritten bill of rights in their
constitutions. Public law and public government were habitually
seen as arbitrary and tyrannical threats to freedom. Freedom was
understood as immunity from interference, and the market where
such freedoms flourished and multiplied became the model of a
free society.

PUBLIC LAW AND GOVERNMENT

It is instructive to consider briefly the controversial readings of
the First Amendment as they bear on the distinction between
public and private law. Elegant and precise as the First Amendment seems to be, the legal reading of it is fraught with complicated ambiguities. There have been and there still are so-called
absolute readings; the proposition means just what it says. But
when these readings are brought into court, their implications in
other branches of the law expose them to controversy. Congress
shall make no law limiting speech, press, assembly, petition, or
religion. This could mean, and has been so read, that the federal
legislature shall not interfere with the states, their legislatures

and their courts, as they regulate or fail to regulate speech, press, assembly, petition, and religion. Or in conjunction with the Fourteenth Amendment it could mean that no legislature, federal or state, shall make laws limiting these private activities of individuals; it is so read in some recent Supreme Court decisions. Or again, since speech, press, assembly, petition, and religion under modern technological and economic conditions increasingly involve properties, contracts, and damages, and these latter can be dealt with in common-law fashion, public statutes should not interfere. Some such unstated assumption must have been in Holmes's mind when he implied that the First Amendment protects the free marketplace of ideas. Frankfurter seems to be following some such presumption when he says that certain kinds of speech must be balanced against other interests. Many of the glosses written on the First Amendment by the Supreme Court in the last forty years can be read as falling within this mostly unnoted doctrine of the separation of powers. Civil liberties, along with many private rights established in common law, must be left in the realm of private law; they are privileges, in the radical sense of that term. This interpretation of the First Amendment gains emphasis from a strict interpretation of the classical doctrine of limited government. The purpose of the human activities listed in the First Amendment, particularly those that affect the family, the schools, and religion, transcend the purposes of government. They should therefore never be invaded by law. It is sometimes added that in principle the law cannot be effective if it tries to abridge them.

Another reading sees the First Amendment as recognizing civil liberties as the very foundation of the realm of public law. Speech, press, assembly, and religion may have transcendent purposes for the individual, but the First Amendment protects their free exercise because they are the essential sources of public thought and legislation; they are the necessary instruments in the field of rational persuasion and common deliberation. Any limitation of them threatens the integrity and effectiveness of the sovereign people. Far from limiting them, the government has a paramount interest in protecting and supporting them if they are threatened or weakened. Civil liberties are not merely private rights, or privileges; their exercise is a duty. The press and all means of communication, education, and the church are indispensable for the discovery and preservation of the common good. Since they are of the highest interest to the government, Congress shall not abridge, limit, or prohibit their exercise. It may on occasion invade the field of common law and private life to free them from rules that choke and impede them, and to make new laws that will ensure them in pursuit of their ends.

I have cited these readings of the First Amendment not to solve the issues that they raise; those issues can probably be solved only by drafting the statutes and establishing the free institutions that the amendment indicates and needs if it is to become clear and effective. Such institutions as now exist are classed as private corporations: some for profit as newspapers, some for charity as universities. If they are to perform their civil functions, they must belong to the public realm where they can be protected and supported and assured in their public function. But we cannot bring ourselves at present to entrust such precious matters to politics; we do not believe that the public realm is capable of carrying out such an assignment. We have similar fears about many other quasi-public affairs that are touched with public interest but fail to get public support. It would seem that we need to imagine, and conceive, and construct a public thing that can discharge the responsibilities that we now vaguely realize.

"It is the legitimate object of government to do for the people what needs to be done, but cannot be done at all, or as well, by individual effort." This statement of Abraham Lincoln may be a good beginning for the discourse that follows. In the last twenty years, it has often been quoted as the answer to the public problems that vex us. But it has been quoted in so many contexts and by so many different persons and parties that it is no longer an answer, but rather a question; indeed, a very complex question, like those questions that the Delphic oracle proposed to the Greeks as they steered their frail ships of state through uncharted waters. For instance, I have been saying that the common law deals with those things that can be done by individual effort. The operations of the marketplace are usually understood to be carried on by individual effort, but some of their agents are voluntary associations. These can be seen as the work of individuals making agreements and using private property. But the results as well as the associations are sometimes touched with public interest, and this interest is at least symbolically recognized in the granting of charters for enterprises that the government wishes to encourage. When this interest appears to be essential to meet the needs of the people, the charter may bring the enterprise into the category of public utilities governed by public laws. In the mixed economies of the contemporary world, some enterprises are judged to fall clearly into the space that Lincoln's statement recognizes as the legitimate operation of government; and these are nationalized. As enterprises prosper and grow, Lincoln's oracle gets more and more attention and our many answers to it get confused. We stop short of making clearly public laws, and we get lost in the temporizing alternatives of planning and questionable administrative edicts. We do not want to face any rigorous application of Lincoln's question; we prefer to explore and experiment under the rules of private common law to see how far such laws can be stretched to cover the novelties. There may be wisdom in this, but the moment of truth will come when we have to answer the question. There is wisdom also in trying to anticipate the answer.

But at the least, Lincoln seems to have laid down what might be called an existence theorem: there are things that need to be done for the people that cannot be done by individual effort; there is a legitimate object of government, of public law. There are things that need to be done for the people, and by the people, collectively, corporately. But Lincoln also laid down another existential proposition, contrasting public and private law: there are things that need to be done, but can be done and done better by individual effort. This serves to sharpen the question, and also suggests that there are in any complex political structure many questions about the allocations of functions to the respective constitutional parts.

In these recent years of Western political experience, the familiar statement of Aristotle, "Man is a political animal," often taken to be a part of dogmatic doctrine but more wisely interpreted as oracular, like Lincoln's, has increasingly come under skeptical questioning. The form the questioning has taken is to assume that it is a simple proposition. We assume that we know what it means and that the only question is whether it is true; more specifically, can it be verified by observation. If the oracle is to be listened to at all, it would be safer to find out first what it means. It should be remembered that the oracle at Delphi often turned out to be a grim jokester, because the quick-minded Greeks often answered the question before they knew what it meant.

We are quick-witted too. We quickly reduce such propositions, sometimes with the help of so-called analytic philosophy, to their lowest empirical terms and then look around for the facts. If we do that with this proposition at present, we conclude easily that man is not even as political as the ants. He may have political impulses, perhaps nostalgic impulses, but in our technological industrial world, these impulses are quickly snubbed. It is only heroic obstinacy, bent on martyrdom, that can provide the evidence for the proposition. That there are persons who call themselves politicians, and by whatever nonpolitical devices they can use "govern" us, is poor evidence indeed. But for the original proposition, even paranoia and corruption are very weighty evidences.

The original proposition has a very rich context, in fact a long history of thought and experience. It is not merely a postulate constructed by a witty man. It is much nearer a middle-range proposition, generalizing a field of evidence for another proposition: man is a rational animal. Politics is a ubiquitous activity of men, one of many other kinds of activity, that shows their irrepressible desire to know and to act rationally. Constant and ubiquitous failure is evidence of a natural power. A single trial and error need be no evidence at all; continual trial and failure against odds is overwhelming evidence. So it is with political struggle as an evidence of rational animality. So it is with speech and tool-using, those other familiar evidences of rationality.

The extended proposition is that man is a rational political animal. The almost universal frustration of political activity in the contemporary world has many causes, some of them new and some of them of very long standing. The present sudden acceleration in the development of speech and all forms of communication based on speech, and the rapid acceleration of tool-making and tool-using in modern technology, promising as they may be for reason and politics in the long run, are for the time being caught in puzzling complications. They are at least temporarily self-frustrating: they are means, but we are not at all sure of their ends. They constitute at present a form of fanaticism, redoubling our efforts when we have forgotten our ends. These are some of the immediate reasons for political frustration.

But there are also permanent reasons for the frustration. If men were angels, say the Federalist Papers, men would not need politics. This might better be put, If men were angels, self-government would be perfect. Laws would be known, understood, and obeyed instantaneously; laws would not have to be made by deliberation, adjudicated in courts, and administered. Reason in its nondiscursive intuitive mode would suffice. But men, because they are animals, know, understand, and act discursively and imaginatively, and passionately. These processes take time, and although they are illumined and corrected by intuition, they can go astray. Men have to learn, confuse themselves, forget, and relearn. And these frustrations are most fateful in politics. Reason is most self-frustrating in the face of novelty, and politics is always deeply involved in history where novelty is the rule rather than the exception. The proposition then further extends itself: man is a rational, political, learning animal.

Seeing this growing series of adjectives, each addition involving deeper frustration, the modern mind jumps to a summary question: why indulge in such a risky self-frustrating enterprise? This question has become for us who are embarked on the most difficult kind of politics, democratic politics, a very acute and crucial question, and the people who are most concerned are at present busy with many escapist answers, many of them under the general heading of political science. The professional political scientist is counseling that we pursue politics by other means. But these answers to the questions are not as escapist, nihilistic, or existential as they seem; neither are they new. They have always been asked when the basic political questions are posed. They show how complex and far-reaching the function of reason is in human affairs, most especially when these affairs are political. The temporary and permanent frustrations are not complete as long as the summary question is being asked.

The preceding verifications of the basic proposition that man is a political animal are admittedly dialectical and paradoxical. In effect, they are saying that continual and ubiquitous frustration of a human activity argues for the existence of a deeply rooted power; the more persistent the frustration, the more irrepressible the power. But there are clearer and more patent evidences. Back of any quasi-empirical verification there is a more basic insight; in this case, there is available an intuitive induction that each man can make within himself. It is usually made in the midst of complex circumstances, although it can be made very simply. It is attested by impressive figures from the late nineteenth century and the early twentieth century. Tolstoy, Dostoevsky, and Gandhi speak out of the depths when they say that each man is responsible for evil anywhere in the universe. They are religious men and their expression is religious. But they have been heard and heeded by ordinary men everywhere. The ordinary men, some of them unsung revolutionaries and martyrs, have translated the saying into political speech and action. They say that each man is responsible for injustice anywhere in his community. The legalist will want to restrict it further and find the responsibility for injustice or injury only when blame can be formally established in a court. But no one will want to restrict it merely to injury or injustice that is explicitly prohibited by law. Responsibility extends to the making of needed laws. The elaboration of the doctrine can be found in Greek tragedy. Tragic blindness is to be found in all human beings, and it is their fate always to be finding their responsibilities for injustice after the fact. It may be that man-made laws should not be applied ex post facto, but it is in the nature of things that the moral law is almost always applied in an ex post facto manner in the course of human learning. This fact is a spur to learning, but it is also the cost of learning. It is by guilt for innocent action that we learn. Tragedy is, in this respect, the great school of reason; responsibility for injustice is the content of learning by suffering.

Justice and injustice are not the only things learned in this way.

Responsibility for freedom and lack of freedom anywhere in the community are associated objects. So it is with peace and war, with order and disorder. These four—justice, freedom, peace, and order—are the parts of the common good. They are the undeniable responsibilities of each man. Such responsibilities are not always immediately recognized or felt, but it is more than likely that they will be so recognized in the course of the ordinary human life. They are evidences of the natural political powers of men.

But there is still another way of seeing and formulating the ineradicable political propensity of men. In an aphorism of F. H. Bradley, it is said that men continually find reasons for what they believe on instinct, but this search is also an instinct. Bradley's remark is an understatement, of course; reason is not only innate and irrepressible like hunger or sex, but it is an essential component of any human activity that is truly human. Again, to be paradoxical, the psychiatrist will bear witness that the uses and misuses of reason constitute an inescapable subject matter of his diagnosis and therapy, no matter how deeply they may be rooted in biological and psychic conditions. This means that man in society will inevitably act in the light of general rules, principles, ideas. The inescapable tools of his actions will be universals. More specifically, if he thinks of himself as a man, he will not be able to escape thinking that other people are men. He will have to entertain the categorical imperative, that the rules he uses to guide his own conduct should apply to other men, to all other men; that the maxims of his action shall be universal. This can be seen as a reciprocity between human beings: treat other men as you treat yourself. But this is to discover justice, and once to discover it is never to escape the concern that it implies. If one finds himself free and cares to remain free, then other men are free and should be respected as ends in themselves and not as means only. It is also to discover a general human responsibility for justice, injustice, freedom, and lack of freedom for all humankind. This finally is to discover the political imperative.

At this point, the two arguments, or the two explorations of the meaning of oracular statements by Lincoln and by Aristotle, cross each other and make a truly crucial turning point.

> The legitimate object of government is to do for the people
> what needs to be done . . .
> Man is a political animal.

The question that grows from the first is: what needs to be done?
This can be answered by a list of the physical, biological, psychic,
and spiritual needs of men as they form cities or political communities. As we are educating ourselves in the so-called welfare
state, there are phases or aspects of all these that fall under some
general political responsibility. But, viewed summarily and
formally, what needs to be done for the people, but cannot be
done at all or as well by individual effort, is justice and the other
parts of the common good: freedom, peace, and order. As stated
in the Preamble of the Constitution they are: union, justice,
liberty, tranquillity, common defense, general welfare—the last
two items clearly further specifications of the four others. But
these are also the imperatives that with the help of Tolstoy,
Dostoevsky, and Gandhi we have found in the irrepressible
powers of the political animal. The needs and the powers of men
in society coincide; they are identical in their simultaneous ful-
fillments. They amount to a common responsibility of each and
all. From each according to his powers, and to each according to
his needs.

Turned another way, the formal demands of the common good
can be seen as the necessary conditions for the existence of any
political community; they are the minimal constituents of any
public government, of the res publica, the public thing. Men who
do not meet these needs or realize these powers are each less
than men. Their lives are nasty, brutish, and short. In Plato's
harsh terms, their community is a city of pigs. Nothing in the
formal, perhaps pompous language of the preceding indicates
that men do not fall to the low status that Hobbes and Plato so
vividly describe. Hobbes is, of course, describing men in an
imagined state of nature where lack of law results in a war of all
against all. Plato is describing a simple state in which a social
contract has succeeded in establishing a division of labor and a
market. Other conceptions of a state of nature have resulted in
varieties of these images from Homer's description of Poly-

phemus's tyranny to Rousseau's community of noble savages.
Perhaps Adam Smith's model of the market as a commercial republic ought to be included as a warning that states of nature
can exist within the jurisdiction of public government. The
doctrinaire partisans of the private law sometimes indulge in the
same confused utopianism and claim that laissez-faire economics
is the essence of the Constitution.

I have juxtaposed the preceding oracular pronouncements so
that the resulting dialectical questions and answers will reveal
their reciprocal meanings. (1) Government legitimately does
what needs to be done, but cannot be done by individuals. (2)
Man is a political animal. (3) Each man is responsible for injustice anywhere in the community. I shall now add another
rather opaque statement from Montesquieu, his definition of
political, as distinguished from individual, liberty: Political liberty
consists in the assurance that you can do what you ought to will.
This has a ring about it that suggests that it is an ethical proposition; for instance, it can be combined closely with Kant's categorical imperative. There would be an increase in the sense of
moral freedom if there were some assurance that the commands
of reason can be obeyed effectively, an assurance that Kant denied
could be guaranteed. But Montesquieu quite explicitly intended
only political liberty. Quite clearly, he is thinking of something
like justice as what one "ought to will" in politics. What then
can be the assurance that justice can be done? The answer to this
question seems to be simple: the laws, laws that are universal
rules with equal incidence on all citizens, presumably based on
some initiative and consent by the people. Laws—their making,
their administration, and their casual adjudication—are the
means by which the individual can discharge his collective
responsibility for justice and injustice. This is consistent with the
Thomistic definition of law: laws are rules of reason promulgated by an authority and directed to the common good; it is also
consistent with Lon Fuller's recent sociological definition: law is
the enterprise of subjecting human behavior to the governance
of rules.

This attempt to explore and to explicate oracular wisdom is a
precarious enterprise. The question can be asked, at this point,

why not settle for the social contract as an adequate and un-cluttered statement of the principles that lie back of our Con-stitution and the polity within which we live politically? All men are born with certain liberties and freedoms. At some point in our lives, we individually or collectively run into enough difficulties, not to mention calamities, to be willing to agree to set up a representative body to discern, deliberate on, and integrate the opinion and will of the people and finally make specific contracts that will serve as laws; and, further, to arrange for the delegation of functions to officers of administration and deliberation. Under this arrangement, elections in part reaffirm the general contract and in part choose persons to fill the offices. As I have suggested above, this is raising an instrumentality of common and private law to perform functions of public law. This may involve, as we now suspect, the confusion of common law and public law and the habits they generate and confirm. It may be that this simple procedural scheme is in trouble now, partly because of the con-fusion of the separate kinds of law, but it may also be that it has allowed us to forget the context within which it was assumed to work, chiefly the conceptions of the common good, justice, etc., that guide the making of good laws.

In the opening words of Rousseau's *Social Contract,* and in Locke's *First Treatise,* it is clear that both were intending to propose premises for government that would replace the terrible tangle of its traditional roots. They wanted to uproot and cast out doctrines like the divine right of kings and the historical accumulations of government by accident and force. The social contract was proposed as the basis for government by reflection and choice. They were protesting against tyranny on behalf of liberty. I have suggested that they did not eradicate the tradi-tion, particularly the common-law tradition; the social contract itself is rooted in the tradition of common law, although it rep-resents a daring innovation. The innovation made, in the style of a generalization, was to provide a framework for a public government that would replace the monarchical public govern-ments of the past, or as in Hobbes's proposal, to constitutionalize the monarchy. It seems now that the social-contract theory worked largely because there were other traditional principles and institutions present and operating implicitly. In quoting Lincoln and Aristotle I have pointed to some of this context, particularly to the common good as it is implicit in the notions of public law and needs of political man. This context is being explored anew by many searchers: some in the field of jurisprudence, some in the field of the so-called living law, where law is understood as the implementation of public policy. My aim so far has been to find the minimal conceptual framework for the erection or restoration of a structure of public law, a place where the promise of a specifically political liberty can be fulfilled under law. Some of what follows will seem quaintly pious and old-fashioned, and some will seem rashly utopian. One should dare to hope that the future will be made of such stuff.

THE POLITY AND THE BILL OF RIGHTS

Hannah Arendt in *Between Past and Future* and *On Revolution* seems to be regretting the two quite different failures of the French and the American revolutions. In spite of their differences, they both failed to provide something that she calls the Constitution of Liberty. The French Revolution made the mistake of letting its strictly political aims get subsumed under what the Europeans call the social question. In sweeping away the feudal and monarchical regimes, it got involved in the heavy business of steering the industrial revolution and remolding or abolishing the classes. In Miss Arendt's view, if I am understanding it, this overloads the political process and denatures it. It starts a never-ending social ferment that will not allow the development of reasonable politics. Hence the succession of republics in France up to the present day.

The American Revolution did not have the social and economic question to solve. It therefore could face the specifically political question squarely, and with the help of extraordinary political craftsmen it drafted a constitution that had many of the requisites of a Constitution of Liberty. The revolution abolished the tenuous remnants of feudalism and monarchy in colonial life, and built a political structure that was innocent of the responsibilities that would accrue to it as the economic and social questions developed.

It was a naïve construction. Naïveté was its virtue, but also its
vice. It has not kept up with the events it has engendered.

Miss Arendt has a very circumstantial and somewhat dark
story to tell in explanation. I shall not discuss that, but rather take
a cue from her discussion of a slip in terminology. In the Declaration of Independence, inalienable rights are listed as "life, liberty,
and the pursuit of happiness." There seems to be evidence that
an earlier version read "life, liberty, and the public happiness."
The pursuit of happiness has been the subject of some study,
most notably in lectures with that phrase as title by Howard
Mumford Jones. Like many such ambiguous phrases, the pursuit
of happiness has had a telling history. It has apparently meant
something like the ultimate aim of a society as distinguished from
the individual. It has also meant equal opportunity for citizens
and, of course, a kind of charter for free industrial enterprise. In
general, it has slipped from a public to a private interpretation.
Public happiness, on the other hand, might have had another
career, emphasizing the happiness of public enterprise and accomplishment. Miss Arendt's guesses about this are not impressive.
She mentions the public man's enjoyment of popular honor and
acclaim, the fun of competition for electoral or appointed office,
and the satisfaction of a public career and accomplishment. She
does not seem to connect this directly with what seems to be her
main theme, the general happiness that free and effective government confers on its society, the deep satisfaction of participation
in good public institutions. To recall the propositions of Tolstoy,
Dostoevsky, and Gandhi, it would seem that the substance of
public happiness might be the satisfaction of discharging one's
responsibility for injustice. This, of course, involves the social
question that Miss Arendt says fatally spoiled the French Revolution. But the French Revolution has made a good deal of history,
not only in France. It would seem that we have a duty to go into
the spirit as well as the letter of the law if we are to find the
Constitution of Liberty that we so far have missed.

The great revolutions of the eighteenth century—French,
American, and British—were very clear in recognizing and emphasizing the basic change that they brought about. They suddenly transformed the individual, the little private man, the

"idiot," as the Greeks called him, the common man molded only by common private law of one kind or another, into the public man. Remembering the pride of the citizen in the ancient Roman res publica, the revolutionary political craftsmen conferred on the private individual a public title—*citizen*. In some cases they made it a matter of constitutional law that there should be no other titles. The title *citizen* was the title of the first official in the public realm. Further, they made these primary officials, working in their new political statuses, sovereign officials. The term *sovereign*, stolen as it was from the monarchic polities, has never had an easy usage in the new regime, but it reinforced the sentiments and confirmed the functions of the new citizens. The title *citizen* and the transformation it recognizes had implications that had and still have to be explored, both in theory and in practice.

The First Amendment, interpreted as the recognition by the government of its obligations to protect and support certain free activities of the citizens, suggests what the primary functions of citizens are. Speech, press, assembly, and religion—each of these have what are called transcendent functions; that is, their ultimate ends are the discovery and dissemination of truths of one kind or another. These ends transcend or differ radically from political functions. But in their civil operations they serve the polity in essential, indispensable ways. Speech is the way a society has of making the first formulation of concrete fact and process; language is the means of naming and ordering things for common human discourse. The press, imitating and elaborating the functions of speech, adds a certain organization of thought and becomes a powerful means of communication and social memory. These reportorial activities can be called the grammatical arts of a community; they provide and maintain the elementary symbolic system by which a human society maintains itself. Crude as they may be, speech, press, radio, and television are the elemental means by which men understand themselves and their fellows. Elaborated and refined, they can be the mediums by which we come to recognize injustice and justice; they are the initial means by which we discover and serve the common good. Their operations arise from mysterious sources in the human soul; their express forms are delicate and easily distorted; they never are perfect. They must be free and they must be cultivated. They should not be abridged and they cannot be controlled.

But speech and press are not merely reportorial. Speech can carry regrets, wishes, and commands; the press interprets, judges, and opines. These mediums of communication are the prime means of persuasion. The rhetorical dimension of speech and press is not merely something added to the grammatical function; it is built in and inextricable. No matter how much a scholar may wish to think that his discourse escapes the rhetorical dimension, his cold or warm speculative discourse persuades. Persuasion may also have transcendent ends, but it cannot escape its essential function in making politics. In fact, the whole public realm may be seen as the enterprise of freeing, canalizing, and perpetuating persuasion.

Assembly is the prototype of the political exploitation of persuasion. Whether assembly occurs at a country fair, in a sports arena, or through a professional association, persuasion is practised with political effects both internal to the group and between the group and the whole community. A great deal of what once was intended as private persuasion, within the family, in domestic entertaining, social gatherings, the suburban kaffee klatsch, the business luncheon, the formal dinner, and the theater party, as well as the niggling of the commercial market, now spills over into an intensely cultivated domain—public relations. Deliberate organization of groups with ulterior public purposes exist under various managers, but a great deal of persuasion of the spontaneous sort exists to tempt the promoter. This is the basis for the much-used political phrase, the *grass roots*. A vibrant democratic society is very much aware of private and public events that happen at the grass roots, and it continually crystallizes and institutionalizes the opinions that grow in this soil of persuasion.

The voluntary associations that Tocqueville celebrated as the genius of American society everywhere imitate the great political association of government. But following Tocqueville's description of their spontaneous generation, we tend to base our understanding of them on their private origins, in sentiments of sympathy and mutual aid. We tend to think of them in their quasi-organized forms as bundles of contracts, making their private laws as they go along. When they grow in numbers and in function, and their freely exercised powers interfere and clash with other similar associations, we tend to defend them as if they were private individuals or, as the law has it, natural persons. This tendency was memorialized when the clauses in the Fourteenth Amendment, which were written to give the freed slaves the status of full citizens, were used to ensure business corporations immunity from interference by the public government.

It is worth noting that the meetings of voluntary associations govern themselves procedurally under *Robert's Rules of Order*. Even a boys' club seems to imagine itself as existing under a charter that states its purpose and as a legislature with a chairman who enforces the rules by which persuasion, deliberation, and legislation take place. *Robert's Rules of Order* provides a little standard constitution universally applied to facilitate and guide mutual persuasion. The voluntary association under this borrowed law is a sort of greenhouse for the forced growth of private into public affairs. It is a seminary for training in the art of formal public persuasion.

It has often been said that our local governments—town, city, county, state, within the national federal pattern—provide a training ground for the citizen who chooses to make politics a career. It is also often observed that this educational base can be either good or bad. There have been periods when local governments, particularly municipal and state governments, have been corrupt, and their graduates on the national level have learned bad habits. It is always a question whether the habits of private common law are transferable to public service . . . without reformation. But, for good or ill, the habits acquired in one locus of exercise are transferred; they are contagious. Since voluntary associations are schools of politics, and they are widespread and constant in their effects on their members, their power to influence the general operations of government, both local and national, and to determine the quality of persuasion that energizes the whole body politic is very nearly fateful for the quality of self-government that can be attained.

This point can be generalized and focused in James Bryce's observation that the instruments and style of the expansion of the British empire begun in the sixteenth and seventeenth centuries were the trading companies. These trading companies, established under royal charters in a period of mercantilism, were in effect put aboard sailing ships and exported, east to India and west to the Americas. Traveling to great distances across salt water, these companies took on a life of their own. Their commercial purposes in a new environment gave them a spirit of independence, and they met ther own needs for self-government, gradually throwing off their dependence on and subordination to the mother government. The spontaneous life within them caught the spirit of voluntary association, but at the same time they invented and incorporated political forms. It is said that John Locke, acting as secretary to the Earl of Shaftesbury, took account of these developments, wrote and rewrote the charters for the many companies, and finally did his *Treatises on Government* as an analysis and critique of the political processes at work in the colonies as they became independent. It was not by accident that he contributed to the writing of the American Constitution by way of the constitution of South Carolina. He was sensing a general line of development, which still persists, of voluntary association into public government. He did not state, but we can now see, that it is an almost natural tendency for the voluntary association to imitate public government by incorporating itself under a charter that becomes either an independent government itself or a part of a government. This tells the story of the genesis of many modern governments. So it is not merely the function of voluntary associations to train their members in the arts of government, but also themselves to grow into governments. It is also true that voluntary associations die, but if they survive they may themselves become public things.

The trading companies were obviously organized to promote trade, but when Adam Smith saw them operating in the British market, he soon detected that they were conspiracies in restraint of trade. He saw them taking over some of the functions of the mercantilist government, through monopoly. Part of his famous book, *The Wealth of Nations,* warns of the bad effects of both conspiracy and monopoly. He was writing at the beginning of a time when the power of the corporations served greed alone and was prophesying their imminent self-destruction, as in the case of the South Sea Bubble. He was speaking on behalf of another voluntary association arising within the framework of common law—the market. His theory helped to make the market understood as the great private institution that could only serve the public community by being left free. Whether Lincoln had this institution in mind in his statement about individual effort is a moot but large, persistent question. But the development of the market was to go through the stages of quasi-governmental organization of the corporation, escaping Adam Smith's condemnation by allowing itself to be regulated. The trading company in this country became the corporation for profit, sharply distinguished from its sister corporation in the private realm as the charitable corporation.

The corporation for profit, the business corporation, because it has increasingly specialized and intensified its functions in the heavy-going affairs of commerce and industry, has developed within itself and in its external relations the style of persuasion that is dominant in the market, the mutual persuasion that we call bargaining. Bargaining can be a peaceful, rational process, a means of arriving at reasonable and fair rates of exchange with the consent of the parties, but it also can degenerate to the level of a contest of power and force. As power—either commercial or industrial, or both—increases, threat can take the place of reason. Competition can take place on many levels simultaneously, and it does—within the limits set by the rules that have developed in common law. Gross force and fraud are ruled out of contracts, but there is an area recognized in law in which the only rule is a warning—*caveat emptor*. The practice of persuasion in the market, as evidenced in advertising, tends to settle to the lower levels of the possible range of the art. It seldom reaches the lowest level of reciprocal threat, but there is always the suspicion of the maximum use of power, with reason estimating what the traffic will bear. This practice dominates the internal workings of the corporation as well as its external relations. It is rather far from the use of persuasion in politics proper.

Although there is a certain contagion of practice between the business and the charitable corporation, the aim of the typical charitable corporation is different; it is not for profit. For instance, the educational corporation gets its charter because its purpose is something that the government wishes to encourage for the common good. For this reason, it is not taxed; in some cases it is a part of the government and is supported from tax funds. When it raises money from private sources or from the government, something like bargaining may take place, but the quality of persuasion is different from bargaining. There is something, at least in the potentiality of the charitable corporation as distinguished from the business corporation, that makes the inevitable pun on *profit* and *prophet* sound a deeper chord of wit. Reason in the charitable corporation can see further than it can in the power complex of the business corporation.

But the ways of statutory legislation and charter granting have never apparently allowed the connection between the charitable corporation for education and the First Amendment. Sometimes the doctrine of academic freedom has operated in the spirit of such an implied connection. The First Amendment grants freedom of speech, press, and assembly to the citizen. In combination these freedoms nicely ensure, almost in cartoon form, the elementary conditions of teaching and learning—Mark Hopkins facing a student with books on a log. Very early the towns made this picture into the little red schoolhouse, and the citizens in voluntary association under a charitable corporation charter built academies and liberal colleges to go with the schoolhouses. Reading, writing, and arithmetic grew into the trivium and quadrivium of the traditional liberal arts. Soon after the turn of the nineteenth century, the states, following the implications of the transformation of the common man into the public citizen, began the building of the first system of universal education in history. This building is still going on: witness the present concern with shortages of schoolhouses, colleges, and teachers, and also the present slow response to the need for a national system of education that does not depend upon the uneven developments of the economic system to support it. Ironically enough, the negative reading of the First Amendment, implying immunity from government intervention, is blocking the legislation that would fully implement the affirmative reading.

The use of speech in teaching, the use of books that fall from the printing presses, the establishment of permanent assemblies in schools and colleges have high aims that transcend the political process of persuasion. They reach to scholarship and contemplation, but it is no derogation of these ends to say that the processes of teaching and learning initiate and develop improved forms of persuasion, and that the habits that go with them are of the highest use to politics. School is the traditional preparation for life, but it is also the basic preparation for politics. In it there is the irrepressible attempt to raise reason from private to public concerns, to raise the arts of bargaining for mutual private advantage to the art of deliberation for the common good, so that combats by force and threat may become subjects for common deliberation.

We often view public education as a device for equalizing opportunity for individuals, and we put emphasis on vocational training for the underprivileged and professional education for the overprivileged; we set up elaborate elective systems to ensure the ordinary individual a free choice from a large variety of careers. Then, seeing the divisiveness engendered in our culture by its trade, class, and caste distinctions, we worry about so-called general education and culture. We see that we are failing in the most elementary initiation of the young into the rights, duties, and freedoms of citizenship; and we end by substituting "social studies," a reduction of politics, for the great common studies in the sciences and the humanities that would school the student in the arts of mutual persuasion that are the basis for perpetual self-education in public life. The liberal arts were once the education of the aristocratic free men who made up the so-called ruling classes. The promise of the eighteenth-century revolution was that common men should become their own rulers. So universal education started in the new republics, and it was liberal education that was to be universalized. But the exclusive addiction to individual liberty of choice, conditioned by competitive economy and industry and their temptation to build wealth and power, forced the competitive system into education, where the young are thus thrown back into the occupations of private individuals without benefit of the common concern for the public happiness. Elected officers are chosen from these frustrated citizens, and they carry their individual causes and habits into public life, which then loses its educational power.

Horace Mann, the first state commissioner of education in Massachusetts, thought and wrote well about the fundamental civic function of liberal education in the school system. He thought of such formal education as the great initiation of the young into the continually self-educating republic of learning, which in turn would perpetuate and continually renew the learning and teaching of the all-pervasive political process of the democratic society. At the same time, he reintroduced the natural sciences to the literary and humanistic curriculum, realizing very fully for his time the importance of basic science to the citizen's understanding of the industrial processes. As the Horace Mann program spread throughout the country, together with compulsory rules of attendance, it ran head-on into the wave of early vocational specialization, individualism, and careerism that finally culminated in Charles Eliot's elective system and John Dewey's progressive child-centered school. Blackstone's *Commentaries,* which had been written as a textbook for required courses in the liberal arts curriculum and used in American liberal arts colleges, was relegated to the reference book shelf in libraries of law schools. Civics courses for secondary schools became exercises in memorizing the bones in the skeletons of local, state, and national governments. Government itself became a rather bad school for the representatives and officers in government service. The ladder of persuasion, which had its bottom rungs in the formal schools and its higher rungs in the hierarchy of government, was broken. For several generations now there have been energetic but unsuccessful attempts to compensate for the failures of education in politics by establishing a universal system of adult education. The Lyceum and Chatauqua have now been replaced by a National Association for Adult Education merged with the National Education Association and Great Books Seminars for citizens, business executives, and civil servants, but an improvement of persuasion in education and government is not taking place; the quality of public persuasion continually worsens as it assimilates itself to the marketplace of ideas and management.

Political science registers the decline of persuasion in our society when it flatly and frankly accepts power as the substance of politics and the essential subject matter of its science. Power is a mercurial term. It can mean the possession of real property and tools; we have learned that these things have great potentiality. But it can also mean the capacity to influence, lead, organize, and control people. It can mean the result of developing and realizing these potencies in organizing organizations. It can mean the so-called monopoly of force that some claim for the government. It is said that the purpose of government is to control power, to resolve conflicts of power. A man, an official, a group, so-called ruling circles, are said to be powerful if they control power, if they can make decisions that will be fulfilled by power or powers, if they can command obedience. One cannot quarrel with such a polyglot verbal usage and the confusion of theory and practice that it produces; neither can one solve the pseudo-problems that it poses. But something like political intelligibility can be provided if all these definitions of power and others that can be added are understood as pertaining to the more or less realized power to persuade. But one must then add the other component of persuasion—reason. Persuasion moves from stage to stage, and each stage accomplished is a power understood and accepted as a basis for further persuasion. Power in this sense involves a belief accepted and obeyed. Power, again in this sense, seeks legitimation, perhaps by reason, but ultimately by law. Power without reason, purpose, or law is insecure, evanescent, illusory. This is the radical meaning of Lord Acton's aphorism, Power corrupts, absolute power corrupts absolutely, and of Woodrow Wilson's retort, Legitimate power ennobles.

No one wishes to deny that persuasion depends on power. Even in the simple case of speaker and listener, there are powers in the speaker and powers in the listener, at first nakedly confronting one another in opposition; but the crucial transactions of bargaining, argument, debate, and negotiation take place in reason. Common deliberation is the typical form that practical reason and persuasion take in politics proper; through it, power and interest find their political ends in the common good, and eventually their true legitimation in law.

But common deliberation, once introduced, takes on a life of its own. It loses its eristic drive, the determination to win the argument. It becomes a true dialectic in which the aim is the discovery of common ends that transcend private ends. It has a speculative end in seeking truth, and this in turn penetrates the apparent, already recognized goods in interest and power to the larger real goods of common life. It expands enormously the conventional freedoms that have their roots in private life. It is often said in defense of the current proliferation of technology that it multiplies possible choices, for instance, in department stores, but the habits of increased common deliberation in the political sphere multiply and fertilize the roots of choice in imagination and thought. There are more undiscovered ends in public life than the philosophy of private freedom has yet dreamed of. The residual poverty of private life with which we are at present fumbling might well find its solution in the discovery of liberty in the public sector.

The immunity and protection for religion that is ensured in the First Amendment has lost much of its meaning, or perhaps never discovered its meaning, because religious sectarianism has allowed its internal quarrels to eclipse the high transcendent aims and its civic functions. Religion has followed its propensity to allow its practices to sink to the level of religiosity; it has often redoubled its efforts as it has lost sight of its ends. When religion is healthy, its philosophical and theological explorations shed light on both individual and common deliberation. Faith seeking understanding stretches the private and public mind. In healthy religions, dogmas are questions that draw all minds into the search. The byproduct is the enriching of deliberation, and religion teaches that there is no end to the possible enrichment. Congress shall make no law touching an establishment of religion or the free exercise thereof because the sources of the citizen's enlightenment must not be cut off. If the decadence of religion continues, and dogmas continue to become devices for closing minds, there may come a day when this part of the First Amendment will have to be rewritten to enable the revival of religion, or some substitute for it, to keep the top of the deliberative mind open.

Included in the First Amendment's list of rights and duties of the citizen, there is the final one, with quaint and somber undertones. It is associated with the right of the people to assemble peaceably, but it is quite different in meaning from that familiar social habit; it is the right to petition the government for a redress of grievances. It is as if the writers of the First Amendment, having seen clearly the elementary and necessary functions of the new citizens in the public sphere and some of the institutions that would be necessary to initiate and perpetuate the new habits, suddenly fell back into the pre-Revolutionary mood of despair about the effectiveness of the public government. Given the elegant superstructure of the Constitution, duly amended, there is the possibility—indeed the probability—that it will not sufficiently deliver to the citizens the justice for which they have "ordained and established" it. Its authors must have remembered the moving occasions when subjects appealed to the "conscience of the King," skipping over and above the courts and parliaments that were his agents. There is something of the spirit of the courts of equity in this, where there were special procedures by which the ever-present discrepancy between the general laws and the unique case could be repaired. But there is also the notion that new situations outrun the laws and still need public attention. Of course, there is also the constant risk of corruption in institutions and officials. How to discharge the responsibility for injustice in such circumstances is the residual question. The older petition to the sovereign had been a remedy—sometimes effective, often pitifully ineffective. The petition, although formal and written, had been addressed to a sovereign but always carried beyond the formality to the human person under the ceremonial robes. In a self-government it is not easy to identify the sovereign in this sense. The President of the United States or the governor of a "sovereign" state is formally given some such official duty in the power of pardon and reprieve for criminals, but this does not meet the whole or the major part of the area of grievances. The First Amendment substitutes the government for the sovereign. Although there have been many petitions to officials, the problem has been solved in practice by assuming that the people, the public, is the sovereign, and the petition takes the form of public dramatic demonstration. Sometimes these dramas take place in theater or hall under cover, but more often the petition is made to the conscience of the people in the street. Recently, the risk of violence in this political act has been avoided in the ways of nonviolent, passive resistance that Gandhi invented and used in India. This has been a great lesson for the whole world in the relation of persuasion to force in public matters. Minimize force so that truth can be spoken to power; this is the meaning of Gandhi's word *satyagraha*. This is the way the people's deliberation makes politics when the established means of persuasion have failed. It can reach to constitutional matters and is connected with the so-called right to revolution, which we are at present seeing exercised at home as well as in other parts of the world.

In this period when little people all over the world are becoming public citizens, some of them for the first time, the right of petition is taking on new meanings, some reaching into the depths of jurisprudence to natural and divine law. Senator Richard Russell said the other day that the power that broke the Southern filibuster in the Senate was not merely his Northern colleagues, not merely the President in his moral appeal and pressure, but perhaps most crucially the ministers who had made what was for him a political issue a religious issue. He was mildly sounding the alarm on the issue of church and state. But he and his Southern colleagues might have used their filibuster time to expound the conservative position concerning the massive shift, on a world-wide scale, to extend the meaning of the civil liberties and the civil rights in our Bill of Rights. In the late 1940's the Political Action Committee of the AFL-CIO drafted a so-called Economic Bill of Rights, which was in effect a petition to extend the assurances of the Bill of Rights to economic matters, particularly the citizen's right to a job. The Declaration of Human Rights, under the aegis of the United Nations, makes similar claims. Both of these documents can be said to have derived from the preambles to the French Republican constitutions of the twentieth century. The work of a thousand and one planning commissions can be understood as petitions to the government for the systematic redress of grievances. As the base from which the petitions are made grows more inclusive of religious, moral, social, and economic considerations, the correlative responses of governments to the social question, as Hannah Arendt calls it, indicate that the right of petition may become the formal means by which governments learn to accept and discharge their growing responsibilities.

This running commentary on the First Amendment cannot end without the grateful acknowledgment that it has been following the thread of Alexander Meiklejohn's elegant argument in *Political Freedom*. His study, lecturing, and writing in the last generation has been in effect a continued amicus curiae brief to fortify the dissenting opinions of Supreme Court Justices Black and Douglas during this stormy period when civil liberties cases have been making constitutional history. His focus of attention has been upon the part that freedom of speech plays in the operation of the Constitution as conceived to be a charter of freedom. He has used Rousseau's version of the social contract as the interpretation of the Constitution and as his premise for a rigorous criticism of the various erratic readings of the First Amendment in the Court, particularly the so-called balancing doctrine, which sees freedom of speech as a private privilege against which other liberties and necessities are to be weighed. Meiklejohn would have us conceive of The People as a fourth division in the government—the very root rather than a mere branch of the government—with freedom of consent, dissent, and criticism, together with all the institutions of thought that support them as the essential structural and functional foundation of self-government. Any invasion of this root by the other branches of government is a threat, perhaps fatal, to the whole enterprise of self-government.

I accept this forthright, cogent argument and its warning. But I have been concerned in my looser and perhaps confusing argument to consider also other organically connected principles in the common good as they bear on freedom, particularly justice. Meiklejohn's use of the social-contract theory is not merely an appeal to the generalization of contracts in common law as I have discussed earlier. He is not ignoring justice in his emphasis on consent and agreement as exercises of freedom, but he does gain much in the clarity of his argument by his sharp distinction between "freedom of speech" and free speech—between the responsible disciplines of public education and debate, on the one hand, and the informal and sometimes chaotic practices of agitation and direct action. There is precedent for this distinction in the Brandeis dictum, derived from common-law doctrine, that says that no speech should be suppressed unless it destroys the conditions in which intelligible public speech is possible. The recognition of the accumulation of injustices in our time and the rush of grievances now in full flood, all over the world as well as at home, raise the question whether the First Amendment is elastic enough to comprehend them.

I have chosen persuasion as a term that will include consent and agreement in the larger, heavier, and perhaps darker political processes that penetrate and enliven the deeply social, economic, and bureaucratic processes that must bear their share of the burden of justice and injustice. Since laws are the means by which we discharge our responsibilities for injustice, and they are also the forms in which our consents and agreements are confirmed, their imperatives must be rooted in as well as carried out in the whole body politic. As I have been stating the thesis, not only must individual men be admitted to the rights and duties of the public realm, but it is time now for us to understand and assimilate many of our institutions, including some of those that we like to call voluntary and private associations, as parts of this political realm. We live much of our lives and form many of our habits as if they were not touched with public interest, and we fear to politicize them because by so doing we risk losing our liberties. We must learn to find the much greater liberties that go with public political life. Among these are not only freedom of speech, press, religion, assembly, and petition, but also the forms of freedom that are inherent, but as yet unrealized, in technological and economic organization.

With the present reading of the First Amendment, its implications, and its presuppositions, many of these liberties are to be found in the full exercise of the rights of persuasion. The full exercise of these rights leads to common and public deliberation by which the things that need to be done, but cannot be done by individual effort, can be determined and agreed upon and enacted as laws. The Constitution was intended to provide us with the public instruments by which this can be done. Many of these are intended in their differentiation and their articulation to maximize reason and to minimize force and chance as they operate in the persuasive processes.

THE CONSTITUTION

It is considerably less than adequate to say that the Constitution is a charter of the Public Thing. But this is no place to embark on another scholarly and critical study of the document; such a study would in any case be beyond my powers. The ordinary common-sensical reading of the Constitution shows that it is compatible with the general principles of the social contract theory. Read at this point in history, it is the map or blueprint of something that exists, no matter how artificial that thing may be. It formulates offices, institutions, and rules for the conduct of these. It laconically, but eloquently, states the purposes of the thing in the Preamble, which recapitulates the traditional formula of the common good. It formally sets an end for the ubiquitous practice of persuasion, more particularly for the practice of common deliberation. It even more particularly formulates rules or laws for the making of laws, for administering them and adjudicating them so that persuasion can be refined in reason and the laws made effective in the free intelligent obedience of the citizens. It says what the ends and means of government are, hence what politics should be.

I am chiefly interested in seeing the Constitution in its function as generating, guiding, and refining persuasion. Persuasion is initially aided by the daily acceptance of common law in the private affairs of the citizens, confirmed by the common-law courts when these affairs come into conflict. The tendency to mutual persuasion is made explicit in the adversary proceedings of the courts, but the judgments of the courts confirm rather than transform the process. Reason is still the handmaiden of private power and individual freedom. The Constitution takes this resulting basic order in the community for granted. But when the interests and powers of individual affairs break through into the community, where public interest is detected, the Constitutional procedures transform private into public affairs. They are thrown into the arena where free speech, the press, assembly, religion, and petition make them subject to common deliberation. They stimulate and educate the citizens to a different kind of thought. The traditional phrase for this process is the formation of public opinion. It is easy to see here why there are two readings of the First Amendment: one reading sees the private origin of the discussion; the other sees the reason that it should be protected for the discovery of the public good, "what needs to be done for the people." The big and important shift is between the habits in which reason aids interest and the habits in which power awaits the legitimation in reason that will make it dependable and intelligible for the public good.

But this new form of deliberation is not easy; it requires discipline and guidance through formal institutions, the political parties, and the branches of government. Although the Founding Fathers did not foresee or provide for the political parties and the Constitution does not mention them, it was inevitable that they would persist from their British originals in the colonies. By 1840 it was possible for Calhoun to point out the character that they have had ever since. They had begun to mix public issues with private conflicts, allowing private interest through wheeling, dealing, and patronage to invade the public sphere. They learned how to generate merely numerical majorities to win elections and bind representatives to powerful, unseen minorities. The political parties had succumbed very early to the strong habits engendered by the regime of common law. At a crucial point in the transition from private to public politics, they reversed the process, so that party politics became a bad school for statesmen. Through party politics, the representatives learn to cultivate and plead for the private interests of their clients, to keep their "ears to the ground," and to ensure their own reelections as payment for favors received. It is only with an heroic profile that the appearance is created that representatives exercise the essential function of public officials, the deliberation of public issues for the common good. They dare to do this if they think their political fences are in good repair; that is, when the private deals happen to back the bill under consideration. It is said by experienced and honest men that no measure is enacted, no persuasion consummated in law, if it is not backed and underwritten by deals and fixes. If this lesson is not learned in party politics, it is quickly learned in legislative halls, both state and national, by those who survive. One might think, as many do, that this is a fine combination of common and public law; it could be the explanation of the chronic stultification of the public thing.

This vital affinity of private and public persuasion, so long established and confirmed in practice, is implicitly condoned both by the citizens and their representatives as long as the private quasi-contracts are kept, and kept silent; but their illicitness is uncovered when the secret private promises are breached, and there is a public exposé or an investigation. This would seem to indicate that the constitutional distinction and separation of powers in private and public law are never really forgotten. Both private citizen and public officer become righteously indignant, both resenting the silent conspiracy that they have been practicing between public explosions. Of course, the canny citizen reads the public news with one eye on the public performance and the other on the symptoms of supporting private affairs. The free press manages to keep us all informed by a style of tragicomic writing, sometimes making events look better than they are, sometimes worse. The self-styled cynical reporter and the satirical columnist are our stock comic characters, never lacking the materials of their bifocal literature.

But there are other evidences that we have not forgotten the distinction between public and private politics. There are party caucuses both before and after elections in the legislative assemblies. Tellingly, they are chaired by moderators who control and manipulate through *Robert's Rules of Order*. The issues are publicly debated. Public agreements and disagreements are publicly arrived at on public issues; numerical majorities and minorities are measured by votes. Public reason is honored; on special occasions, it is even celebrated ceremoniously. But almost always, the elaborateness of the celebration is proportionate to the degree of compromise that has been achieved in private, not compromise between the issues but between the private power and the public principle. This reality of underlying compromise is often publicly reported and justified by appeal to the practical political principle that politics is the art of compromise, or the art of the possible. "Possible" in this sense most often means what the private interests let the public government do—for a consideration.

The power of persuasion in a free society may seem very small and ineffective, and the notion that the substance of politics is persuasion may seem idealistic and pious—not realistic, as the practical politician says. But if persuasion is the varying combination of power and reason that I am contemplating, persuasion is the sum of effective political power in a community. The Constitution seems to recognize this, and to propose the methods and devices by which it can be maintained and improved. But some of these methods and devices are often viewed with impatience and irritation because they seem to break up the structure into ever smaller fragments and episodic actions until the power is, from the point of view of efficiency, made ineffectual. If the government were better organized to produce results, it would be an unmanageable monster, so we are often warned; but it is actually worse than that—an uncoupled, unstrung leviathan, each of whose parts is a trap that catches and stifles any political impulse or energy that reaches it. One of the recurring themes in political science is the contention that one or another branch or subbranch of government is usurping the functions of other branches and is on the way to tyrannical power, pursuing its ends by nonpolitical means. Ironically enough, the rest of society imitates this style of disorganization in the name of pluralism, and claims to find freedom in the manifold choices of competing purposes in its separate parts.

Montesquieu said that the only solution to the problem of freedom in governments of large territories and populations would be the federal principle, which is perhaps most simply stated in an extension of Lincoln's oracle. The legitimate object of government is to do for the people what needs to be done but cannot be done or done as well by subordinate parts of that government; what needs to be done, and can be done by subordinate parts of the government, should be done by them, and not by the larger parts or the whole of the government. But the American federal scheme of government goes beyond this obvious hierarchical distribution of powers. It breaks the connection and separates the powers of the parts, so that each exercises a maximum of autonomy. This is obviously the case in the relation of state to national governments, as it is expressed in the doctrine of states' rights. It is applied at the top in the separation of powers in the three branches of government: legislative, executive, and judiciary. It is applied in the division of powers between the House of Representatives and the Senate. All of these divisions, together with many variations, are repeated in the state governments in relation to counties and townships. Straight lines of command and management are seldom allowed to continue anywhere in our system. Not even parallel lines of authority are integrated when they traverse the same territory or population. There are no trunk lines of information between the parts within the government. This is the drastic criticism of our disjointed public thing.

The writers of the Federalist Papers are at pains to show that, although the division of powers is often sharp, there are always stated provisions in the Constitution for bridges between these parts, bridges that are almost like treaties between sovereigns. The joint committees of the House and the Senate are typical. In these there is a principle of mutual veto or unanimity. In these bridge procedures, there can be discerned perhaps the fundamental principle that will explain the paradox of the federal principle.

There is plentiful evidence that the drafters of the Constitution were aware of the temptation to use the constitutional system for the building of power, or the tendency as we say now, to see government as a concentration of power. Montesquieu had warned them of this in prescribing the federal device to cure the evils of bureaucratic empire in large nations. John Calhoun says that the constitution-makers were aware of the dangers that lurk in the use of numerical majorities to conclude deliberations.

There are many devices, not all genuinely political, by which numerical majorities can be generated as merely numerical majorities. Party whips and machines are not the only agents of factitious majorities. We now have many names for the secondary means of persuasion, short of bribery: the bandwagon, the steamroller, railroading, pressure groups, lobbies, riders, etc. Even the committee system, which was invented to ensure thorough deliberation, can be used for horse-trading, logrolling, passing the bacon, and feeding the pork-barrel. These devices are often used to moderate the friction of private interests by paying off deals and fixes of secret negotiation. These frolics and detours offer themselves as manipulative devices by which power is built and maintained—power to win a vote by numbers. We have learned to tolerate them, even to accept them, in the comic spirit as the great game of politics.

But John Calhoun very early saw them as subversions of the political process, and he saw the checks and balances of the separation of powers as the constitutional remedies. The power of mutual veto between the branches of government could stop the power drives. But such checks provided only the occasions for the recovery or discovery of the deeper constitutional process. The occasions might provide opportunities for further dickering, but the implied end of the veto power is the approximation of something like unanimity through deliberation directed to the common good. The effect of the veto in a Quaker business meeting is often the stalling of action, but its aim is to allow and to encourage continued persuasion that will lead to a deeper and more reasonable consensus. It seems that Calhoun must have been right in discerning some such, perhaps implicit, intention in the minds of the founding fathers. It may be that Calhoun's failure to persuade his colleagues of this and to invent the procedures for the proper bridging of the separated powers is the crucial default in our failure to maintain adequate persuasive processes under the Constitution.

Seen from the point of view of an efficiency manager, this process seems mischievous; no self-respecting business would tolerate such procedures for arriving at decisions. Why not abolish one legislative house or merge the two so that the business of the country can be expedited? The answer must be that the Constitution does not see government as a business. It is interested primarily in seeing that justice is done, and this end calls for a different kind of persuasion and deliberation. The legislature is not set up to make particular concrete decisions; it makes laws that are as universal as possible and can therefore have equal incidence on all citizens. Persuasion that does not reach this level of abstraction and generality should fail. Disagreements between the two houses and their constituencies should be accepted as problems in deliberation that need full consideration and inventive solutions. The system of checks and balances was conceived as a filter by which chance and force are eliminated and reason refined. The best case that can be made for aristocratic governments is that the legislative process should be in the charge of cultivated minds that can practice reason for the common good. Democratic government must provide the ordinary mind with the disciplines and the institutions by which it can acquire the habits of thinking about the common good, and these habits must be as good as, or better than, those claimed for the aristocratic mind. All this was implied in the deliberate intention to bring the individual into the public sphere as a citizen. The system of checks and balances, so generously distributed throughout the structures of government, accepts the implication in the idea of citizenship and its elaboration in the First Amendment. It dams up and rechannels the flow of persuasion in the community, letting in light and air, and raising it to higher levels so it can be released to invigorate the legal process. The proposition that it poses is most difficult and glorious; it is not refuted by the fact that it is only partially fulfilled so far.

We must now return to the proposition that laws are the means by which the responsibility for injustice is discharged in the community. So far I have been concerned with outlining the course or the courses by which persuasion rises from man-to-man conflicts through learning, disciplines, and institutions to the level of law-making. The courses pass through so much noise and apparent disorder that the outcome seems unlikely. As Coke said, the law is a second reason. If this means that many individual reasons interact and combine to create a public reason, it seems unlikely. Not even the professional lawyer, or perhaps least of all the professional lawyer, seems to believe that. But there is a complementary saying—that citizens, lawyers, legislators, executives, and judges find law. This seems to be implied by the legends of the origin of common law; it seems even more supported by the experience of law in the public realm. It is, of course, the common teaching of many religions. It should not be necessary to recapitulate here the arguments about the brooding omnipresence in the sky, natural or divine law, for and against. It is enough to note that the operating or living law in any community or in any case has a context in traditions and precedents and that any legislation, application, or judgment extends the precedents into something that is new. Law is made and found as we think about what we do; it is inescapable, and it marches forward with us.

In discussing persuasion as a combination of power and reason I have been setting a tough problem. I have said that as persuasion reaches one of its ends, the making of laws, it progressively purges power and refines reason. It is often said that when persuasion finally becomes law, it achieves a monopoly of power that it then places behind reason, which then exercises authority with sanctions, coercions. This is the tempting solution to the problem that current political science seems to have accepted. This quite clearly is not the case. It is true that law has great power, the power of persuasion, a preeminent power of persuasion. But it is not the power to seize and to dominate. It is rather the power to see, to penetrate, and to pacify. There is obviously an amphiboly, an ambiguity, in the term *power* in the last two sentences, that needs clarification. The power of persuasion that I have been following dialectically for some time in the foregoing is a potentiality, a tendency with a purpose, which is realized slowly in the process of persuasion. If law is its end, its realization transforms the potentiality into an act. A power realized is an act. The power of persuasion is realized when it is legitimized, when it becomes a law, an act as it is called when a bill is passed in Congress. And it is an act of reason.

As acts of reason, laws have many aspects, or facets. In the first place, they are ways of understanding, concepts that reflect and measure the affairs of a community against purposes and ends. There is a moral for the social scientist in this. Law is the architectonic of the social sciences, the social sciences will remain merely tentative hypotheses and programs of action until they refer their systems of principles to laws. Or, put otherwise, the behavioral sciences are now consultants to the persuasive process that makes laws, awaiting their places in the community's body of law. Law is the community's way of getting a true understanding of itself.

But the theoretic or speculative aspect of law has its true place in practical reason, as one of the premises or imperatives that direct action. In this aspect, law is the act of a rational will, of a general rational will that finds its true end in the common good, chiefly justice, but also freedom, peace, and order. Here the interests and powers that have gone into the persuasive process are transformed into intelligent, voluntary obedience to the law. The law is hypostatized into the authority that promulgates rules of reason for the common good. The body politic is the true rational voluntary association. The law is the people in common action, commanding and obeying themselves for the sake of their highest common ends.

But, although the proximate end of persuasion is fulfilled in law-making, this is not the entire end of the matter. The Constitution in its function as the institutor of offices and institutions, and as an application of the ancient maxim, Divide and rule, establishes another branch of government to execute the laws. A legislature might, through its committees, conceive itself as a board of administration; knowing the intent of the laws it makes, it might assume that it is fit to administer them. But the Constitution does not allow this, although the committees sometimes spontaneously exceed their powers as overseers. The administration and enforcement of the laws is given to the executive branch. This division of power is often thought to be made for the purpose of braking and limiting the processes by which power is accumulated and concentrated, as merely a baffle for the efficient working of the government. The President and his cabinet are often compared with the British prime minister, who is an operating link between the legislative and executive functions, acting as agent of and reporting to Parliament. But our Constitution breaks the link in order to recognize explicitly and concretely a difference in style of function proper to the branches.

A better reason than mere brake, baffle, or limit on power—either of the legislature over the executive or of the executive over the legislature—is suggested in the power to veto legislation granted to the President. This is one of those bridges or treaties that bind together what has been separated. It stops the final passage of a bill pending further persuasion; it dams up the power in order to refine it and release it in an improved and more potent form. The concern for this is ostensibly measured by the demand for a two-thirds majority to override the veto, but this is not the substance of the procedure. Its aim is to continue public deliberation, or, to be sure, to prevent passage of a bill that does not induce better deliberation. It is also always in the power of the executive to administer regular partial vetoes to bills that Congress passes by the discretionary manner of this execution of them. This again allows for administrative deliberation, a form of persuasion that is different from legislative deliberation. It suggests that laws are still instruments of persuasion, persuasion of executive officers and the whole chain of administrative agents that deal finally with free citizens and their associations. The careful analysis of various styles in which the executive branch exercises this kind of persuasion is to be found in Richard Neustadt's *The Presidential Power.* Quoting President Truman, Neustadt says that the first thing a new President learns is that issuing an order is only the beginning of a long and sometimes futile process of persuading his subordinates to carry out the laws that are their and his responsibility. It is a great illusion to suppose that the executive power rests on the hypothesis that the President is the commander-in-chief of the armed forces, or indeed of the police force.

The division of powers between the legislature and the executive branch is based on the great difference between two kinds of persuasion: the public deliberation that goes into the making of law, and the persuasion of law that gets the obedience of the people. The will and power, the concern for injustice, that sets the persuasive law-making process in motion would seem to ensure the assent of the people to the product, but the transforming effect of executive deliberation on the law as a command is surprising and highly educative to self-governing people. There has been an upward dialectic refining away private interests, and then there has been a downward dialectic that has to take account of side effects unanticipated by the voter—and indeed by the intermediary representatives and officers. For a new executive, there are many new facets to the adage that politics is the art of the possible.

Overseeing congressional committees offer feedback from the administrator to the legislator. Legislative persuasion and administrative persuasion mirror each other in many ways, but the two differ enough to justify the separation between the two powers, both troublesome and salutary as they may be. The laws sit, as it were, at the top, with lines of legislative persuasion leading up to them and lines of administrative persuasion leading down. These lines are punctuated by knots: the legislative line by congressional committees, the administrative lines by agencies or bureaus. These knots are forums for persuasion to take place, primarily of constituencies and clients, but also of each other. A recent foreign observer, Herbert von Borch, in his book *The Unfinished Society,* has summarized his observation of these organs of government by characterizing American society as a very permeable one, as compared to European communities. Europeans in general are shocked by the orgies of persuasion that our government allows and stimulates. They see in them all the risks of corruption that we also see and worry about. But von Borch also finds in it a commitment that we have made, at least in principle, to the full play of persuasion. Like Tocqueville, he is appalled at the sparse utilization of these processes at present, but he sees in them an almost infinite resource for recovery of health, vitality, and reasonableness in our public life. Too many citizens and officials let their present frustrations eclipse this vision.

This is no place, and I have no intention, to make a detailed study of the thousand and one joints and disjoints in the constitutional structure like Woodrow Wilson's study *Congressional Government* or the quasi-sociological studies of opinion-makers, decision-makers, and conflict-resolvers. These have had their valid specific purposes. As I have said, my intention has been to see the Constitution as a kind of flow sheet for the circulation of the lifeblood of body politic, persuasion. It may seem that the term *persuasion* lacks sharp definition and loses any useful meaning that it may have had. But I have aimed at some generality that would show the basic function of the whole structure. If the common good is to have any meaning, there must be some operation that is proper to its nature. Persuasion, ubiquitous and continual, up to laws and down from them, and finally around, returning on itself in the people, would seem to serve the general discursive requirements. The analogy with the circulation of blood in the human body is apt. The blood carries nutriment as fluid fuel through arteries, arterioles, and capillaries to power the organs, tissues, and cells of the body. It also carries oxygen to release the energy of the fuel wherever it is needed; and enzymes, catalysts, hormones in subtle balances to control the rates and places for the release of the energy. The digestive vegetative organs dissolve and refine the food for the selective absorption of the fuel into the blood. Could this be the analogue of the apolitical domain of the custom? The venous system draws off the wastes of combustion that would poison the body and then returns the clarified medium for recirculation. Each organ has its own sub-circulatory system with some of the autonomy of service to itself and to the rest of the body that is suggested in the European notion of subsidiary institutions.

Then there is a system of nerves that report and direct the business of the body. There is the so-called autonomic system, with many centers of coordination—the ganglia or half-brains—that report their activities in the semiconscious signals of the emotions and exert a massive general control over the central nervous system, with which consciousness is associated. If the nerves are the legal system of the body politic, then the autonomic nervous system is the common law and the courts of common law. The central nervous system is the great system of public law rooted deeply in the elementary processes of persuasion, speech, press, assembly, religion, and petition of the First Amendment, and elaborated in the higher level institutions of the public government. Its afferent and efferent nervous channels carry electronically the sensitive and motor impulses that are coordinated in the three parts of the brain and at the same time mysteriously transform themselves into the rational processes, and give the body its arts and its wisdom. It is easy to overdo this analogy from W. B. Cannon, but it helps keep the abstraction with which I have been dealing alive.

For the third great branch of government, the judicial system, singled out and especially protected from the cruder forms of persuasion, and yet concentrating and formalizing its most essential rational practices, I can find no obvious physiological analogue. Perhaps the analogy is confirmed by its apparent failure. The highest rational powers in the individual man have never been satisfactorily identified, localized, and articulated in the central nervous system, not even by the subtlest skills and thought of the brain surgeon. The search is still on. Just so is the search still on for an adequate analysis of the judicial process in jurisprudence. The best view of the process is afforded in the courtroom, where it can be seen in full dramatic form. The case is a human situation that has complicated itself and needs clarification. The natural persons who come into the court become dramatis personae, with dramatic roles partly assigned. There is the plaintiff and the defendant. Each has legal counsel, armed with knowledge of the laws. One or more judges sit at the bench; they preside as directors of the action, but perhaps more importantly as hearers of the adversary pleadings. In addition, there may be a jury of ordinary citizens, perhaps the prototype of the citizens in the modern state, who take on a highly public role of judging the case under the law as it is submitted to them by the officers of the court. The substance of the proceedings is still persuasion, mutual persuasion, formal deliberation, with the assigned aim to come to the decision that the case falls under the relevant laws. Evidence is presented formally; the law is expounded; both law and fact are under judgment. No crude majority rule is invoked in the final judgment of the jury; it must be unanimous or there has been no trial. Cases may be appealed up to the Supreme Court, where arguments between judges about tough cases may end in majority decisions.

The court system, from the courts of common law up through

the state courts, with their parallels in the federal system, to the Supreme Court, would seem to be carrying the heaviest burden of rational persuasion that any human institution has ever carried. The only comparable burden would seem to be that laid on the academic institutions of disputation in metaphysics and theology in the Middle Ages. But even there, the responsibility to do justice to any and every human individual was seldom present.

Both the difficulty and the concentration on the solution arise from the oldest philosophical problem—how to bring the universals of human reason, the reason of the law, to bear on the individual case. The individual is always richer in reality than the universal, as the universal always outruns the individual in implication. The same philosophical problem arises in each of the professions—the slippery diagnosis in the medical clinic, the casuistry in the confessional, and the case in the court—as it also arises in the ordinary individual's conduct of his life. The situations all demand humility before the demands of human persuasion and the ultimate search for wisdom. It is remarkable that human society should have discovered so early and continued so long the customs and rules of the courts of law, where the highest human powers are regularly loaded and stretched to and beyond their limits in the attempt to discharge the responsibility for justice.

It is not clear that the legal officers of the court always understand or remember the high rational process that they assist, but it is worthy of note that the formality and ceremony of the occasion is always there to remind them.

THE PATHOLOGY OF THE PUBLIC THING

It will be well to keep the physiological analogy alive as we turn now to the pathology of the body politic. I have myself been indulging, in a somewhat disorderly manner, in the tragicomic art of the newspaper columnist, describing current political men, struggling to govern themselves, as better or worse than they are. This is inevitable if politics is, as I am saying it is, substantially persuasion, which can be either violent or rational at its extremes, and variously both between its extremes. But even within this latitude, persuasion can be to one or another degree sick or healthy. To see how sick or well we are at present in our body politic, consider the alternative remedies we have considered in the project called the Political Process. We have been giving a most general diagnosis in terms of the citizen's failure to participate in the process into which he was thrown by the eighteenth-century revolutions. If we do not attribute this breakdown to the perversity of the overrational Constitution, we cite the inordinate size of the government structure and process or the enormous proliferation of knowledge, particularly in science and technology, as the causes of our alienation and malaise.

There have been two notable prescriptions of remedies. I shall overstate them for purposes of emphasis and clarity. The two diagnoses agree in two respects. They note that the functions of the federal system of checks and balances are not fulfilled, that the citizens and their representatives do not use the separation of powers to introduce and induce increments of persuasion, but rather find them traps for their goodwill and occasions of mischief. They further note that partly because of this disability, but more importantly because of the great weight and pressure of the affairs to be dealt with, the legislative and the judicial branches of the government have defaulted and abdicated to the executive. Their prescription is to make the de facto failure of the legislative and judicial branches the occasion for the de jure strengthening of the executive or administrative powers.

The proposals for the reorganization of the executive branch is borrowed from the model that is used in schools of business administration, and the acceptance of this model indicates the acceptance of the translation of the governing process into the managerial process to which the business corporation aspires. On close view, the essential image at the heart of the business company is a man with a pencil doing the arithmetic of the balance sheet. This central image is projected to the executive business structure, which reaches at one end to the empirical research of the market analyzers and at the other end to the strategic maps of the sales force, with the middle range of operation given over to the blueprints of manufacture. But suddenly the picture of men with pencils transfigures itself into the model taken from the strategic bombing practices of the Air Force in World War II. The men with the balance sheets become the computers into which intelligence reports are fed and out of which issue detailed assignments for bombing flights. The Rand Corporation and its proliferating satellite organizations translated and elaborated these computerized managerial systems first for application to business organizations and then to society in general. When these systems have not yet been put into hardware, they can be applied to men who then appear as organization men, once invidiously called bureaucrats, now styled "the new professionals."

The ideal, already realized in segments of the political process, is the streamlining of persuasion, or in European terminology, the rationalizing of managership. For what I have been calling the refinement of persuasion, the reduction of power to reasonable deliberation, another reduction is substituted—that from the noise and confusion of speech, press, assembly, radio, and television to the quiet click-click of the black box into which are fed the opinions analyses and out of which come the party platforms or the bureau plans. This is also rationalization, new style.

So, in the last presidential election such a black box was offered to the Republican Party at the beginning of the campaign, and on the Republican refusal, it was accepted and used by the Democrats. The precinct analyst, once the ward heeler, fed data to the box. The Democratic candidate with charm and skill translated the numerical computer language back into the poetry and rhetoric of the party platform and campaign promises. We voted, mostly by machine, and elected the top executive, who then collected his organization men with their subordinated bureaucratic aides, who in turn fed the items of policy into the executive computers. The fact that the program had to be ritualistically detoured through the legislature and the uncomputerized agencies, and was all but stopped, only confirms the argument for the streamlined executive; it was not streamlined enough to avoid the noise and waste of the constitutional ritual.

The preceding was one of our prescriptions. The second prescription agreed with it in finding the executive branch the comparatively sound surviving medium of political action, but it emphasized the wastefulness of another part of the federal structure, that part made up of the state and local autonomies. These should be abolished or perhaps better absorbed into the national government, so that another streamlining can take place. Again, the picture is derived from the managerial model. States, cities, and counties and small towns become departments, in the French sense. In the absence of the formal legislative machinery, the elections aim primarily at choosing officials who perform their representative duties not as legislators, but as administrators. The programs that are administered originate in the expert technical offices of the executive bureaucracy. The bills that may pass through the pro forma proceedings of the vestigial legislature are essentially plans that are laws only in name. The aim is administrative efficiency for the nation's business; "laws" are the edicts or directives of quasi-business managers.

In this scheme the mooted question of administrative law is solved totally; all law becomes administrative law. But there is a remnant of the question about unchecked governmental power that so exercised the Founding Fathers, and has been inherited by their descendants. To ensure participation and responsibility, a massive system of checks and balances is set up to parallel the single integrated executive. The idea for this system is borrowed from the office of ombudsman long established in several of the Scandinavian countries. In its original, the office of ombudsman is conceived as a separate branch of the government, and its function is very like the Roman office of the tribune of the people. The ombudsman watches over the operations of the government, accepts complaints, and is enabled to report them as grievances to any office of the government and annually as a general statement to the legislature. Reporting is usually enough to get attention and remedies, but there is the residual power to bring suit against the government officials.

This invention of the Scandinavian countries was obviously an anticipation of trouble in the operation of the constitution and the laws, trouble that would gain attention and clarification in the operation of the office. In the American proposal, it is assumed that the trouble is present and clear enough to indicate its massive elimination and cure. So the ombudsman solution is also massive. At each administrative level, and perhaps in each administrative office, there should be representatives of the people present and participating in the administration of the "laws." They should continually be supplying the facts and the arguments for grievances suffered by the people, individuals or their organizations, as the laws are applied. These representatives should in some cases, at least, have the power of veto on the decisions of the bureaus. They should courageously maintain some of the force of the separation of powers in the present Constitution. It seems more likely that they would be drawn into the powerful process of keeping the nation's business running, and would possibly become public-relations officers of the bureaus, to keep the people persuaded. In order to make their function effective, there probably would have to be a massive popular organization that would filter and order public opinion, inform it by widespread adult educational activities, and back the grievance machinery as the labor unions back their business agents in collective bargaining. But it should be noted that the function assigned to the public government is managerial, and the tendency is to let law, such as it may be, develop from administrative practice.

I do not cite these proposals in order to refute them, but rather to use them as diagnostic probes to indicate the troubles that lie back of what is called nonparticipation or alienation. They show not only the withering of consent and the atrophy of some of the main channels of persuasion but the invasion of forms of power that would once have started liberty bells ringing all over the country. (Perhaps the bizarre antics of the extreme right should be attended to as the quacking of geese once was on the Palatine Hill in Rome.)

Some of the inventiveness that is going into the administrative innovations in the organs of government is imitated from models in business. In the literature that deals with the corporations and the economic order being built on them, the terminology of trust-busting takes on a new, literal meaning. Firms that combine in restraint of trade were once called private governments. The muckraking zip of that rhetoric, we should remind ourselves, came from the contradiction in the adjective *private* being associated with government. We now read long and tedious articles exploring this phrase as a serious description of our pluralistic

society; we have public governments and we have private governments, and the more the better for our liberties. We now have a
theory of administered prices that mutually support one another
through cartels, hidden treaties between apparent competitors.
When quasi-open agreements between large firms pass the
approving eye of the Sherman Antitrust division of the Department of Justice, sometimes because they are in the national
interest, the corporations file their plans with the cognizant
government agency. Oil is the subject of such an agreement.
Airplanes and computers, mining and agriculture make combinations that receive government subsidies. Currently we have in
the inventive works of the State Department a new corporation
for international communication based on Telstar, which will
have private investment, government investment, and international investment. But this kind of concatenation and integration of corporations is only the tip of an iceberg. Thousands of
smaller corporations are operating more or less independently of
one another, but most of them feel their dependence and obligations to the few at the top and are bound in tight relations by
the credit system.

The majority of the massive government buildings in Washington house bureaus that have been established by law to regulate
the private corporations. (Perhaps there should be a tingle along
one's spine in response to this combination of the words *private* and
corporation.) But it appears that these public bureaus regulate
best when they join the regulated; it would seem that they have
been set up to initiate the private corporations into the public
sphere. Like the new citizens of the early modern republics, they
have to learn the habits of public responsibility under law. They
may be forgiven for looking awkward, even corrupt, in their new
roles.

But it should be noted that the assimilation works in two
directions. As the private corporation takes on its public role, the
government bureau takes on the habits of the private association.
It is often said that the private business corporation could not
tolerate the democratic procedures of a republican form of
government in its own management. The moral of this may be
that the government bureau should not tolerate the procedures

of business. The partnership may be mutually corruptive, but the actual developments seem to indicate that the government bureau is more easily corrupted when it takes on business habits. Without taking over the private sector, the government bureau often finds itself managing, not merely regulating. The style of persuasion between the two is administrative persuasion. Perhaps the best evidence of this is that the managerial tasks of both can be done better by computers. At present there is a stubborn political reluctance to make any formal hookup between the private and public bureaus, but particularly under military urgency the collaboration accelerates. The most versatile of the devices in the armament of common law—contracts—supply the legal forms. Government contracts show the invasion of public government into the private sector and the infiltration of private government habit and custom into the public sector, and we are warned by a departing President that the military-industrial complex is the locus of attention for those who watch over the deeper changes in the living Constitution. ("Government contracts" is another combination of words that should have the attention of the keepers of the political lexicon.)

But it may be late for us to study the jurisprudence of corporation law. If we pierce the corporate veils and look behind the legal fictions to find the natural persons, we shall not be too surprised to find that the man with a hoe, a pickax, a crowbar, a scythe, a chisel, a hammer, a saw, a brace and bit, an ax, a lever, a wheel, an ox, a horse or a mule is seldom present. Instead there is a waterfall, a steam engine, a diesel, a dynamo, or an atomic-energy plant transforming and transmitting power through wheels and wires to machines and tools. Men are still bio-mechanical links in this complex, but we are told that tomorrow, if not later today, there will be no men involved at all. Judgment and skill, as well as power, will be delegated to hardware. It may not be long before Andrew Hacker's picture of the corporation, stripped of stockholders and workers down to the board of managers with papers in hand, will be black-boxed. But this apocalyptic vision should not be surprising to us; technology has for a long time been the working substance of the corporation. The efflux from the black boxes has been informing our industrial and commercial and governmental behavior for a long time.

Furthermore, we should not linger too long on the tangible machinery of the automated factory. If we are to pierce the veils of the whole of our corporate life, we must quickly see that the most eerie, whimsical genies of the intellectual and imaginative disciplines have popped out of the academic bottle, and have been embodied, mainly under government contracts, in institutes of research and development. It is the equations of the mathematicians that pull the strings, not only for the industrial puppets but for the dramas and games of organization and management of men. It may be a relief for those who find Ellul perverse and falsely prophetic to read Sola-Price, as he reports that it was not only the disciples of Descartes but also the mathematical pundits of ancient Alexandria who made their first applications of their findings to automatons, animals, birds, and to men who, moving mainly by water power, told time by imitating the stars, acted plays, and practiced the arts for the amusement and entertainment of the idle. It is still an unsolved riddle of history why the Greeks did not bring off the industrial revolution that Descartes's algebra accomplished in the modern world. It may be that Roman law was not yet able to sustain it, as it is now doubtful that our law will be able to contain it.

Several points should be remembered as we watch and marvel at this march of industry into the puppet theater and the seventeenth-century formal garden. It is not, as is often said, that mathematicians and mathematical physics are reducing the artificial and natural world to number and quantity. As long ago as Leibniz and George Boole it was clear that the reasoning that goes into mathematics can also deal with words and qualities. It is another kind of reduction that is taking place. In any human art there is a segment that is operational; human discourse as well as hoeing, machine tending, and human management proceed by moving things about, and if these disciplines are sufficiently elaborated, they will run themselves. Human beings that are disciplined beyond a certain point become automatons. Raymond Lully in the fifteenth century transferred much of the dialectical dance of categories that had been developed in late scholasticism to cardboard and metal machines. Peter Drucker has recently made the same point about automation; we are much further along in the process of automation than we think, because in the factory and the university, as well as in the industrial laboratory, which is a combination of the two, men have been acting like automatons. We are now teaching the machines to act like ourselves. It is not a joke that machines are now able not only to think like high-school students but to write better Ph.D. theses than graduate students have recently been doing. Here is another of those contagions of the arts, like the confusion of management and government. The university has been feeding modern science to the industrial establishment, where it has turned science into technology so thoroughly that many scientists have lost the distinction. But the assimilation has worked the other way, too. The university is now finding it hard to distinguish itself from the industry that it has been serving so well. We may be glad that human beings are being freed of the burdens of labor, both industrial and academic, but another question arises: are human beings being obliterated by the industrial process even as they contemplate their obliteration by the bomb, which was also produced under government contracts?

REMEDIES?

It will be noted that in the last few pages I have been indulging in a new and fashionable style of discourse. Its popular form is science fiction. It chooses some theme in recent scientific investigation that is a mixture of fact and hypothesis, lets the facts act as a launching pad for the orbiting of a hypothesis, and then by poetic, novelistic imagination constructs a world. Human beings are usually invited for the ride, but packaged instruments might just as well have been the passengers. We are so fascinated by the spectacle that we are debating now whether to send men or instruments to the moon. This actually is an old art revived; Lucian in the ancient world wrote *True Histories*, and Swift in the eighteenth century wrote *Gulliver's Travels*, and it is not long since H. G. Wells became a prophet with his *Time Machine*. There is perhaps novelty in the present fashion in that both authors and readers view it with alarm rather than enjoyment. There is perhaps a closer causal connection now between the growing concern of science and the withering of the literary imagination, to say nothing of the absence of philosophical criticism. In philosophical terms, there is to be discerned in the methods of science a trick, valid in its own terms, illusory in its general employment. The trick consists in reducing a concrete situation to one or a few of its aspects in special observation, catching the abstraction as it leaps to the eye as a hypothesis, and finally extrapolating the hypothesis as a heuristic guide to find new facts. When the search, or research, is on, it is easy to supply quasi-facts from imagination. Thus, from some new chemical fuels and some tables from space dynamics, we go to the moon on some classical Newtonian trajectories. So we can predict the population explosion, the hunger implosion, the reduction of the government to purely executive managerial mechanisms, and the elimination of human beings by the automatic industrial process or the bomb. That we are actually behaving, as individuals and as sovereign citizens in public affairs, as if these things were true, either verifies the fictions or gives us a sense of unreality. Such is the enchantment that binds the two cultures, scientific and humane, together.

The disenchantment is not easy to achieve. The amateur can imagine growth curves running on all sorts of categories, education, poverty, race violence, transportation, cities, chewing gum, cigarettes, and crime. Each of these has its apocalyptic transcendental, infinity. Then the amateur can invoke the saving spirit of what is yet nonexistent science, ecology, in which all growth curves are integrated in some hoped-for homeostatic environment for human existence. These are disenchanting in that they introduce a measure of skepticism about the method, but they do not reveal the realities that have been left behind in politics, the unsolved problems of the present. We can say with the journalists that we have seen the future, and it doesn't work. That is a measure of wisdom; we know that we do not know the future.

We do know that the reduction of self-government to the executive function is not an accomplished fact. We even know that the executive branch has not been completely reduced to bureaucratic administration, that the corporations are not yet perfectly managed, that technology is not yet automatic, and that the black boxes are not yet sealed. It may be that the cussedness of human nature is blocking all these programs from the swift accomplishment of their appointed rounds, but this may mean that the political animal refuses to be reduced, that he still struggles to find himself in the provisions of the Constitution.

But at the same time, we must admit that the managerial society that has attached itself to the executive branch and looms so large in the midst of the body politic is real, and we can raise the question whether it can be reduced to the terms of the Constitution even though it may force a redrafting. In undertaking this task, it may help to note that the managerial instruments of the bureaucracies have been extensions and constructions from elements in the common law; they are inventions in property law and contract law. With the help of social-contract theory, these elements have been woven into the charters and bylaws of the corporations. The bureaus by which the government has regulated the corporations has filled the forms with machinery, as industrial development filled the forms of common law. This means that the economy, guided and formed by common law, has broken through into the public sector.

The rhetoric of this breakthrough has always tried to persuade itself, with the help of Adam Smith and his economists, that it is all a private matter, and for a long time it denied the allegation that it was touched with public interest. It has resisted regulation by public law, preferring to rely on the rules of common law. It learned to live with the Sherman Antitrust Act because such intervention seemed to be strengthening the wall that separated it from public law; the statute itself seemed to be reinforcement of common-law freedom of contract. But the rhetoric got thin in the Great Depression, and is used now only to supply an ideology in the cold war.

At long last, it now seems clear that the managerial society must ask itself Lincoln's question. Is it doing for the people what needs to be done, but cannot be done at all or as well by individual effort? At least in part, the answer must be that it is pursuing the legitimate object of government and that it must be recognized in its legitimate function. In short, it must be politicized, given its explicit rights and duties, its responsibilities for justice.

There have been many answers to Lincoln's implied question, and these answers have made much politics. Marx, more than a hundred years ago, made a very glib answer, as it now seems: nationalize the means of production, the tools and the organizations of capitalism, the corporations and the labor unions. This has been called the immaculate conception of socialism; it does not specify and explicate itself, and where it has been tried it has made the questions of allocations of functions among institutions more complicated and acute. In the first place, state capitalism and incipient tyranny resulted, as Marx had warned in his theory of the dictatorship of the proletariat. In some cases, it has produced both chaos and paralysis, and a slow recovery of function in mixed economies. Russia seems not to be sure whether it has passed this phase and entered into an orderly communism that had to be invented to spell out what Marx had meant. The Russian picture is confused because it did not even have the initial capitalist organisms to take over and maintain. In all these cases, there seems to be a residual bureaucratic problem, the governmental, military, industrial, technological, scientific complex whose structure and operation depend upon managerial rules. Government has grown, while consent has withered.

It may be too early to eliminate the simplistic socialist answers; there still may be clarifications and inventions to come. But it would seem wise to see if there are other alternatives, some other way or ways to answer Lincoln's question, some other way to recognize the obvious public interest embodied in bureaus without sacrificing true politics. As I have suggested above, the complex is not yet integrated; it is hardly organized at all. It is possible to see it as the model for all the other pluralisms that are so much admired by private citizens for the so-called liberties they provide. This suggests that there is a new natural division of powers emerging among the bureaus, and therefore a new problem in federalism to be solved. And perhaps there are new points of entry for the persuasive process. The opportunities for inventions in the federal democratic process seem worth exploring briefly, in principle.

In the first place, we should not restrict our attention to the military-industrial-scientific complex. Important as this is under conditions of the cold war and its consequences, it has many implications for and fringe effects on other institutions, and these may turn out to be helpful in seeing the whole problem. There are many private voluntary associations that are touched with public interest and need to be initiated into the public sphere. It is not hard to identify and list them. In fact, much of this assessment has been made by the sociological political scientists who have developed the doctrine of bureaucracy in a pluralistic society. They have recruited and prepared the candidates for the great initiation. They have even given them names with implications; they have called these quasi-corporate entities *subsystems*, systems that are subordinate to the inescapable large system, government. There are sub-subsystems, and there are suggestions of a horizontal and vertical order among them. I shall not attempt a review or make a critical appraisal of the classification and the ordering.

Presumably, there is a distinction that any answer to the Lincoln question must draw. Some of the substructure is ready to be recognized formally as subsidiary to the government; the rest is not yet ready for its reception into the public status, and falls into the category of private voluntary association, where it is adequate to the needs of the community. The line between them will always be a matter for prudent pragmatic determination, as society develops and the persuasive process changes.

As a working benchmark at the start, it might be well to admit above the line those organizations that are already chartered. These are the organizations that the government needs for its own health, that it wishes to encourage, as Justice Marshall says in the Dartmouth College case, or those that, left to their own devices, wax too strong or too weak to survive or to serve the public needs. These should be invited to apply to the federal government for new charters in which their purposes would be made explicit, and assured that they have the powers to do what they ought to do. This means that they should be given the powers they need to govern themselves without interference; to quote the Constitution, they should be assured of a republican form of government. This does not mean that they all should have exactly the same form of government to the last detail, but whatever the variation that is needed to fit their functions, they should imitate the federal government as far as possible; they should separate the powers of legislation, administration, and adjudication; they should be obliged to get some degree of consent from their members, by votes, representation, and review.

In an earlier section of this paper I gave some attention to the exercise of persuasion as it leads up to the formal making of law, and in another section to the other exercise of persuasion that leads to the administration and enforcement of law. The present distinction between charitable corporations and corporations for profit suggests that we already make a rough correlation of these categories of chartered associations with the functions of law-making on one hand, and of law administration on the other. This distinction and correlation of function were not intended at the start, and they are too rough for application now. But they suggest that there might be roughly two quite general categories of charters, one for the institutions that cultivate and promote the activities listed in the First Amendment—free speech, press, assembly, religion, and petition—as these might be elaborated in the office of ombudsman. Or perhaps the whole educational establishment, including a system of universal free adult education, would fall into this category and determine the detail of its organization. Then there should be another category that would fit the business and technological world. Under federal charters there would be ensured the kind of freedom that is required in commercial and industrial organizations. It seems clear now that these organizations are no longer primarily concerned with profits; profits are mostly plowed back as capital investments and are therefore means rather than ends of organization. The outstanding features of such organizations even now are the teams of experts who devote themselves to research, development, and management; they are engineers and technologists groping for professional statuses and functions. As they discover these functions, they will look for organizational patterns that will approximate the guilds and professions of the past and that are now partly forgotten. Their charters should take account of and encourage this development from managerial know-how to truly professional practice and public service.

The charter, upon which I am relying here both as a mark for

the identification of existing institutions that are touched with
public interest, and as a legal instrument that can be elaborated
and extended to provide the formal conditions of independence
and self-government for subsidiary institutions, has an interesting
history. The idea of a charter probably got its original meaning
from its application in the polity of the church. In order to give a
cathedral church or a collegiate church, or a monastic order or a
knightly order, the authority required for its autonomy, the
superior authority gave it a charter. This was more than the
establishment of a subordinate office with duties and responsibility
to a superior. Because its functions implied a high degree of dis-
cretion and freedom in order to discharge its responsibilities, the
charter carried with it licenses and franchises and a maximum of
immunities from external interference and direction. When the
charter became the chief instrument of the mercantilist monarchy,
it was like a patent given for the practice of skills in a trade. The
monarch wished to increase the wealth and trade of the nation;
he offered patents and charters to groups of tradesmen, sometimes invited from abroad, so that they would contribute their
activities to the realm. The charter sometimes took the form of a
contract between the monarch and the guild; the charter was said
to be granted for a consideration in the contract of a promise of
service to the realm. Then as private companies were formed,
they came to apply for charters of incorporation so they could
collectively act as legal persons with limited liability. It seems
that the charter has always been used as a middle term between
the government and the individuals in bodies politic. Charters
give autonomy and form to what is called the substructure or
the subsidiary voluntary associations, in European usage. American corporate organization has been so loose and free-wheeling
throughout its history that the charter has been almost a negli-
gible consideration. Nevertheless, it is there waiting to be used
when the occasion arises.

We should see just what takes place when a charter is granted
and accepted. In a politically organized community, the government accepts from the people, both individually and collectively,
the formal responsibility for doing justice. Part of this responsibility is discharged by the government as such through its laws.

But some of the responsibility, either deliberately or by chance, is left or is delegated to subordinate or spontaneous organizations and individuals. For some of these that need stability and continuity, if they are to carry out their purposes, charters are granted that state the respective purposes and ensure the means that are required. For the people and the government, this is the ensurance that they can do what they ought to will; it is the establishment of a measure of political liberty according to Montesquieu. The statement of the purpose and the specification of the means constitutes the institution; it is a constitution conformed to the proper function of the institution. It is the embodiment of a part of the common good. It ensures freedom as well as justice to the institution and its members.

As American institutions come of age, we are seeing the need for better charters, charters that will give stability and continuity, but also charters or constitutions that will ensure orderly and effective self-government to which members can give assent. As a consequence, there is a new sense that the members must understand their responsibilities better, and this amounts to a new demand for the legitimation of functions. This is now being expressed as a concern about ethics, but it is better understood as a need for a professional understanding of duties and privileges, and the need increases as science and technology accumulate. Professional understandings mesh with the chartered means and extend the intelligible structure and function of the organizations. This is my understanding of Admiral Rickover's recent plea for the professionalization of the bureaus. The constitutionalization of the bureaus depends upon the professionalization of the personnel, he seems to say.

But in my rough division of the substructure into two categories, the educational and the economic, there seems to be a further organizational problem. The institutions that fall under the list of activities, or liberties, of the First Amendment, speech, press, assembly, religion, petition, are numerous. At present, they glory in their pluralism, but they are not discharging their responsibilities, and they do not feel free. They violate even the principles of individual freedom; they interfere with and destroy one another. Competition sometimes destroys function, and for this reason the competitors have to be regulated, sometimes in ways that seem to violate the First Amendment. If these institutions have the charters that I am proposing they will need some kind of reasonable coordination. An obvious example is the allocation of channels for radio and TV. A less obvious but more pressing need is something like a reasonable system of public education. Again, the Constitution provides a model for imitation. Let the chartered institutions establish a federal scheme of coordination.

Although economic institutions, particularly corporations, have, it must be added, gloried and waxed strong in their pluralism, they have also sought their own self-government and coordination, sometimes by their own efforts and sometimes by open request for or acceptance of regulation. The increasing search for understanding of their public responsibilities and their increased professionalization provide some ground for developing their own federal association.

These proposals for chartered institutions could be understood as pleas for the wholesale acceptance of the corporative state so egregiously demonstrated in the last generation in Europe. Set up a real department of education (and propaganda) and a corporate managerial bureaucracy, each hinged to a cabinet officer in the executive branch. Thus we shall rationalize our educational and economic establishment. But this is the powerful, apparently inexorable, drift in the public affairs of our time, which I have been criticizing. Of course, it may be that the wave of the future has already broken over us and that it is too much later than we think to do anything about it. Then again, it may not be so.

My proposal of a subconstitution, federating chartered subsidiary institutions, is a kind of monster. It is, in fact, an analogue of those monsters that the writers of science fiction construct. But I am extrapolating on the Constitution, not on an engineering formula. Nor am I joining the managers. Far from putting the new federal monster in the executive branch, I am rather proposing that the subconstitutional federation be set up, or imagined, as a new branch of government, independent and autonomous, related to the superstructure by a Calhounian power of mutual veto with whatever bridges of mutual persuasion may be invented. I confess I have no detailed blueprint.

TWO PROBLEMS

I shall desist now from the further projection of hypothetical solutions. Such exercises are chiefly valuable for the posing of questions that may help to clarify problems. I should like to try to state two urgent unsolved problems, each of which epitomizes the puzzling relations of the public to the private realms— planning and the city.

If I have been right in letting the common law define the private, nonpublic part of the community, and in noting that the activities in this domain tend to cross the line between it and the public domain, falling more or less awkwardly under public law, then at any given time there will be a set of legal and social problems to be solved. Since the late nineteenth century, there have been problems of this sort arising around the part of the economy that is incorporated for profit. These troubles have been variously described, first, as conspiracies in restraint of trade or competition; then, as the threatening power of the trusts; then, as concentrations of economic power; and finally, in our time, as a syndrome of symptoms, such as corporate irresponsibility, cartels, administered prices, collusive contracts, and the government-industrial complex. Each of these titles has marked the occasion when the public government has had to intervene, usually when the corporation has been "touched with public interest," a phrase that euphemistically indicates danger to the community. Paralleling the crises, and continuing in the intervals between them, there has developed an almost continuing debate about the government responsibility for the regulation or control of the economic system. How might the government anticipate and prevent the recurring crises? One of the answers that is always proposed is planning.

It should be recalled that planning has long been a feature of the managers and directors of the corporations, each for itself, but this has often been planning for fellow corporations that depend on key firms for their survival in the competitive world; hence, collusions, cartels, and concentrations of economic power.

The notion of common public planning has been associated with European economies, which have feudal, mercantilist, and socialist practices still extant in the modern domain of the market. We like to think that we have no such foreign habits and ideologies operating in our laissez-faire system. The fact is, we practice planning in private, while we eschew it publicly. As I have said above, we choose to rely on the devices of common law, property, contracts, and torts as our charter of free economy.

But planning in its first appearance is practiced as the negotiation, acceptance, and fulfillment of many-sided contracts. It partakes somewhat of the theory of the social contract, but is primarily the employment of private contracts. Plans are made partly on the basis of business prediction, partly on the basis of needs and the allocation of resources, and partly on the basis of the received theories of economic science. They are made for a limited period of time and for limited sectors of the economy, though not always for single corporations.

But at the same time, the plans often take into account public needs, and they comprehend common purposes that go beyond goals that can be fulfilled by the separate efforts of single corporations or individual businesses. The plans often incorporate government regulations and even data and statistics that the government supplies to the citizen. The plans are often made by government bureaus and offered to members of the substructure as statutes to be proposed to the legislature, or as administrative law made by the executive under due authority. The outstanding example of this practice is in the Department of Agriculture, which presides over a part of the economy that gets out of hand during a war and then never recovers control by its own efforts. There are many other examples, many of which came to light in the Depression. There will be many more as automation works its way with labor and industry.

But the best-laid plans of mice and men gang aft a-gley. The planners often account for the failures by the very plausible claim that fragmentary plans are not enough; plans must be comprehensive and general. One fragmentary plan alone cannot control the conditions that are necessary for its success; plans are like scientific experiments; they depend on controlled conditions. The anti-planners cry feudalism, mercantilism, and dictatorship, and during the cold war sought metaphysical arguments to show that planning is rationally impossible. The human mind is incapable of comprehending the affairs to which planning applies. The mixed economy ferments and boils over between inflation and full employment, or between boom and bust. These matters, no matter how poorly understood, are so important, so much matters of life and death to the community, so loaded with the issues of justice and freedom, that they demand the attention of the public government. They are the typical problems that must be dealt with by public law.

But the procedures of planning, begun in private organization and now continued in government bureaus, sometimes appearing as edicts of administrative law, do not fit any of the procedures familiar in any of the branches of government. The legislative branch follows the rules for public deliberation, but its aim is statutory laws that have generality and equal incidence to ensure justice and freedom. The executive branch, in spite of many present exceptions, tries to apply the statutes without invading the realm of private management. The judicial branch, no matter how commanding and legislative it has to be at times in its judgment of cases, stops short of acting as temporary receiver for businesses that are in bankruptcy. Lon Fuller, following Michael Polanyi in his argument that economic, like scientific activity forms essentially an open system in which decisions have to be made in many centers, associations, or individuals, says that it is a mistake for administrative agencies to undertake judicial functions on cases that arise around their plans. The reasons for this judgment are that the cases cannot be briefed for adversary proceedings; they are not two-sided but many-sided—polycentric, as Polanyi calls them. I am not sure I understand the logic of planning and the logic of judicial procedure well enough to agree, but I do see a dark spot in this confrontation of the private and public spheres.

In answer to a question from me, Harvey Wheeler has generously formulated the problem in my terms. He writes:

> When the cumulative institutional effects of private contracts is such that in fact private law (contract) is achieving the effects of statute law (that is, creating rules which have general govern-

mental effect rather than private contractual application), then
the private law of contract becomes empowered (through governmental guarantee of the obligation of contract) to achieve not
only the effects of statute law but also the effects of unconstitutional and improper statute law. That is, it may in fact be applied
unequally, retroactively, and particularly. When this happens, it
is clear that the proper sphere of contract is being exceeded and
the sphere of statute (public) law is being invaded. At this point
(in theory) some correction and/or regulation is required—either
to exclude contractual arrangements from improper governmental effects or to permit the invasion of the sphere of statute
law and regulate its incidences, so that the canons of statute law
are maintained even though the law is private and contractual in
origin and in theory. It is this latter case that comes under the
practice known as "planning." This is the only theoretical defense
for planning so long as the distinction between private and public
law is maintained.

Harvey Wheeler continues:

> When one "plans" for an economy, one intends to use govern-
> ment and law as tools to control an entity which implicitly re-
> mains a somewhat autonomous social function. Before the
> political problems associated with "planning" can be solved,
> some way of eradicating the implicit disparity between the two
> functions must be found. Perhaps your analogy between economic
> behavior and the law of contract will provide the lever—turning
> Lon Fuller on his head, so to speak.

I have only one thing to add. It would seem that planning is a
kind of purgatory through which the economy and some other
activities in the private sector, such as education, will have to
pass and transform themselves before they will appear fit to come
under public law. It may be that only part of planning will
survive in the public sphere, and a residue will remain private.
It is also possible that public and private law will be clarified and
strengthened by the ordeal that now seems inevitable.

The second problem is the city, and it bristles with ironic
questions. Perhaps the deepest irony consists in the historical fact
that politics originated in the city, the *polis,* and it is now in the
city that the whole political enterprise is and has been for a long
time most in doubt. Lewis Mumford says that the city happened

as the implosion of several ancient organizations of human beings: the market, the temple, and the palace. The bumps and grinds of this meeting were explosive, inwardly, and the history of the city shows power struggles between these forces. Since the citizens were human, the struggle slowly and episodically transformed itself into the orderly methods of rhetoric, debate, and dialectic—the mutual persuasions that became common deliberations and law. The Greek city-state was almost a miraculous result; Athena was born from the brow of Zeus. Plato and Aristotle, and the citizens of that city-state, almost equally miraculously, were able to give a rational account of the politicization, the civilization, that the Athenians and others suffered or accomplished. But the irony is explicit in their accounts. Until kings are philosophers and philosophers are kings, there is no hope for the political enterprise. This is not Plato's application for a job; it is nearer a comic reductio ad absurdum of the political enterprise, and this reduction, repeated over and over again, is the history of politics and civilization.

Our contemporary city is an epitome of this accumulation of experience. It is the city that opened up the possibility of the Public Thing and in its collective thought promised its existence, as this paper discusses. But if the city did not exist, we would have to say that it is impossible. In its modern form, the city is a corporation, the public municipal corporation, and its history is the chief theme in the long history of corporations in general. The modern city starts over again as a spontaneous collection of persons and institutions, roughly the same ones that Mumford designates in his story of the ancient origins. It exists for a time in solitary splendor in an almost unorganized environment, sometimes as the capital of an uncivilized territory with unmarked boundaries or with domains that are variously felt as spheres of influence: commercial, religious, or military. Just as it is about to make a polity of its community, a town with walls, it comes under the stronger influence of another city, or it is itself that stronger city and dominates the life of its satellites. At this point, it either writes its own constitution, or it applies to the superior city for a charter. It becomes a fully or partly self-governing borough. As the polity follows the lines of its influence the city becomes involved in the larger community; it is a

municipal corporation in a nation. When the government is
republican in form, as in northern Italy and Germany during the
Renaissance, there is a tendency for several such cities to form
leagues or federations; the political energy runs high and refines
itself. But the usual tendency is to allow the influences of commerce and war to form hierarchies, provincial cities bowing
before metropolises. In the end, the municipal corporation
becomes subsidiary to the metropolis or the nation over which
the metropolis rules.

The American city, ruled partly by the county, partly by the
state, from which it gets its charter, and partly now by the
federal government, has almost forgotten that it is a political
entity. The municipal corporation is only one of hundreds of
corporations, charitable, for profit, and public, in a vast corporate
tangle that is embodied in the sprawl of its houses, its factories,
its public buildings, and its streets. The physical city, once a high
composite work of art, is now the outward and visible sign of an
inward political and spiritual disgrace. A large city like New
York or Los Angeles is a conglomerate of 1,400 public corporations and thousands of private corporations, each claiming self-
government, but in practice making deals with absentee, im-
personal landlords and unidentifiable officials. You can't do business with city hall, nor can the city hall practice politics with
the citizens or with its equal or superior public corporations. In
desperation, for more than two generations now, the city as a
public entity has tried to contract out its obligations, first to a
commission or a city manager who would apply the methods of
business management, latterly to private corporations who will
do the day-to-day housekeeping and services, and to the planners
who will supply research and development. The city, the inventor
of the public thing, is abdicating all its functions to the many
private things that operate in the habits of common law.

I shall make no further attempt to clarify this problem; if I
did, it would most likely refute the main thesis of this paper.

Perhaps the proper ending for this paper would be another
attempt to state the main thesis. For the sake of the argument, it
accepts the American doctrine of common law. This doctrine
teaches that a fundamental, continuous, universal law develops

in all human communities through the procedures of courts, first set up informally, and progressively formalized in the course of time, which find law in the reasonable resolution of conflicts that arise in the course of human affairs. Judgments in one or several like cases become precedents for guidance in later cases, and these likenesses lead to the accumulation of laws and doctrines that in our tradition gradually fall under the topics crime, property, contracts, and torts. With the instructive exception of crime, these topics and the laws that fall under them seem to deal with private affairs.

Crime is an exception because very early it singled out conflicts that threaten the existence of the community. It required appeal to the superior authority of the community, to some form of public government. Whenever other kinds of conflict in private law likewise threaten the community, there is a similar tendency to appeal to public government. Thus the accumulation of property under corporate forms leads to the theories and practices of socialism; when contracts deal with heavy matters, there is the theory and practice of the social contract, sometimes to set up the public government itself, sometimes to establish subsidiary institutions that serve the common good; when blames for wrongs suffered become diffused and hard to trace, insurance becomes social security legitimized and administered by government under statutes.

The public government arises because there are things that must be done for the people, but cannot be done at all or as well by individual effort—or under the procedures of common law. Preeminently, the individual's responsibility for injustice throughout the community cannot be discharged without public law, statute law, arrived at by mutual persuasion and common consent. Modern governments began when revolutions brought the ordinary private individual into the process of making and administering public statutory law. He was made a citizen. Our Bill of Rights, particularly the First Amendment, stipulates the rights and duties of speech, press, assembly, and petition, which enable the citizens to enter into continuous and increasingly formal processes of mutual persuasion which issue in law under the Constitution.

Formal self-government of this sort is always a precarious enterprise. Its processes are powerful and delicate, like all the processes of human reason. They can be degraded and prostituted for other purposes from government. Persuasion is a complex of reason and force. If it is to be adequate to the needs of government, it must continually replace force by reason. The provisions of the Constitution, especially the large division of powers in the legislative, executive, and judicial branches, and also in the federal division and combination of local, state, and national parts, formalize and channel the persuasive process so that public laws can be found that will carry the burdens of justice and freedom.

To a great extent our Constitution has not been fulfilled in practice. In particular, the essential division of powers, and the consequent system of checks and balances, has been found annoying and frustrating. The body of common law has cradled and cultivated the powerful processes of the industrial revolution, and it has been found difficult to rule the powerful energies of technology, business, and corporate organization. The inventive and accelerating use of property and contracts has generated persuasive powers that have been understood as private affairs, but that have increasingly been found to be touched with public interest. Public law has not developed, or indeed been trusted, to deal with the consequent threat to the community. Consequently, private affairs have had recourse to the arts and sciences of management. In its attempts to control and regulate, government has increasingly turned to the instruments and styles of management.

It may not be too late to take account of the accumulation of the multitude of subsidiary corporate institutions, styled private, and to assess the possibilities of transforming their managerial forms of organization into the legal and political forms of public government. The Constitution has many models of such forms waiting to be used. The future of justice and freedom depends upon our ability to find the assurance that we can do what we ought to will in public law—in short, to put our confidence in political liberty.

7

SO REASON CAN RULE: THE CONSTITUTION REVISITED

═‖‖

> We the People of the United States, in Order to form a more perfect Union, establish Justice, insure domestic Tranquility, provide for the common defence, promote the general Welfare, and secure the Blessings of Liberty to ourselves and our Posterity, do ordain and establish this Constitution for the United States of America.

THE PREAMBLE

THE words and phrases of the Preamble to the Constitution are not accidents, and the statement that results from their composition is not a work of idle rhetoric or propaganda. "We the People . . . do ordain and establish this Constitution" condenses into a few words the essence of the revolution that gave birth to the United States of America; it confirms the principle of self-government, that governments derive their just powers from the consent of the governed. It was a resolution written in the eighteenth century, but it was the announcement of a discovery of a principle that had always been true. Kings as well as the newly made citizens had known the

Originally published as A Center Occasional Paper, Vol. 1, Number 2 (February, 1967).

deep practical truth of the principle, no matter how far they may have been from conformity to it.

Something similar can be said about the other phrases in the Preamble. They are authentic in the language of the eighteenth century, but they are stating truths that had been hard-won in previous revolutions and had been confirmed in long experience of the vicissitudes of government. They are variations of the traditional conditions for the existence of a political community. Through long usage they had been formulated in the brief abstract language of the common good as the purpose of all government: order, justice, peace, and freedom. The authors of the Constitution knew that they were building on the foundation stones of a long tradition. When they added "common defence" and "general Welfare," they were merely adding some implications of the traditional formula, and they could have added others, as if to say "and so forth."

It is fashionable today to read these phrases as the statement of ideals or values, and then to think of other possible purposes and "goods" that ought to be added and thus constitutionalized. For example, in some more recently written constitutions world peace or a guaranteed income for each citizen has been added. But it would seem that such additions, though worthy of common concern, are subsumable under the terms of the traditional constitutional formula. They specify things that would be brought about if the laws and politics of the time conformed to the principles of justice, freedom, peace, and order.

It would take a long and complicated demonstration to show that the traditional formula is both necessary and sufficient as the statement of our highest political purpose. Part of such a demonstration would consist in showing that the rest of the Constitution supplies the specific means that the grand purpose implies. Another part would try to show that any needed amendment or improvement of the Constitution is authorized by the preambulatory goal. It may be recalled that some years ago there was an attempt to conduct a great debate about our national goals. It is noteworthy that none of the contributions to that discussion reached any novel purposes that transcend the statement of the Preamble; most of them fell far below. This is not to say that the

Preamble contains all the possibilities that will ever be discovered
in the common good; it is to say that novel proposals should be
tested to see if they are equal to or more universal or more profound than those we have inherited.

The logic of the common good and its formulations is worthy
of note. Its terms *justice, peace, freedom, order* are mutually
implied. Each one requires the others if it is to be realized. None
can be suppressed or ignored if the others are to be saved. It is
therefore not possible to treat them as alternative ideals or values
to be balanced or bargained away. There may be times when one
of them is deficiently cultivated or realized, or it may be that a
new problem may throw one into a higher immediate priority,
but both in formal thought and in the logic of events the realization of one entails the realization of all the others. It has been
guessed that the cold war is a rivalry based on the apparent fact
that the Russians are devoting themselves to social justice and
that the United States is devoting itself to freedom. As the cold
war wears on, it appears that both countries are bringing these
concerns into balance; the Russians are discovering the claims of
freedom and we are discovering new depths in our failures of
justice. And this is happening not merely because of the pressures
of competition and propaganda. It is a part of justice to recognize
the freedom of men and it is a part of freedom to will that justice
is done.

It may be true that the Preamble would be more effective
pedagogically if it spelled out some of its implications so that the
officers of government as well as the citizens would be continually
reminded of the high functions of the laws they make and use.
But by the same token, a citizenry well educated in the law might
better read and understand the formula in its present elegant
expression and in its perennial truth. The Preamble may not be
the best possible statement of American goals, but its brevity and
comprehension stand as a challenge and a warning to those who
are ambitious to improve it. For those who find it formal and
cold, it may be noted that the general-welfare clause has enabled
and continues to enable an infusion of charity into the community's concern for the good of its members.

Another clause in the Preamble, "in Order to form a more

perfect Union," had a very special meaning when the Constitution was drafted. The Articles of Confederation had not provided the unity that the new nation needed. The need had become pressing for the purpose of ordering the commerce of the thirteen colonies. When the drafters met, they were known as a committee of commercial gentlemen. But it took little deliberation for them to discover that unity or union had more extensive implications. It contained the need for a basic political order. Meeting this need raised the question of federation to the level of primary attention. The War of Independence had led the colonies to recognize themselves as sovereign states, and this recognition was so vivid that they feared that submission to even a federal union would result in the loss of the independence for which they had fought. Thus, the very purpose of the Constitutional Convention seemed to threaten the thirteen common goods of the constituent parties, and the principle that had gone by various names, usually called states' rights, but now amplified and called pluralism, was uncovered. The tension between this principle and the principle of union made the politics of the young republic and came to a crucial climax in the Civil War. The tension has risen and fallen since then, because resort to arms was not a resolution but rather a hardening of the convictions on both sides. Because modern political science and the behavioral sciences have been pursuing politics by other means, the federal problem has been watered down into a weak procedural pragmatic defense of what is called our pluralistic society.

The revival of politics depends to a great extent on finding both the theoretical and the practical meaning of the purpose expressed in the clause "in Order to form a more perfect Union." The theoretical issues can be seen in recognizing that there is a necessary counterpart of *e pluribus unum* in a reversal of the phrase, something like *ex uno plures*. We cannot establish a "many" without laying the basis for founding a unity, and this is a continual process. In a living society, the finding of the unions and of the relevant "manys" is the life of politics. It comes down to Lincoln's principle that what needs to be done but cannot be done by the individual or the parts by themselves can and must be done by the government as a whole. Finding the units of government and legitimizing their respective functions is the main business of government. And this is begun and continues by the making and remaking of the Constitution.

The current use by the Supreme Court of the Fourteenth Amendment to give uniformity to the provisions of the Civil Rights Act, the reapportionment of electoral districts, and the procedural codes for criminal trials in the states has the appearance of imposed unity, but it has not yet been stated that these will lay the ground for an increased variability in these matters. New problems have been posed by these judgments of the court, and they will blossom in many diverse solutions of local problems. The codification of law by the Romans forced local invention and variety of interpretation. Thus, also, new achievements in legal justice provide new liberties and rights. So the perfection of union is a permanent dedication of the Constitution to the process of political progress as history poses new questions for political solution. This suggests the evolutionary order over which the Constitution presides. Order as an imperative of the common good implies the continual ordering of the parts of the community, the perennial dividing and ruling that government requires.

So much for the Preamble. Much, much more could be said about it as laying the foundation for the complicated provisions of the Constitution. I have chosen these comments as an introduction to the discussion of two principles that pervade these provisions, the principle of representation and the principle of federation.

REPRESENTATION AND FEDERATION

Representation of one kind or another has always been a necessary and pervasive principle of government. In most general terms, it is the solution of the many diverse problems of the political union; it is always the guide in the process of making a more perfect union. Even in the direct democracy of the Greek city-state it was necessary to elect officers to carry out the decisions of the assembled citizens. Even in Rousseau's radical proposals for the expression of the general will without intermediaries, there had to be magistrates who would think and act as agents of the people. But representation in the experience of less democratic regimes had been a more complicated and subtle device. The many things that have to be done for the people, but that cannot be done by merely individual effort, require many different kinds of representation, and some of them involve functions that are not adequately described as carrying out orders or executing the will of the people. At a crucial stage in the development of parliamentary institutions, Edmund Burke seemed to invert the notion of representation when he pointed out that his duty as a member of parliament was to ignore the literal expressions of the will of the electorate in order to discover his and their responsibilities to the common good. In fact, he was not denying his responsibility to his constituency, but rather demonstrating his and their common, underlying search for the general good of the community.

Representation has its roots in the distinguishable powers of the individual human being, most particularly in what is known as the reflective power of reason. We sense, think, feel, and will, but we also know that we do these things. At first, in children and adolescents. this knowledge can be confused and confusing. It takes years of sophistication and education to bring it to focus and articulation in the mature adult. When it reaches a kind of stability and clarity, it becomes the means by which the individual teaches himself and the base from which all the rational powers realize themselves in the playing of games, in customs and rituals, in dramas, in institutions, and, of course, in politics.

As a corollary, the arts, the institutions, and the organization of society provide the individual with the occasions for observation of himself and others in which roles are imitated, propagated, and invented, and are internalized in habits. The sociologists have recently abstracted role-playing for the understanding and ordering of all social behavior. Such theories are obviously borrowed from two familiar institutions, the theater and the political state, both of which in their respective styles enable men to see themselves as others see them; that is, to represent themselves to themselves.

When a man becomes an actor, the playwright gives him a role in speech and in action. The actor has to learn his part and to make it his second, or third, nature. His performance holds a mirror up to himself and other men; he holds a mirror up to society and re-presents it. Of course, all the fine arts partake in this representative function, and they, including the theater, are subject to the familiar criticism of simply representative art. But they are highly selective in what they represent and their projections are full of imaginative extensions and distortions; and as they distort what they represent, they also transform it.

In the sociological theory based on role-playing, the long history of social, economic, and political institutions appears as the interaction between dramatic models and individuals and groups. The family, the market, and government are continually making and remaking roles for individuals to play. Before the young take on the stations and duties of adult life, they play roles in both formal and informal education and thus acquire the habits on the basis of which they graduate and are initiated into the responsibilities of adult life. If this education is truly liberal and has awakened the intellect to its many dimensions of sophistication and insight, adult life will retain the capacity of playing roles, but it will also include some of the detachment that will enable it to invent alternative roles and therefore to shift roles easily and freely. Since the liberal arts deal in symbols and universal ideas, the playwright in every man not only will reflect these separate roles but will reach theories and make rules for action. The exercise of the liberal arts will transcend the merely dramatic and find laws of society, and even of natural objects.

Dramaturgy and government may seem to be pretty distant analogues of one another, and the reduction of political representation to playacting would seem to be a satirical trick. But if the liberal artistry of the playwright is taken into account, it is not too difficult to see a constitution and its attendant laws as a plot writ large. It is possible to see a benevolent despot or a fanatical dictator as the playwright and director of a great drama; we have in fact seen such spectacles in our time. It is possible to see a constitutional monarch as the protagonist in a living drama; historians have often used this dramatic machinery to give force to their narratives. John Stuart Mill, though he does not use

dramatic terms, shows how these forms of government have fit
the stages of development in historical or backward societies; he
seems to say that these forms fit not only because they adapt
themselves to the respective conditions of men but because they
also have led to more adequate forms of self-government.

The dramatic analogy would seem to get confused and to break
down as democracy develops, for the citizen is not only an actor
playing a role but also playwright and director as he is elected or
appointed to public office. It would seem that the political life of
the community as a whole becomes the improvisation of many
author-actors. On second thought, however, this means that the
drama has become genuine politics under a developing constitution, and confusion is avoidable if the citizen-actors understand
their parts in the thickening plot, in other words, their offices and
their duties.

I have taken this detour into dramaturgy in order to suggest that
the reduction of the notion of representation to a kind of agency,
according to which the representative has orders from his constituency that he is obligated to carry out, is a misleading analogy.
Representation has many dimensions, and there have been other
well-known analogies that reveal them. Plato's laborious roster of
the human arts under the master art of government is a classic
example, one that we should be reminded of as we try now to see
technology redistributing men and work and roles under our
Constitution. Likewise, the division of society into classes, and
their varying relations to the class of classes, the body politic, has
been a perennial reminder of the never-ending problem of representation. As we approach what we like to call the classless
society, we ironically discover groups and interests in conflict and
requiring decision-makers to resolve the conflicts.

While all these analogies and more that might be adduced warn
of the danger of oversimplifying the device of representation,
they have recently in the hands of the sociologist tended to displace the political problem that they were originally intended to
solve, or at least clarify. Since they are not mere fantasies but
describe real political problems, at least partially, and seem amen-
able to empirical verification and even measurement, they have
become the favored materials in political science. But it should

not be forgotten that they are analogies and therefore somewhat risky aids to political thought, realistic though they may be. They may be even more risky in the practice of politics since they seem to legitimize many forms of political corruption.

So far, representation has been shown to be the extension of that reflective power of the human mind to know itself, to know itself not merely in its individual mode but also in its articulation with other minds. Society knows itself in its representatives. But political representation proper has another intention. Society by nature wishes to know its goals, its ends, its goods, its common good. Sociology tends to show only the apparent goods, what men think they want. Liberal politics used to be concerned that the representative, the politician, be responsive and responsible to public opinion, but it was also concerned that he should be a statesman too, who would practice the political arts in order to discover the real common good and to make not only himself but also his constituency responsible to that. Politics would then be not mere playing a role in a theatrical representation; it would involve both a practical and a speculative dialectic, as in a Platonic dialogue, to expose sophistry and special interest, to penetrate private and public opinion, to expose the impostorship of group power and interest, and to discover the real common good in the process. This process was not conceived as a pleasant ballet of pure spirits but rather as the most difficult and energetic effort of men of goodwill to raise themselves together to the level of political intelligence. As the Founding Fathers said, if men were angels they would need no government, and if they were beasts, they could not attain it. Being men who could learn, they might achieve it through discipline.

So, in this most difficult of enterprises, the roles that men play must be turned into learning disciplines; there must be a curriculum, and this is supplied by a constitution and laws. A citizen in a self-governing society is enrolled in that school; his rights and duties launch him on a course of lifelong learning. But a representative by election or by appointment must both learn and teach. The great comprehensive assignment is to learn and relearn the common good and through the laws to teach it to succeeding generations of citizens.

If we consider the learning that goes on in the daily life of the citizen under the common law, it seems that this learning is concerned chiefly with men's private affairs, but that because of the continual process of development in common law that expands it into the field of public law the individual discovers his public life as a citizen. If, for example, one gives the First Amendment of the Constitution a positive reading, it provides the citizen with the institutional means by whch self-government can be generated and continually improved. However, these First Amendment institutions—free speech as practiced in the press, in assemblies, in education, and now in radio and television—are preparatory and subsidiary to the great institutions of public government that draw all roles, all classes, all groups, all arts, all interests together and articulate them for the effective discharge of the citizen's responsibility for justice and the other goods that are common in the community. The U.S. Constitution and the laws penetrate the body politic, give it intelligible form and viability. Through them the government itself is the representative of the people.

In a representative government, constitution is a continual process. On the elementary level it makes citizens out of natural persons. The process is not merely nominal: the citizen is an elementary officer, an epitome of the reflexive relation of self-government. This means that he has a duty and a right to judge his own concerns, his acts and their effects, as they bear on the common good. If they entail the common acts of the community, he again has the duty and right to contribute to the common deliberation by which the acts of the community are decided. Common deliberation, or mutual persuasion, happens on all levels of society, and the common judgments to which it leads result in agreements, promises, rules, roles to be played, the learning of the useful and liberal arts, and the organization of institutions. On all these levels there are imitations of the offices, the laws, and the constitution of the strictly political government. It is from this political paradigm that penetrates the whole society that the preceding analogies derive their plausibility. And to this paradigm—the constitution, the laws, and the offices—the analogues should contribute their meanings.

As political science and philosophy are architectonic to all the social sciences, so is the Constitution architectonic to all subordinate institutions. It names and defines the offices of government and then establishes the procedures by which the officers make, administer, and adjudicate the laws. Although a citizen is already an officer by virtue of the revolutionary transformations of the eighteenth century, his rights and duties have further constitutional implications. He may be elected or appointed to public office, and he undergoes a transformation; or perhaps a stronger word should be used: he is transfigured. Grover Cleveland's aphorism "Public office is a public trust" underlines the transformation. The officer represents the interests of his constituency, but with a difference. He must revise the simple notion of a mandate, or of acting as an agency, so that his essential duty is to make, administer, and judge the laws that serve the common good. He must see the interests and needs of his clients under the aspect of the common good. Justice must be done, freedom extended, peace kept, and order discovered. He must ensure the legitimation of power throughout the community. He must always understand that it is through this kind of representation that the citizen participates in self-government.

All of this may seem to be a highly artificial, purist, or idealistic interpretation of constitutional government. But two considerations should be kept in mind. The first of these is the distinction between private and public law. Private law developed its rules primarily in the courts of common law, where the interests and needs of individuals were adjudicated by adversary proceedings. In this setting, the lawyers are said to "represent" their clients, and the full power of their pleadings is devoted to the separate interests of their respective clients. It is only the judicial process of the court that reaches anything like the transformation of the case into a general rule of law. But public law under the Constitution is different. It has been invented and supported to meet the need discovered in common law for a different view of society, a society that continually searches for a more perfect union, a social contract, a super-personal instrument for dealing with crime, a developing general welfare, and a social security, all these as the conditions for its existence.

The second consideration is that the invention of institutions able to fulfill these conditions is rooted in the natural power of the human mind to know its natural social processes. Even when we fail to realize these ends and to provide the proper means, we need the assurance that they are possible of attainment, and that they are in part, at least, continually achieved. The Constitution provides us with the machinery of laws and representative offices that ensures us as a people that we can do what we ought to will.

All constitutions break down the whole governmental institution into parts with specific limited powers, but the U.S. Constitution is well known throughout the world for its unusually drastic separation of powers. Although it establishes a national unitary government, it follows Montesquieu in applying the federal principle throughout the structure. Historically, this was easily accomplished because the formulation was accepted when many new colonies were jealous of their new independence. They persuaded each other to make a more perfect union on the condition that they retained many of their own original powers. The language of the Tenth Amendment seems to express a resolve that each new proposal for the delegation of powers to the central government would be scrutinized before it was made. But there seem to have been other reasons for adherence to the federal principle. The reasons usually given express the fear of centralized power, a fear that was inherited from the European experience of monarchical imperialism. But there seem to be still other, more philosophical reasons that are derived from the application of the principle of the division of labor in economics and psychology.

Adam Smith's argument for the division of labor was not new; it had been made by Plato and often repeated. It claimed that both productivity and skill were progressively enhanced when the product was distinguished sharply from others and the respective skills in production were separately cultivated. It has also been argued that human freedom is increased when the various specializations of human activities are multiplied. We have cause to wonder about where the argument leads since Taylor applied engineering analysis and broke down work into hand and eye movements, and perhaps unknowingly ground down jobs to operations that automatic machines can do better. Freedom in work may result in freedom from work.

But short of the extremes to which the argument leads, there seems to be a stage of specialization that fits the human condition. Human beings suffer frustration when they try to do everything at once. Special attention to the product and the operations that its production requires does develop the proper art, and its practice establishes relevant habits and skills. It is an easy inference from this that the practice of an art is the realization of distinguishable natural human powers. And this argument from the arts applies to the understanding and discipline of human conduct in general. It also applies to the art of government.

So the division of the powers in the Constitution fit and correspond to the powers of the human being. This view of government is at present under heavy skeptical criticism: the division of powers in the great institutions of government— legislative, executive, and judicial—is held to be too rationalistic; the actual conduct of government does not and cannot respect the distinctions; the living Constitution upon which our political life depends is quite a different thing from the formal written document, and we pay sentimental homage to a myth, while we follow custom and improvise an American way of life in our exploitation of persons and institutions. But this is to say that we choose not to use all of our powers of intelligence, particularly the higher powers that the Constitution invites us to use. The point can be put crudely and comprehensively by saying that we honor and cultivate the powers of the human mind, even the rational powers, when they are engaged in the invention and tending of the technical processes, while we allow similar powers to wither when they are engaged in the making and tending of the laws.

The reason that the Constitution distinguishes and allocates to the great divisions of government is practical reason. It has some important similarities to theoretical or speculative reason; likewise it is implicated in modern science and technology, which combine the theoretical and the practical. But the aim of practical reason is different from the aims of theory and science, and its criteria of rigor and validity are different. It necessarily aims at the good, and cannot escape questions of value. Although it needs to know how events take place and must take account of causes, it is directly concerned with the ordering of means and ends, with final causes. It has many subject-matters. It deals with human beings, more particularly with individual human beings in ethics and rational psychology, but perhaps its noblest science is politics, which deals with human associations, where the ends are common goods and the means are the rules and the laws of organizations, including the state.

The classical definition of law sets up in most brief and elegant form the field within which practical reason operates as political reason: law is a rule of reason propagated by an authority and directed to the common good. Our Constitution is such a law or body of laws. "We the people" are the authority that propagates the Constitution, a master law that in turn establishes other authorities or offices that in turn propagate other laws. Following Locke and Montesquieu, the Constitution distinguishes three great offices, powers, or functions: the legislature, the executive, and the judiciary; and to them are assigned respectively three uses of practical reason: the making of laws, the executing or administration of laws, and the adjudication of laws. Furthermore, the Constitution not only divides these functions but also separates them by making the institutions equal and independent. They are, as it were, insulated from one another, on the ground, I am claiming, that their confusion would frustrate their efficient service to the various ends of the common good, not only freedom, as Montesquieu argues, but also justice, order, and peace.

THE LEGISLATURE

For some reason that I am not able to discover, there are no studies of the legislative process comparable with the many studies that have been made of the judicial process. This apparent neglect may have something to do with the current decay and denigration of legislatures all over the world. It would seem that the disappearance of legislatures or the forfeiture of their functions to other branches of government would be a most fateful development. Yet the present tendency in that direction is commonly viewed without alarm, and it seems that it has been observed and condoned for a long time. John Stuart Mill in his

Representative Government says that no one should expect legislatures to make laws. They should debate issues and inform the public, but the actual making of laws should be assigned to small legislative commissions that would be competent to carry out such a difficult task. This suggests the American solution, which is for Congress to give the major and essential tasks to congressional committees, who then report out bills for final action.

There can be no doubt of the difficulty and importance of the process. It cannot be concealed or dismissed by saying that it is the function of the legislator to express the will of the people. The reverence given to the heroic law-givers of the past—Moses, Lycurgus, Solon—and the lyrical outburst of Rousseau when he thinks of the miracle of law-making in a self-governing society, are at least reminders that the legislative proceess needs special attention. The following paragraphs could be another modest reminder in any adequate study.

To begin with, it should be recalled that laws have other origins than from legislatures, namely, courts of common law, and that statutes are often extensions of those laws. But common-law courts do not primarily aim at legislation; the laws that result are byproducts of the judicial process. Statutes are supposed to result from the deliberations and mutual persuasions of legislative bodies, and the formal procedures are supposed to consummate the massive political processes of the community. The question, then, is, what are the intentions and the chosen means by which such a remarkable result—law—is achieved.

On first thought, since law is a rule of reason, it would seem that some kind of induction is involved in law-making, some kind of generalization from concrete facts, events, or actions that need further understanding and direction. This clue could lead to a reexamination of the rules of induction for science, as they have been formulated by John Stuart Mill, David Hume, and Francis Bacon. This is not the place to follow this clue, since the thorny problem of scientific induction is not the aim, but it may be worth noting that these three philosophers had other careers that immersed them in disciplines more closely related to law and politics than to empirical science. Mill was a civil servant, Hume was a historian, and Bacon was a judge. There may be an im-

portant truth in the witticism that Francis Bacon thought about
science as a lord chancellor; similar comments would be applicable to the other two. Bacon and Mill made observations that
have puzzled their followers in the criticism of scientific method.
Bacon said that in the observation of facts the form or law of facts
leaps to the eye. Mill asked a question that he never answered:
why is it that the great discoveries in science are generalizations
based on one single observation?

They all seem to agree implicitly with a later distinction of
stages in the process of induction: primary and secondary inductions. They seem to be admitting that the rules they formulated
were secondary to an initial intuitive induction such as Aristotle
described in a simile. Aristotle saw facts as slippery, hard-to-catch
data fleeing like a retreating army. The army rallies and falls into
order when one soldier turns and takes a stand on a point of
vantage, a hypothesis, upon which his fellow soldiers form ranks.
These puzzling remarks are not analytical solutions of the problem
of induction, but they do suggest a crucial stage in law-making.

A law-maker is faced with a mass of slippery, hard-to-catch
information, pressures, and troubles that threaten order in a
society. He seeks a strategy and a rule that will reduce the chaos
to order. He with his legislative colleagues seeks further information and opinion. At some point in the deliberation, a legal
hypothesis leaps to his eye. He takes a stand and proceeds to
persuade his colleagues. His insight may come by way of analogies
with other laws, to which he turns as lawyers do in their court
pleadings. The process may have started outside the legislative
chamber and it may involve hearings of lobbies by one or more
committees. Trial drafts are made and amendments considered.
The bill may be voted down and restudied for further action. It
may be shelved for later consideration.

This is a rough description of a very complicated process, but
one feature of it seems to be crucial—the first grasp of the legal
hypothesis. This corresponds to, if it is not identical with,
Aristotle's intuitive induction. Without this, there is no deliberation, no persuasion, no vote. (The political computer has no
program.) Of course, the legal intuitive induction happens in a
context—complaints by citizens, pleadings by lobbies, and the

other varieties of persuasions, more or less reasonable. But the crucial context is the body of other law already passed and operating, and the demands of the common good. These produce something like a conversion in the representative law-maker. Because of the exigencies of election campaigns the representative starts his career in the role of an agent of his constituency, but he realizes as he deliberates on prospective laws that his assignment is to translate the conflict and strife of citizens into a rule of reason for the common good. His intuitive induction—the generalization of the information—is demanded, but it is also helped by the imperative to do justice, make order under freedom, and restore peace to the community. His agency and his insight are like those of a judge. He must see the justice and injustice in the complex situation and find the law that will discharge the community's responsibility, not only in the instant case but for all similar cases.

This means that a legal hypothesis is not merely a generalization from facts and verifiable by facts; it must meet additional criteria. If it is to become a law, it must transcend the welter of facts and pressures of persuasion and become a rule of reason that will persuade free human beings to cultivate new behaviors, actions, habits, and even new institutions as means to the common good. Too often legislative reason tries to meet these criteria by simply adding a penalty to the primitive legal hypothesis. There is some semblance of validity in this appeal to force, since behavior and habits can be formed by coercion, and it is said that a political community has a monopoly of power to accomplish that. But for any human community, it is a cruel regression to the lower levels of civilization, and it is merely an illusion to suppose that coercion is the basis of law and order.

The leverage of persuasion is the reasonableness that can be imbedded in the law, and it is to this that the consent of the governed is given. This consent can be reduced to the superficial consent that exists in popular opinion, and it is in this sense that a law seems to be the generalization from particulars. There is an illusion in this as there is in the use of coercion. The literal expression of the will of the people, processed through agitation and the ballot, can be very deceitful. If the law is to take root in the habits of free citizens, it has to be framed so that it is available to the intelligence of everybody. As a good teacher must respect the intelligence of his pupils, so the law must appeal to the sense of justice of the community. A law exists in the reasonableness it brings to the people, and it is to this that they consent. So, the legislator has to reach for and refine the formulation that amplifies his initial legal hypothesis in order to draw out the consent and win the obedience of the community in the future, as well as in the present. The final verification of the law is given only in the settled habits that it induces in the citizens. Ultimately, this is the meaning of the consent of the governed; all the other preliminary expressions of consent—polls, caucuses, party platforms, citizens' ballots, and votes in legislative chambers—are only the external conditions for the generation of the internal substance of legality in the habits of the community.

This distinction between external laws and internal habits comes from two kinds of ethical thought. There is the theory of conduct under rules of reason, or codes of ethics. This reaches its climax in Kantian ethics where there is a hierarchy of imperatives, culminating in the categorical: make all the maxims of your action laws universal. Under this master rule, there are hypothetical imperatives that take time, place, and circumstance into account; then imperatives of skill that govern the practice of the arts. Under these rules, the individual governs himself as if he were a polity.

Then there is the ethics of the virtues. Adherence or obedience to the imperatives develops habits. When the habits are achieved and are properly ordered to valid ends, which are ensured under good laws, the habits are virtues and good conduct is free and accompanied by pleasures.

These kinds of ethics can be cultivated separately, and the independent cultivation is necessary at certain stages of education. But the legislator, he who makes the rules of reason for the common good, must know the reciprocal relations and the influences of each on the other. Perhaps the most important knowledge and skill that he exercises in law-making concerns the timing of these relations. It is said in the legends concerning Solon and Lycurgus that when they had drawn up a code of laws for their respective polities they got an agreement from the people that the laws should not be changed for ten years, and during that interval they absented themselves from their communities so that the requisite habits could be generated in the people. Sure enough, they got the promise of the people to abide by this legal stasis, but they were under no illusions that they had thereby gained their substantial consent. That could only be recognized and judged after ten years of practice; only then would they know what new laws or amendments were needed.

Whether attention of this sort is given to law-making, this process is always present. In the political thought of the ancients, these legends were honored by Plato, Aristotle, and Thucydides in their rule that laws should not be changed rapidly. This is often taken to mean that these thinkers were simply conservative; they feared the open society. But their true meaning is that the real existence of law is not in enactments or books but in the hearts of the citizens. This kind of wisdom was well known to monarchs and aristocrats; it has usually not been known by democracies. It may be impossible to give it respect under modern conditions, but it would seem that legislators should be aware of the dangers in its neglect. Consent of the governed becomes a mockery if it is interpreted, superficially and literally, in terms of the mechanics of representation and participation.

This somewhat plaintive appeal to the wisdom of the legislator suggests some other jurisprudential depths that we might wish to invoke. In this country, we have become familiar with the eye the legislator has to the likelihood that his work will be reviewed by the Supreme Court. Part of this caution is due to a prudential care to avoid having his law judged unconstitutional. But another part of it appeals to the cultivated wisdom of the justices as they view a new law in relation to the rest of the body of established law. The notorious side effects of the Prohibition amendment upon the rest of our body of law illustrates the problem, and similar problems arise around almost any statute that single-mindedly seeks a remedy for clear evil, but at the same time brings unforeseen effects in other branches of law; for instance, the apparent effects of the income tax on corporations-for-profit, which in order to protect themselves from the tax have set up thousands of charitable corporations where their assets are

sequestered. This is not to say that side effects are always evil,
but only to raise the question of what might be called legal
ecology. The ramification of corporation law raises these questions in great complexity, so great in fact that foresight seems
overwhelmed.

But it is time to return to one of the basic themes of this essay,
namely, that persuasion is the all-pervasive life of the body politic.
There are various kinds of persuasion on the low, high, and
middle ranges. On the level of production and trade there are the
adversary proceedings of the courts of common law that formalize
the business of the marketplace. In the so-called voluntary
associations there are the more or less chartered organizations
that practice the arts of debate and management under *Robert's
Rules of Order* and tables of organization. Under the enabling
immunities of the First Amendment, free speech is practiced
with its elaborations in press, assembly, and petition, and these
are further developed in our system of free and compulsory
education. In all of these, the intent is to increase the ratio of
reason to force. Contrary to much current theory, truly effective
and dependable power is increased as reason prevails. Free
speech is the ensurance of persuasion, and without it power is
evanescent. But in order to bring persuasion to its full realization,
it must be transformed into laws or rules of reason, and it is for
this consummation of politics that the Constitution establishes the
machinery of representation and legislation.

The transformation of persuasion into law, whether begun in
the House or the Senate, becomes final by the Congress only after
both parties have approved a piece of legislation. Under our
bicameral system, members of the Congress have the responsibility to find in mutual persuasion and deliberation the intuitive
induction that results in a legal hypothesis; for instance, the
insight that leads to a social security law, or to a criminal law.
The process is essentially a generalization from problematic
conditions and needs of the society in all their variety and complexity. The result must represent these concrete particulars in a
reasonable and just pattern; in this sense, it must be responsible
to the community and the electorate.

In the normal course of particularly significant legislation, the

House and the Senate have their own bills before them, and when the first to act sends its bills to the other for concurrence, agreement is reached through floor discussion and action, or following a recommendation by a joint House-Senate conference committee. In both bodies, the procedure involves the wisdom of legislative experience. It is this wisdom and experience that is employed by the legislators in finding the locus of a prospective law in the general body of existing laws, in considering the constitutionality of the proposed legislation, in judging the power to induce new habits in the community with concern about the side effects that may result with respect to other laws, and in considering the fitness of the new legislation to serve the common good.

I realize that other reasons are given for a bicameral system; most of them bear on the usual concerns to limit the respective powers of the two houses by allowing them to check and balance each other. But these considerations can and ought to be subsumed under the imperatives of jurisprudence mentioned above.

When the bill passes formally into law, sometimes aided by the joint committees of Congress, a new entity exists, not yet the achievement of a living law existing in the hearts of men, but a relatively permanent power of persuasion. Stated in universal language, it is an entity of reason voicing the will of the whole community. It approximates the positivistic definition of law, the command of the sovereign to be enforced by sanctions. But this formula contains a great temptation to identify a law with the so-called monopoly of force that is supposed to be exercised by the state. This would imply that the legislative art consists in the manipulation of groups and their interests into some kind of coalition so that their combined force can coerce the compliance of the rest of the community. Too often the behavior of politicians seems to verify this account of the legislative process. However, this description is far from the actual process.

The political process of persuasion, it is true, has its roots in the play of groups, interests, and forces in the community, but when a bill becomes a law, it has been divested of the powers that went into its making, and the decision has been made to entrust the common good to a rule of reason, the only power that can penetrate and permeate the body politic. It becomes the law of the land. This is the truth that lies behind the myth of the social contract: the citizens have made a contract to surrender their individual rights to the popular assembly or its representative parliament, which in turn has agreed to abide by the process of deliberation and the rules of reason. It does not change this fundamental constitutional process to admit that the results are sometimes imperfect and have to be supplemented by police action. The sanctions are not the basis of law; they are auxiliary aids of law to deal with the gap between reason and habit. If the law turns out to depend for its effectiveness just on force alone, it is not a law.

THE EXECUTIVE

The final words of the previous section indicate that the law has passed the line separating the legislative from the executive branch of the government. Austin's phrase "the command of the sovereign" is in the executive or imperative mode, and the passage to the executive department is recognized in our system in the President's act of signing the bill. This has two effects: it is a final act of legislation and it is the acceptance of his duty to execute or administer the law. That he can veto the bill and return it to the legislature for further deliberation is an indication that the act is not merely formal. By his signature the President certifies that the law has become a command and that he pledges his obedience to it, not only his own obedience as an officer of the government but the obedience of the whole executive branch. He also reasserts the proposition that this is a government of laws, not of men, and this means that the law has reached a moment of independence and superiority; it and no person or combination of persons is sovereign.

It is of course true that the mere promulgation, or publication, of a rule of reason does not by itself constitute effective government, just as it is true that issuing an order, no matter by whatever authority, police or military, is not necessarily effective. Richard Neustadt in his *Presidential Power* tells how Truman pitied Eisenhower when the latter became President. He said

that the general would be shocked when he discovered that when
he issued an order from the President's office, nothing would
happen, that the only power of the President is the power of
persuasion. To be sure, the President's power of persuasion is
very great because he is acting under law, but it is still only
persuasion. So it is throughout the executive branch.

The executive mode of persuasion is different from the legislative mode. Whereas the legislator operates under an assignment
to find a universal rule that will bring justice and freedom to the
whole community and its many interests and pressures, the
executive operates under an assignment to administer a general
rule of reason so that it can be carried out by many groups and
individual citizens. If the rule merely dealt with inanimate or
nonrational things, the persuasion might follow the analogy with
formal logic. From the general rule as a premise succeeding rules
of less and less generality might be deduced until they are
applicable to concrete particulars. Superior officers could issue
orders to inferior officers of administration. Tables of administrative organization would seem to indicate that this is the process.
But although ours is a government of laws rather than of men,
the laws operate through animate, rational, and therefore free
men. The men who fill the offices of government, as well as
the men in homes and on the streets and in the factories, have to
understand in order to obey, and they have to understand well if
they are to enlist the obedience of other men. The sequences of
Hegelian logic would seem to be more apt: the superior officer
issues an order or a thesis; the lower officer or officers assert an
antithesis that is more specific and full of circumstantial considerations; and these are followed by executive deliberations
which result in a synthesis.

However, both of these models are only borrowed from
theoretical reason, and although they are relevant as guides in
practical reasoning, the actual process of administration is
different in several respects. The major premise of practical
reason is the statement of an end or purpose that requires the
discovery and ordering of means. The law may indicate what
these are, but the application may involve the invention of
institutional and technical means and their actual management

in order to achieve the legal intent. Experts in engineering and administration may have to be enlisted, and each of them will have to find his official duties amidst many contingencies. If the enterprise is novel enough, there may have to be new skills acquired on the job. Know-how will have to be added to expertise. Goodwill and morale will have to be added to patience and fortitude.

So, although the executive branch and the President as chief executive suggest a hierarchy of offices and lines of command, the business of administering and enforcing the laws is much too complex to be contained in such a scheme. The creation of the President's cabinet, which was not explicitly provided for in the Constitution but was obviously needed to exercise the powers that it delegated, demonstrates the point. In effect, the President's next act after signing a bill into law is to pass it on to the proper secretary, who then organizes his department to carry out the legal intent.

In the case of the Department of Justice, this may call for the immediate application of the police power, but even in this case the attorney-general may have to bring a case before a federal court before he can literally enforce the law; and this may become a recurrent necessity and involve the development of a strategy to deal with a series of novel and difficult cases, such as those that have arisen chronically under the Sherman Antitrust Act. The other members of the cabinet obviously preside over much more than simple law enforcement, even much more than the appointment of under-secretaries and their staffs to promulgate and superintend the carrying out of executive orders. They are involved in kinds of persuasion and deliberation different from those of the legislative branch. They have to build bridges from the law to the citizen, from the office to the institutions that form the infrastructure of the society, and these bridges themselves become large and powerful institutions. The Treasury Department provides currency and collects taxes, but it also has to deal with the banking system and its controls of credit; the Labor Department has to discover the consequences of labor laws that enable the development of labor unions.

But perhaps the Department of Agriculture demonstrates most

fully the function of the executive branch. In order to carry out the legislative intent of an Act of Congress, this Department had to initiate the scientific research that has transformed agriculture from the bundles of crafts and trades that make up the small farms into industries and technologies and economies. To aid in this, it partook in the development of educational institutions, the land-grant colleges and universities, which would combine research with training for the citizen-farmer. It also aided in the establishment of county agents, who carried information and skills to every village and farm. It has to deal in many variable ways with the granges, farm bureaus, and cooperatives that have sprung from voluntary associations. It has always had most complicated relations with the separate states and their agricultural interests and sovereignties, choosing when to enlist their cooperation, when to check their provincial enterprises, and when to circumvent their jurisdiction and deal directly with concrete problems. Since the agricultural empire has always been a major factor in the national economy, recurrent economic depressions and the disturbance of the market by world wars have induced the government to intervene by varying devices of regulation and control of production, prices, storage, and subsidies. This has generated a body of law and a system of administration to aid the farmer, protect the consumer, and advance the public welfare.

The other departments have had similar if not as extensive developments. They all tend to invent new institutions within the executive branch, and these in turn stimulate the development of responsive institutions in the so-called private sector of society. Sometimes the private sector itself spontaneously generates new institutions that need protection or aid from the government, and the government responds by establishing the so-called independent regulatory agencies, which do not fall under the categories provided by the cabinet but nevertheless belong to the executive branch and fall under the general powers of the President.

In the early days of the republic the offices of the executive branch were filled by appointment, some with approval by Congress but many without. There consequently grew up the so-called spoils system, in which the President rewarded the

members of his party with executive jobs without too critical an
eye to fitness for the office. Although this system cost a good deal
in inefficiency and/or corruption, it made for lively politics both
in the election campaigns and in the operation of the executive
branch. But as the weight and complexity of governmental affairs
increased, this form of political vitality had to be sacrificed for
the need of efficiency. So gradually the lower executive offices
came to be filled by examinations and judgments of merit in a
new system of civil service. As the standards were improved, the
executive branch was manned increasingly by persons of experience, education, and training; the offices were filled with experts
who could look to careers in government and expect increasing
education on the job.

It is common now to refer to the executive departments as
bureaus, and this means that a new kind of reason has appeared
in the art of government. It is often assumed to be the kind of
reason that is customarily imputed to the professions, but it is
actually the expert and technical reason that is exercised in
management. As the civil servant or bureaucrat is often experienced in business and industry, so the arts of government are
now borrowed from the current technology. It would seem that
technique has taken the place of both law and politics in
governmental administration. This transformation has gone so
far, it is said, that the present progressive introduction of computers and automation into the executive offices will not change
the present operations except to increase their speed and eliminate
the possibility of corruption. It may be recalled that the current
word for the combination of automation and computation, cybernation, is derived from the Greek word for government.

But this progression from the spoils system through the civil
service and the bureaus to cybernation ignores an aspect of the
executive art that is very general throughout the executive branch.
This process might be called executive legislation because it has
produced a vast body of administrative law. Such legislation is
implied in the powers and duties of the executive. Statutes that
flow from the legislative branch are general in intent and therefore
must be made more and more particular as they are applied to
cases. In the middle ranges that descend from the President and

secretaries and chiefs of bureaus, each office formulates rules to
be followed by lower offices and finally by the citizen. But each
step in this quasi-legislative and quasi-judicial process involves
persuasion, consultation, even trial and error, to make the rule fit
the case. When the persuasion becomes complicated it develops
friction, the lower official or the citizen may challenge it, and in
acute cases may take the rule to court. The judges and lawyers
have trouble in dealing with this kind of adjudication, and as a
result there arises the problem of administrative law.

On first thought, as was noted earlier, it would seem the
difficulties in the administration of a law would be merely problems in deductive formal logic: the subordinate rules flowing
from the general law are constructed from middle terms in
syllogisms, or those long series of syllogisms that are called sorites.
But the difficulties come precisely in reducing the complex
operations of the law in the society to rigorous terms.

Such reductions are attempted in hearings, say by the regulative
agencies, in which representatives of the organizations that are to
be regulated appear with briefs before representatives of the
bureaus. Something like lobbying takes place in these hearings,
something like collective bargaining, something like the adversary
proceedings of the courts, something like negotiating for contracts. Sometimes the bureau sets up a court with full judicial
formalities, as in the tax courts under the Treasury Department.
When the hearings are less formal, it appears that the officers of
the bureaus, having been chosen in the first place from the
knowledgeable members of the private organizations, are acting
in collusion with their former associates, and the regulated are the
regulators. Some see in these confusions a creeping bureaucracy
hungering for power, and some see a creeping socialism. To those
concerned with the rule of law and reason, administrative law
presents a vast problem in jurisprudence in an increasingly
bureaucratic and technological society. Can technology and
organization be brought under law? Shall law become a technology?

These questions have in the last generation been cast in a new
form. The large industrial corporations that have rapidly assimilated science and technology to their manufacturing and market-

ing operations have found it necessary to make comprehensive plans. Likewise, the developing economies in the new nations have found it necessary to make plans on a national scale with the help of their governments. This has resulted in the apparent reduction of most of the problems of both economics and politics to the problems of management and administration, both public and private. As they are increasingly turned over to experts and their quasi-professional methods for solution, teams of researchers and developers are assigned to find the facts and to rationalize problematic areas that need organization, direction, regulation, and government aid.

When the plans are drafted, they are recommended to voluntary associations, to corporations, or to various levels of the government for action. But there is no commonly held mode for the acceptance of these plans. A voluntary association may accept a plan as a temporary policy and carry it out. Corporations may hire their own experts and build the plans into management programs. A team of experts may work for many firms in an industrial complex, and the members may agree to follow the plans in cooperation, as if they had made a contract. The government bureau may draw up a plan and offer it to a sector of the economy, or a sector of the economy may make a plan and submit it to the government. In these latter cases, there is a question about the legal status of such plans and possibly about the sanctions that will be used in their enforcement.

Plans have profound effects in the society and in the body of accepted law, but in themselves do not satisfy the requirements for statute laws. They are sometimes formally made by bureaus that are called authorities, like the Tennessee Valley Authority or the Port of New York Authority, and are ad hoc edicts or directives. There may be the usual hearings granted to the affected citizens for ascertaining their consent, but the courts have difficulty in dealing with cases that cannot be treated in the customary adversary proceedings unless they are broken down into citizens' suits against the government. Permission may be granted for citizens to sue the government, but such permissions are exceptions to the general rules, and the suits deal with the administrative problems in only a piecemeal way, leaving the problem of general legitimation of the plan untouched. There is, in general, a struggle between the technicians and the lawyers, and there is no procedural solution for this in sight, even though public opinion is slowly coming to accept the necessity of planning. The legislatures have as yet found no way of incorporating plans in conventional statutes, except by delegating more and more authority to the executive agencies. The effect of such delegation is to defunctionalize the legislature and give at least the appearance of plausibility to the widely held opinion that government has now become almost wholly executive, administrative, bureaucratic, and impervious to democratic control.

No doubt there is reason to view these developments with alarm, and there are many signs that the alarms are getting attention. Perhaps there is not attention enough to the political processes that have developed within the bureaus themselves; that is, the mutual persuasions and deliberations that go on inside the bureaus, between the bureaus, both inside and outside the government, and with the general public. It should be remembered that it took many years, even centuries, for the common law to comprehend the phenomena of the industrial revolution and to transform itself into public law. It now should be recognized that public law is only beginning to transform itself to deal adequately with a bureaucratic and technological society.

THE JUDICIARY

It is said that no man is worth his salt if he was not in his youth a socialist. In a similar aphoristic style, it can be said that no one devoted to the rule of law should be trusted if he is not sympathetic with the anarchist. These mild paradoxes indicate the judicious temperament and the judicial function in government.

If a law is a rule of reason directed to the common good, its terms will be universals. It will apply to what is equal in men, it will apply equably throughout the community, its jurisdiction will be coterminous with the community, and it will reach to the concrete case. These properties of law provide part of what is meant by the legitimacy of government; they are part of the ensurance that law is the means by which the responsibility of the citizen for justice can be discharged. They are ensurances that men's potentialities as political animals can be realized in political action.

But, reassuring as these virtues of law are, they also mark the limits of its powers. Rules of reason may penetrate the concrete cases, but since they are abstract they cannot exhaust the infinite variety that exists in the concrete individual, or take full account of the infinity that exists in the contingencies of his place, his time, or his circumstances. No matter how good the law, no matter how imaginative, honest, and diligent the officers, no matter how thorough the legal process, every case will hold a residue of contingent fact and circumstance that is not comprehended in the terms of the law. Such a residue may or may not be relevant to the determination of justice, but when it is relevant, it calls for mercy and even charity. The anarchist sees this discrepancy between law and fact, and on it makes his case against all law and government. The judge in a court of law sees the discrepancy and presides over a process that will reduce it to a minimum and therefore increase to the maximum the degree of justice that is humanly attainable.

The jurist and the anarchist are not alone in recognizing the precarious role that reason plays in human experience. Both the ancient and the modern scientist, who devote themselves to speculative reason, are familiar with the cussedness of empirical fact and the corresponding clumsiness of reason in arranging the data for verification. Measurement, that most characteristic art in the sciences, is accomplished only with increasingly complicated instruments and experiments, and the results are announced with coefficients of tolerance and margins of error. The laboratory and industry deal with these residues of reason by strict controls of the conditions of experiment and measurement, which eliminate irrelevant and sharpen relevant observation, but their chief reliance is on a kind of second artificial reason, the calculus of probability.

But in a court of law, as in the medical clinic, the concrete individual case is the focus of attention, and the reason is not primarily speculative but practical. In the legislature and in the executive branch, the main objective is the making and administration of general rules that will preserve and improve the life of the community; but in the courts the aim is to provide justice to the individual, and the issues are often matters of life and death. Therefore, the fact that most citizens will obey the law or that the law is probably just for the great majority of cases is not enough. The meaning and intention of the law must be found in the case, and a judgment must be rendered on the individual case if the common good is to be faithfully served.

Throughout the long history of the courts of law there have been many discoveries, inventions, and accumulations of devices to discharge this most difficult of functions. If the appearance of two parties to a dispute before a judge is the original prototype, the formality of adversary proceedings with the accompanying distinction between the plaintiff and the defendant may well be the guiding thread of the historic development. As in other phases of the political process, competitive interests and partisan pleadings were accepted and encouraged not for their own sakes or for what they would demonstrate of their powers to prevail in the contest, but rather for what they would provide in the way of relevant and competent fact to aid the judge in arriving at a just judgment. The court soon discovered that interest and even passion, irrelevant as they may be to the final judgment, can be turned to account as engines for rooting out the details of the situation that are necessary for an objective view of the situation. The full play of adversary proceedings may complicate the process but they tend to prevent quick judgment on the prima facie case.

But the need for evidence goes beyond the naked pleadings of the two parties to the dispute. At an early time, there had been attempts to acquire evidence from higher and lower sources outside the court: ordeals by fire, water, and even combat. These were bizarre, and they led to bizarre results. Slowly but surely, other, more rational procedures were substituted, chiefly the admission of witnesses testifying under oath and the aid of trained legal counsel in questioning the witnesses to educe further information and to put their testimony in order. The lawyers were members of the court under the supervision of the judges as well as agents of the parties. They were allowed to question not only their own witnesses but also the witnesses of the adversary. These

additions to the court led to the formulation of rules of procedure
for the judge to enforce on the parties and their counsels, particularly the rules that govern the admission and treatment of
evidence.

The inquiring amateur, viewing the apparent growth and
complication of the court, expects to find some steady improvement in the intelligibility and rationality of the procedure. But
this is not obviously the result. Teachers of the law of evidence,
for instance, find that the rules have grown like Topsy without
rhyme or reason, at least on the surface. They are filled with what
appears to be proverbial wisdom, old wives' tales, old men's saws,
and scraps of ritual. The young lawyer has to memorize the rules
and hope to understand them as he pleads. There have been
monumental attempts to see deeper into possible principles of
human psychology and morals that would put the fragments
together in some rational code as well as to assimilate them to
strictly legal thought. But the treatises that have resulted are
heavy tomes that do not yield to systematic consolidation and
simplification.

The moral to be drawn from this puzzle should not be unfamiliar to the philosophical critic. It would seem to be that
practical reason, the more rigorous it tries to be in dealing with
the concrete case, deploys its searching questions in more and
more complex patterns. The law is no exception. It gives itself to
the so-called system of casuistry and equity as it increases its
concern to bring justice down to earth.

Perhaps the most impressive illustration of this general insight
is to be found in the development of juries. A court of law,
whether it be primitive with adversaries in a quarrel and a judge,
or formal and sophisticated in a politically organized society, is a
dramatic microcosm of the whole community. It differentiates the
roles of its members along lines that sharpen rational functions.
But the result depends on, and through the jury expresses, the less
rational thought, will, and passion of the immediate social environment. In this respect, the court is like Greek drama in which
the chorus was so prominent. Classical scholars were at first
puzzled by the presence of the chorus. The choral odes and
dances could be seen as embellishments of a spectacle, but for

the most part they seemed to be dull and functionless additions; they did not advance the action. On further study, however, it became clear that the chorus fed new persons into the drama as it developed and responded on its own to the main action in telling ways. The scholars finally concluded that the chorus was the mainstream of the play in which the actors floated and magnified their roles. In more literal terms, the odes and dances provided the context of ritual and custom in the community without which the play itself would have no substance, no persuasive force.

This does not imply that the courts imitated the dramatic model, although the parallel may suggest a hypothesis that might be explored. It seems probable that the chief, or king, or the self-appointed judge needed the ritualistic and moral support that a jury provides in order to make the court effective. It seems that there has always been in the Anglo-Saxon tradition something like a jury accompanying the business of the courts. Sometimes jurors act as witnesses, sometimes in grand juries as advisers to the prosecution, finally as petty juries who make the final judgment and render the verdict.

The Greeks and Romans used juries, but they seem to have been large assemblies of citizens chosen at random to hear the pleadings, presided over by moderators, and rendering their verdicts by majority votes. They were organs of direct democratic government without the sophistication of later representative government, and therefore without the beginnings of the distinction between legislative, administrative, and judicial functions. In the Anglo-Saxon tradition, juries seem always to have been small bodies of citizens—twelve, fifteen, or twenty-three members—who serve under oath, and under increasingly formal rules. Perhaps the most striking formality is that they are required to reach unanimous decisions and are given unlimited time for deliberation in achieving their conclusions, a procedure that is considered impractical in any other democratic institution. A court trial with a jury is thus a peculiar combination of highly technical and professional procedures and of submission of the formal result to the collective judgment of untechnical, unprofessional men of common sense. The theory now is that the jury judges only the issues of fact, but it is known and expected that it also judges issues of law. Because laws as well as men are being tried, the jury has a quasi-jurisprudential function. And yet the verdict is rendered laconically—guilty or not guilty—and no reasons are given.

In the present climate of opinion, it is not surprising to find the jury viewed by both the lay and professional communities as a peculiar institution. It has never been generally accepted on the European continent; it is gradually being given up in England; it seems to persist in the United States because the right to a jury trial is guaranteed by the Constitution. The thin rational criticism of the social and behavioral sciences is beginning to raise questions about its validity, and it is being proposed that a computer might well be substituted for these mysterious and almost secret procedures. The traditional defense of the jury varies from sentimental appeals to the role it has played in the development of democratic institutions to the general defense of small local institutions against the encroachment of big central government. It would seem wiser to see these as partial statements of a larger concern that is intrinsic to the political use of practical reason.

Law has been called a second artificial reason, which is partially hypostatized by being formulated. Habit is often called a second nature, which has been deposited in the human psyche by practical action and experience. The proper combination of these two entities is essential to the life of law and self-government. A jury judging a case is one of the places where this combination becomes effective. It is true that lawyers appeal to the emotions and passions of the jury; it is true that juries can be deceived by false rhetoric and histrionics, as students can be misled by the subtler arts of teaching in schools and universities. But imagination, emotion, and passion are the concomitants of both habit and formal reasoning, particularly the formal part of practical reason. The fact that a jury of twelve good men and true deliberates behind closed doors that protect their freedom of speech, sifts the noisy expertise and artful pleading of the courtroom, and comes to a unanimous decision may be something to remember as we submit our democratic institutions to a relentless critique.

So far we have been commenting on some of the schematic

trappings of the court of law. They are fragmentary and external
to the judicial process in which they play a part; they are like the
stage set, the properties, and the list of dramatis personae of
the theater. Concerning the judicial process itself there is a
voluminous literature, which is still growing. But for the amateur
critic much of this literature is unavailable because it is written
by and for the lawyer whose training and daily practice is the
reading and pleading of cases. The best treatises seem to have
been written by judges who have heard the cases and rendered
opinions, often without the help of juries. But even these more
detached commentaries are in the form of legal doctrines, first-
order abstractions made from bundles of cases, which aid the
legal mind to get from one case to another and build the bodies
of law that accumulate like coral reefs and persist as quarries
from which precedents are selected and used in further pleadings.
Even if I were able to do so, I would not presume to add to these
commentaries.

A new venture might perhaps begin with the distinction that a
judge makes when he delivers his charge to the jury. He instructs
the jury in the law that is relevant to the case and implies that
they are to accept his account of the legal issues. Then, separately,
he summarizes and comments on the facts as they have presumably been established in the testimony of the witnesses and in the
pleadings of the respective counsels. He may go further and point
out the unanswered questions that the jury must consider in their
deliberations leading to the verdict. Issues of law and issues of
fact may have been distinguished in the pleadings, but the presumption is that these two kinds of issues may have been confused
in the minds of the jury. This confusion may be more probable
since it is a part of the art of vigorous partisan pleading to
anticipate and lead to the final judgment that applies the law to
the facts. The chief function of the judge's charge to the jury is
to raise the level of rhetoric and mutual persuasion to the level
of clear dialectic.

The distinction between law and fact suggests that there have
been in the arguments by counsels two kinds of hypotheses: one
that acts as a plot and tends to throw the facts into a narrative
pattern, and one that selects laws and precedents to make a legal

doctrine to fit the instant case. Actually, because of the adversary proceedings, the attorneys for the prosecution and the defense multiply these two into four hypotheses, one of fact and one of law for the prosecution, and one of fact and one of law for the defense. These hypotheses are the threads of thought that are spun by the pleading and lead from the indictment to the verdict. They are often announced at the beginning of the respective pleadings, but they may not be clearly formulated until the counsels deliver their summaries at the end.

In a factual aspect the parties to the litigation appear as characters in search of authors. The attorneys are the authors. Their briefs are preliminary scenarios with blanks to be filled in on the stage of the courtroom by other characters acting as witnesses. They are sworn to tell the truth and their testimony must be "material, relevant, and competent" as it is cross-questioned by the attorneys and scrutinized by the judge for admissibility. Real evidence—that is, physical objects identified by witnesses, signed documents, and expert testimony—may be admitted; much testimony that is offered is not admitted because it is immaterial, irrelevant, and incompetent to advance the narrative or eventually to fit under the terms of the legal hypothesis.

Although the rules of evidence are many, complex, and detailed, they are not merely restrictive; in skillful hands they can be powerful tools to search out the facts that will fill in the blanks in the narrative. Much legal history has been made by research on the part of attorneys who have known how to construe their findings not only to gain their admission to the court but also to expand and deepen the judgment of the judge and the jury. But, as historians and fiction writers know, narrative is a very high and difficult art. When it is practiced under the conditions of the courtroom, where the life, liberty, and property of individuals are at stake, the imperative to do justice gives a new depth to the imperative to tell the truth.

Witnesses are sworn to tell "the truth, the whole truth, and nothing but the truth, so help me God." This phrase expresses the heaviest burden placed not only on the witnesses but on the court. It should be remembered that the truth that is sought is in the mode of practical reason, and that its meaning is spelled out in the elaborate rules of evidence. When the many testimonies of the witnesses are put together under the factual hypothesis, it must be clear that the total narrative is something less than the "whole truth," the actuality. It must be the whole truth that is humanly available. Some events must be left out, some must be inferred, and the continuity must be supplied.

Even without the rhetorical and histrionic arts of the respective attorneys, there are many possible openings for argument about the facts, and it is these openings that give the conditions for the competing narratives of the adversaries. In the laboratory, where measurements are plotted on graphs, it is said that an infinite number of curves can be drawn through the plotted points. The rule is to draw a smooth curve. So, in pleading, the testimonies and other items of evidence are like these points. The counsel can draw many narrative lines that compose the facts into the narrative. The rule here is that the story must be credible and persuasive to the jury, or the judge when there is no jury. As a result, the pleadings often struggle with truths that are stranger than fiction.

So it comes about that a court of law, from which the words judicious and judicial get their meaning, is the political institution in which persuasion reaches its highest passionate, imaginative, and verbal development in rhetorical, dramatic, and dialectical forms. These forms are most fully developed in the summaries of the attorneys at the end of the trial. These performances seem to confirm the worst suspicions of the layman about the corruption of the legal profession, for they seem to be mockeries of the function of the courts. This, however, is to misunderstand the judicial process. Part of the explosion of argument is due to the pressure of the assignment—to do justice—and part of it is due to the pressure of the formal confines within which the trial takes place; but most of it is not only allowed but encouraged by the court and can be understood as practical reason stretching the whole human being to his utmost powers of comprehensive judgment. There are times when human reason does its best in the cool, even cold, contemplation of its object, but there are also times when the responsibility of reason, particularly practical reason, involves it in the struggle to mastery of human life.

Another part of the judge's charge to the jury deals with the development of the legal hypotheses that have been guiding the pleadings of the lawyers. The beginning of these legal hypotheses is, of course, in the indictment, the allegation that the defendant has violated one or more laws. But the law is general or universal, and the case is concrete and individual. Therefore, the application of the law will involve the particularization of the law to fit the case, and this may involve a complicated course of argument. In this the judicial process is like the administrative or executive process. It would seem that both processes could be carried out by syllogisms or sorites, but even if this were the case, the finding of middle terms is a laborious process. In the executive process, these middle terms are found in the course of negotiation and experiment, and the result often is rules and edicts that may serve to guide an officer or a bureau in carrying out the intent of the law; but there is often a residue of indeterminacy or ambiguity that has to be taken to court. In effect, the judicial process has to complete the executive process in novel and difficult cases.

Although the philosopher or logician may be able to discern a syllogistic thread in the legal reasoning of the court, this is seldom, if ever, the form that the lawyer sees or follows. Rhetoric, rather than logic, is the legal style, and this is the legalist's habit not merely when he is appealing to a jury but also in his own private study or office. The reason for this is hard to find and to justify. There is no intrinsic reason why a lawyer should not be adept in grammar and logic as well as rhetoric, and there is much to be said for the thesis that he ought to have a comprehensive liberal education in which mathematics, as well as the verbal arts, plays a part. Perhaps the computer will teach the lawyer to acquire and use the whole arsenal of intellectual arts, on pain of having all of the judicial process computerized.

Rhetoric is most ofen associated with figures of speech, metonymy, synecdoche, metaphor, etc. But the figure that takes the main burden of legal reasoning is the analogy. Those rows of drab books in dull blues, dull reds, brown, and gilt that line the shelves of a lawyer's office contain cases or abstracts of cases that have been recorded in courtrooms, and the textbooks of the law schools up to fairly recently have been case books. To the layman this is a vast compilation of pedantic detail. But besides the dates and jurisdictions of the cases, the intelligible links between the cases are analogies. Some history-making case contains an archetype, or ruling pattern of relations, to which a later case provides an analogue, and these two points of reference set up a line along which many other cases are assimilated by analogy. When the instant case, for which a brief is being prepared, falls into this line or near it, the whole previous series provides the precedents. Each case will have varied the original and the preceding patterns, but the variance will not be enough to have broken the analogy. The present case may seem to stretch the preceding analogies, and then it will be the task of the lawyer to argue it into the series. The pleading may fail and the case may be lost if the step from the past to the present is too great, or it may be won if the new step is admitted and the law is reinterpreted to cover it. This movement of the reasoning from precedent to precedent constitutes the essence of judicial legislation and the growth of the law. Sometimes the original archetype is given in a statute, but the mediation of precedents will be an aid in making the law effective, in keeping it alive in new circumstances, and in approximating justice in the judgment of the case.

Obviously, it would be an oversimplification to see the instant case falling into a single line of precedents as the last term in the series. This may happen in a simple case, but the harder cases will have facets that lead to many archetypes and series of precedents. The headnotes that precede the opinion in Supreme Court reports aid the reader in following the legal hypothesis of the case, and these references must reflect the notes from which a pleading lawyer has written his brief. The selection and introduction of precedents are the work of the attorneys, but there are occasions when the judge makes such a contribution, particularly when he completes the legal hypothesis in his summary and charge to the jury. Not all precedents offered in the pleadings are admitted; many are offered and few are chosen. There is something like the struggle for survival of precedents in pleadings, and their persistence through the ordeal is decided first by their fitness in the series of analogies and finally in the credibility of the whole argument.

After the final arguments of the counsels have been made, it is the task of the judge to clarify the issues that have been developed in the course of the trial. Although he may have made rulings in the course of the arguments, taken notice of the laws and the precedents cited and the admitted or excluded evidence, and in general kept order in the courtroom, his review at the end will be needed if only to counterbalance the strong partisan pleadings of the counsel. But actually, he must bring into play the means by which a synthesis of the arguments can be made in the minds of the jury. Presumably, each counsel will have made in his summary a consolidation of a legal hypothesis and a factual hypothesis, together with precedents and evidence, and he will have "rested his case" in a final plea for a verdict. The rule is that the judge must in his charge state the issues that have emerged in the legal hypotheses of the two sides and make his judgment on these; in effect, render a legal, professional judgment on what the relevant law is for the case. He passes this judgment on to the jury for their application to the evidence. Then he has a further legal task to review the evidence and give its items their respective weights insofar as the rules of evidence apply. One might say that he clarifies an additional evidential hypothesis as a part of the major legal hypothesis. Thus, the judge provides the jury with as clearly specified a body of law for the instant case as is possible.

It remains for the jury to make the final judgment, which combines the legal and factual hypotheses, together with their own view of the facts, and this pattern may include a revision of the weights that the judge has assigned to the facts. It may seem from the layman's viewpoint that the burden put on the jury is more than twelve good men and true can bear and that the legal profession is defaulting its duties in submitting its laborious preparations and procedures to the final judgment of ordinary men. But this is to miss the function of both the legal profession and the public. The court is a representative institution to which is assigned the most difficult of political functions. It brings its professional aid to the judgment of the public. Compared with the legislative and executive branches, it is a model for the bringing of reason and deliberation to the business of self-government.

This account of the judicial process has omitted, so far, a major theme in Anglo-Saxon jurisprudence, one that is most often memorialized in the charge that the judge delivers to the jury. In all criminal cases, the defendant is assumed to be innocent until he is proved guilty beyond any reasonable doubt. We often forget that this rule is not honored in non-Anglo-Saxon jurisdictions. Together with other rules that flow from this as a premise—for instance, that no defendant shall be compelled in any criminal case to be witness against himself—it sounds a deep note of warning concerning the precarious nature of the judicial process, and indeed about the total effect of the legal process on society. Montesquieu says that one of the ways to judge the quality of any society is through its criminal code. He is chiefly concerned about the degree of liberty in a society and the connection this has with a limited constitutional government. But he is also thinking about the other aspects of the common good, and the ways in which a society assimilates and distributes the "spirit of the laws." The presumption of innocence and the burden of proof that this throws upon the prosecution is, to be sure, a safeguard of liberty, but it is also setting limits on the use of practical reason in general.

In all too brief compass we have been taking a narrow and almost microscopic view of the court of law. If the institution were not so widespread, we would have to call it extraordinary. It is one of the wonders of civilization with respect both to the rational ends that it seeks and the rational means that it invents and maintains to achieve those ends. But we should see the individual court and the individual case in its broader context. We have already noted the part that precedents play in its procedures. These are chosen from centuries of records; by implication the whole body of court records is in principle brought to bear on the instant case. Precedents from foreign jurisdictions may be introduced by lawyers and judges in American courts. If the law in this form is not a brooding omnipresence in the sky, it is a body of world law. The Romans discerned this when they identified the law with the *ius gentium*, and reached beyond it to the law of nature and the logos.

Again, the individual court operates within a context of appellate courts. The supreme courts of both the federal government and the several states supervise systems of courts to which cases already tried by the lower courts can be appealed, and the Supreme Court itself functions at least in part as a segment of the appellate system. This means that, although the cases in the lower courts are carried through to decisions, the trials can be reviewed and rejudged, and there may be a series of appeals from the lowest courts up through the appeal courts to the highest courts of last appeal. Errors of the lower courts may be found and corrected, decisions may be reversed by taking note of new evidence or even of new precedents, cases may be remanded to the lower courts for retrial.

The appellate court follows the pattern of adversary proceedings. Briefs are submitted and pleadings heard from opposing attorneys, but seldom, if ever, are new witnesses and their evidence directly admitted, unless the amicus curiae briefs can be so construed. No juries are employed, but more than one judge sits on the bench, and their decisions are arrived at by majority vote. But perhaps the most striking difference from the lower courts is in the reasoned opinions that accompany the appellate decisions. These opinions still show a deep concern with the justice that must be brought to the individual case, but it seems that the law as well as the defendant is being judged. Some of these decisions have made legal history and are essays, if not small treatises, in jurisprudence.

In spite of the fact that the many judges on the bench act as both jury and judge, the whole appellate establishment is made up of legal officers carrying out highly professional functions. It is often said that these appellate courts are the least democratic of any of our governmental institutions, but it can also be said that they are the highest and most trusted representatives of our society. We entrust to them the highest duties of a democratic society. We do this because the courts, particularly the appellate courts, are like the traditional professional guilds. They are made up of men who have a body of practical scientific knowledge, and they belong to a professional society, the bar, which is devoted to the common good and can protect the individual acting together with his colleagues in doing their duties. There is some such rationale in the trust we grant to juries in courts of first instance, and the higher courts confirm our trust the more they bring professional integrity and independence to the exercise of the authority that has been delegated to them.

The notion of the professional guild is further emphasized in the hierarchical agreement of the courts of appeals. A lower court knows that its procedures and decisions are subject to review; that its defects and errors can be improved, corrected, and amplified by other members of the guild; that its decisions may be reversed if greater knowledge and wisdom are available and needed. We are aware of this trust in the care we exercise in the selection and appointment of judges, in the life tenure that most appellate judges enjoy, and in the independence that we wish them to maintain. The trust is not only in the persons but also in the bar and the institutions of the judiciary.

Our own Constitution carries this delegation of authority further than most modern constitutions do in the establishment of the Supreme Court. In addition to its status as the court of highest appeal or last resort, Chief Justice Marshall in one of the earliest acts of the court conferred on it a power not mentioned in the Constitution, the power to judge the constitutionality of acts of Congress and of administrative laws that arise from the operations of the executive branch, as well as laws that arise from judicial legislation. He did this under a general principle that he discerned working in our form of government. If the Constitution establishes ends to be achieved, it must also be authorizing the means by which the ends may be gained. The powers to authorize such means are the implied powers of the Constitution. In Justice Marshall's opinion, the principle of implied powers acted immediately upon the court itself. All officers of the government swear to uphold the Constitution, but this oath has a special incidence upon the Supreme Court; it must uphold the Constitution judicially. As the court of last resort, it must affirm all laws that come under its cognizance that are consistent with the Constitution, and it must strike down all those laws that are inconsistent with the Constitution. It does not make declaratory judgments of this sort, but judges the laws that are relevant to the case in hand, thus following the usual judicial process.

Thus, it becomes literally true that the judicial system as a whole is continually judging laws as well as men, and the laws themselves are subject to correction and improvement. The Constitution itself is living and growing in the judicial process, finding its implicit meanings and making them explicit in the cases that develop in a growing society.

The widening perspective that opens out from a given case in terms of the reliance of the courts on precedents and in the system of appeals has a still further dimension. A case may have gone through both the lower and higher courts and reached its final disposition. But similar cases can still arise for such treatment in the future, and the arguments of practical reason may be brought to bear on a continuing theme. Earlier judgments may be reversed or extended to new but similar matters. Although the matter of a given case may be disposed of, the body of law continues and grows. The familiar aphorism of Hippocrates concerning the art of medicine applies to the art of law: Life is short, the Art long, the case fleeting, the trial treacherous, judgment difficult. The judge must be ready not only to do his duty, but also to secure the cooperation of the attorneys, their clients, and the juries. There is the short view of the case, the longer view of the appeals, and the longest view in the growth of the law.

I began with the intention to describe the respective functions of the separated powers of government in order to justify their constitutional separation. I am not sure that the intention has been served, but I seem to see now that the separation shows the progressive clarification and improvement of reason that is intended in the three liberal arts of the trivium: legislation formulates laws after the fashion of the philosophical grammarian; the executive turns laws into the instruments of persuasion and action after the fashion of the rhetorician; the judiciary generalizes and abstracts the law until it becomes the dialectical mode of understanding not only the law but the whole society. Under our Constitution the law divides itself so that reason can rule.

8

THE
TEMPORARY
NATURE OF
ECONOMIC THEORY

‖‖

I WISH to propose and partially defend a thesis, namely, that economic theory, in its classical formulation and its later variations, arose as an apologetic for the commercial phase of the industrial revolution, that it continues as the basic strategy of industrial development, and that it will disappear when the world is industrialized. I shall take a long but rapid running start.

We forget the debt that Western civilization owes to the nine-hundred-year cold war between Christendom and Islam. In the course of those years, there were many challenges and responses, many threats repelled, and many filtrations through the military curtain. The legacy of armored knights was chivalry and the code of the gentleman; Muslim learning left rational science and the universities; and the Crusades left trade. In the later stages, part of the power of Islam consisted in a navy of small lateen rigged boats that navigated the Mediterranean and the Indian Ocean by dead reckoning. The final coup was given this Islamic power by navies of large square-rigged sailing ships, navigating by magnetic compasses, owned and supported by Portugal, Spain, Holland, and England. The result in Europe of this cold war was called the Renaissance. Among other things, it led to the birth of nation-states and the expansion of Europe to the four corners of the globe.

Presented for discussion to the staff of the Center for the Study of Democratic Institutions on January 12, 1961.

The sailing ship epitomizes the victory in that cold war. In encircling the Islamic navy, it circumnavigated the earth, and, as it extended empire, it built trade. It renovated politics, and it created the object of economic theory by establishing the market as an institution. It made the crucial combination of technology and commerce that would increase the wealth of nations.

During the period of this earlier cold war, another institution, the monastery, made for the first time in the West the crucial combination of the intellectual and the manual arts that planted another seed of the industrial revolution, and as a byproduct set up the accounting system that would measure the growth of capital in collective enterprise, both free and communistic.

By the middle of the eighteenth century, the sailing ship, the monastery, and the nation-state, through their various disciplines and influences, combined to form the framework of the market and the factory that Adam Smith described in *The Wealth of Nations*. In this treatise, he supplied the accounting system and the rationale for the market and the factory. It is this rational accounting system that forms the economic model of the modern world.

The style of *The Wealth of Nations* is, for the most part, descriptive and historical; it is often noted that it is in effect the public announcement of the industrial revolution as we now understand it. But Smith practiced his descriptive art so intensely that an abstract theory emerged, and this is to say in modern terms that he based his theory on very rich empirical data accumulated by shrewd and sharp observation. He detected in the complex workings of the production and exchange of external goods a set of abstractions: the economic man, the market, and the accumulation of profits that could be turned into capital. The economic man produces for the market for the sake of profits, and he reinvests these for the sake of further profits. After two hundred years of practice, observation, and description in these terms, we can reduce all this to the theory of the perfect market and the price system, and we can imitate the mathematician by stating the theory as a set of definitions, postulates, and theorems, to be verified or refuted by the historical and/or statistical facts.

Very early, in fact, as *The Wealth of Nations* was being written, there were incorrigible facts, conspiracies in restraint of competition, which Smith detected whenever he saw two entrepreneurs having lunch together, corporations with the smell of mercantilism about them, and government interference. These distort and spoil the smooth working of the market. It may be noted that these phenomena arise from the disciplines and the influences of the institutions that established and framed the market, tendencies to cooperate and organize rather than to compete.

The economist has always had a choice of strategies in the face of these facts. He can retreat from them and apply his theories only to the smoothly operating parts of the market, or he can invade them with his theory. Both alternatives have been chosen, but on the whole, invasion has been preferred. Smith's words were directed to parliament at least half of the time. He advised controlling conspiracies, abolishing corporations, and refraining from interference. And his aggressive argument was that the general welfare would best be served by the free operation of the market, even if it invaded the corporation, the government, and the university as well. He showed how these organizations could be improved if their operations were brought under the rules of business. For instance, teaching would be improved if professors competed for students and salaries. His advice has been followed, and economic theory has prospered and grown; the economic system has become the model for our society as a whole.

But, as this conquest has taken place, there has been an equal and opposite recoil effect on the market and its theory. Conspiracy, cooperation, organization, although they have been reduced to business management, have clogged and frustrated the market. Monopolies, cartels, and regulation, not to mention advertising, ideologies, government subsidies and contracts, depressions, and wars have removed large parts of the so-called economy from the market mechanism. Another mechanism, the dynamic mechanism of technology, sets the conditions and supplies the reasons that the market does not know, but to which it has to respond.

It was originally said that the market, if left to itself, would justify the ways of the greedy economic man to the general welfare, that self-interest was God's secret weapon against sin. But if the market is a disappearing phenomenon, as it seems to be, other invisible hands will have to reveal themselves, and they probably will not be called consumer sovereignty, or revealed preference in the marketplace, or even the blessed consensus. They have already been identified as the hands of the managers feeding programs to the corporate computers, the press, and the government bureaus.

This raises the fundamental question of what the original purpose of the economist was. We can no longer believe that it was the general welfare or the wealth of nations. It seems rather to have been the building of the industrial system. Taking his cues from the sailing ship, the factory, and the market, he was feeding the program of the industrial revolution to the commercial community and to the general public. But when he has accomplished that purpose, he finds that the public has been corrupted, and that the managers have taken over. It is then the economist's business to serve the managers, and he finds that the accounting systems, or parts of them, such as cost-accounting, will serve well to measure and control input and output, and to make industry hum and grow.

It may be time to recall the adage, Economy is the management of things. Perhaps we ought to call the men aside, the men who are caught in this management, and ask them if they would not like to manage, or rather, govern themselves. The socialists have been looking for a century in this direction, but all they report is that the common good and the rule of law in the state have withered away before the invasion of the market. The democratic society has still to find its Res Publica.

9

SCIENCE, SCIENTISTS, AND POLITICS

‖‖‖

T HE implication in discussing the nature of science and technology is that a distinction should be made between science and technology. Such a distinction is almost wholly unrecognized in our scientific cultural environment. In a recent seminar in which I participated, the question of the difference between science and technology came up, and the answer was: "There isn't any. We no longer separate them." This is a shocking statement. It is sobering to think that there is no possibility of distinction.

C. P. Snow has said that scientists and technologists have become soldiers. They are not working for themselves: they accept orders from others. They are not able to take responsibility for their own strategic judgments in science, to say nothing of the uses to which their work will be put. Whether the decisions are being made on the scientific or the technical level, scientists are not making them.

President Eisenhower, in his farewell speech, pointed out two things that needed to be watched: the hookup among the military, the scientific community, and the industrial community, and the hookup between the scientist and the administrator. We may have heard more about the scientist-soldier than about the scientist-manager, but the latter is equally threatening to the political community.

From "Science, Scientists, and Politics," An Occasional Paper on the Role of Science and Technology in the Free Society, published by the Center for the Study of Democratic Institutions, 1963.

When a scientist is a soldier, he is subject to direction and is a means to an end established by someone else. When he is a manager, he sets the goals and directs other people. But this may not be as deep a paradox as it first appears. Both as a soldier and as a manager, the scientist is involved in practice, in practical activity. He is working in what a traditional philosopher would call the realm of practical reason. Usefulness is the standard by which he judges his work. Thus it is difficult to distinguish between science and technology because part of the meaning has gone out of science. The scientist has diminished not because he has become irrational, unreasonable, or arbitrary but because he has become a technologist.

Limiting science to the practical realm is comparatively new. Science was not born in the fifteenth or sixteenth century. The word *science* has had a long usage—about three thousand years— and until modern times its meaning contained concern about truth, pursued by speculative or theoretical reasoning rather than practical reasoning. These, too, are diminished words. Speculation has become something done on the stock market, and theoretical means "academic" to the general public. To the technical scientist, theory is simply a means to an end. But there are some slightly old-fashioned scientists around who feel that the essential nature of science is not involved with practical reason. They say the scientist's work is to discover the truth, formulate it, and make it a matter of public as well as professional knowledge.

In Thorstein Veblen's striking phrase, "A scientist is addicted to the practice of idle curiosity." This defiant definition states in a humorous way a high dogma about what science is. This is the origin of the popular notion that the scientist is neutral on questions of utility or on the affairs of practical life. Idle curiosity means that the scientist is concerned only with truth. The results of the search for truth may be used for good or evil, but it is now said, even by scientists, that judgments about their use cannot be made by science.

If the scientist's concern is truth, it is his responsibility to be sure that science is not misused so that something false comes out of it. The burden of maintaining the activity of discovery implies a responsibility for academic freedom, but few scientists have defended academic freedom in this country though it has been in danger for the last generation. Perhaps this is because most scientists do not distinguish science from technology. Academic freedom may not be essential to questions of application and use. There is not much point in defending it if truth is not the object. If there is any absolute reason for academic freedom, it is that the search for knowledge of truth is an activity of human beings essential to everything else they do. The heaviest responsibility of the scientist to society may be to refuse to make himself useful.

Several kinds of sharply different judgments are to be made about the whole range of science and technology. The scientist, as a man concerned about the truth, makes one essential judgment about his findings: whether they are true or false. The technician, as an original inventor or as an adapter of something already discovered, makes a judgment of usefulness or fitness. He decides whether it works, and need not judge whether it is good or bad in any other sense. Business or industrial interests make different judgments from those of the scientist or technologist, which partly explains the difficulty of communication between the laboratory and the industrial manager. A much more general judgment about the utility, validity, and desirability of scientific work is made by society and imposed by social pressures.

But there is something missing in this series of judgments. The purposes of science may be considered by the scientist as a professional man. *Profession,* as it was once understood, meant more than a specialty. Universities were founded in Europe to educate and certify those who aspired to the professions, and the training included more than science. Students were taught the liberal arts, and achieved a realization of a larger theoretical, speculative body of knowledge in which the sciences are placed. From this point of view, it is possible for a scientist to stand before the community and say yes or no to the alternative applications of science. But we no longer understand what the liberal arts are. We call them philosophy, but philosophers have shrunk into departmental academicians. The professional man, in fact the whole society, does not have a good philosophical background, and as a result there is a kind of judgment that is not being made. It is the only kind of judgment that could distinguish between science and technology.

Although medicine has lost a great deal of the philosophical professional integrity that was expressed for an earlier time in the Hippocratic oath, physicians as individuals and as a group still make professional judgments. They do not prescribe poisons indiscriminately; they do not let commercial pharmacists dispense certain drugs without prescription; they judge malpractice. Although these judgments seem to belong to ethics, they are not primarily ethical. They are based on the professional theoretical knowledge of the physician. If the natural and social sciences wish to become professional, they need to discover and formulate such judgments both for themselves and for society. But in order to do that they will have to become philosophical enough to distinguish between truth and workability.

10

TECHNOLOGY AS A SYSTEM OF EXPLOITATION

≣||||||||||||||||||||||||||||||||||||||||||||||||||||||||||||||||||||||||||||||||||||||||||||||||||

T HE current discussion of technology in books and journals, both learned and popular, can be heard as a
desperate clamor for a definition of terms. The reader or listener
would like to call a moratorium on argument until the authors
come to terms with one another and ideally with their common
subject matter, or less ideally with their separate subject matters.
Each new author is tempted to respond to the clamor and legislate
clear and distinct definitions. There may be wisdom at the present
stage in refusing to yield to the clamor. There have been many
definitions in the past that simply do not comprehend the problematic phenomena of the present. There are always attempts to
make loose and general definitions that do not penetrate and
articulate the problems. There perhaps is need at present of a
more patient, ruminating discussion that will identify and arrange
the materials for a later definition. I would like to offer one strand
of such a discussion. I hope it may throw some light on the cause
of the confusion that delays definition.

THEORIES OF THE ARTS

The discussion of technology is very old, and it is almost continuous with the Western intellectual tradition. I suspect there is
a similar continuous discussion in the Oriental tradition. *Tech-*

From *The Technological Order*, ed. Carl F. Stover (Detroit, 1963).

nology is a Greek word. Unlike many apparently similar scientific terms in modern languages, it is not just stolen from the
Greeks and recoined to fit a scientific novelty. It was a part of
their discussion of the human arts. It meant the prescription of
rules for the arts, and the context for it was a rich, subtle, and
technical discussion of all the arts.

Plato is famous for his theory of ideas. He should be equally if
not more famous for his technology, his theory of the arts. He is
fascinated throughout his dialogues with the origin of the sciences
from the arts. The modern notions about technology are elaborations of parts of the ancient discussion torn loose from the ancient
context and developed independently because of the novelties of
modern industry. I would like to trace very briefly and diagram-
matically this separation and development.

The Greek word for art was *techné,* and it signified the power
or capacity, the habit or skill, and the intellectual virtue of a man
to make a product or an artifact. This formula is a highly con-
densed and for us oversimplified conclusion of the Greek discussion, which continues through the Roman period in somewhat
degraded form and finally reaches its most subtle elaboration in
scholastic thought. It belongs to the tradition of rational and moral
psychology that we have honored more by neglect than cultivation
since the eighteenth century. It emphasizes three distinct things:
man the agent-artist, the end product, and the ordering of means
by rational rules. A man realizes his natural capacity by acquiring
a second nature in habits that are ordered rationally to the ends
in the things he makes. Art is an intellectual virtue whose function
it is to deal with contingent and empirical things by reasoned
opinions or rules.

The Greek discussion begins and develops in a context wider
than this compact humanism. The preceding analytic formula
applies clearly to what the ancients called the intellectual or
liberal arts, and to what we call the fine arts, but it also applies to
the useful arts or crafts, those arts that make useful things. The
habits and skills of the formula are involved in the selection and
acquisition of natural materials, what we would call raw materials,
and in transforming them into the product.

It would seem that the scientific distinction between matter and
form had its origin in the analysis of the arts. Matter is that which

is fitted to receive forms that exist first in the artist's mind. The artist's or artisan's act is essentially putting such a form on this malleable matter. The means by which this is done is first the hands, but soon the extension of hands in tools or elementary machines. The typical example of the artistic act is the imprinting of the seal on wax, then the fashioning of the statue out of marble by the chisel, and then the making of a chair according to a pattern. These archetypes are easily extended to agriculture, carpentry, cooking, and building; some with many tools and an order of applications; and some subordinated to others as wood-working to flute-making to flute-playing. There is also the art of tool-making to serve the arts which use the tools.

The tool or the hand operates between the form in the artist's mind and the raw material, but form also demands the training of the human capacity in skills that are learned. Some of these skills seem to be learned by rules that can be taught, some only by repetitive practice, some by the maturation of instinct, some apparently by inspiration, some by close attention to the material and its fitness to the end product.

This matter of skills and learning was the mysterious subject matter of great fascination and thought for the Greeks, and it led to one of their more familiar contributions to the tradition. They concluded that art imitates nature, that nature is the great teacher of men. This conclusion came at the end of a long period in which they believed wonderingly in the many legends in which the gods were said to have taught men the arts and still presided over the practice. All the wonder was finally precipitated in the doctrine of the four causes, first applied to the arts and then to nature. The causes of any end product were first in the matter that could be fashioned or formed; then in the form in the artist's mind that could be impressed on the matter; third in the hands, tools, skills, and energies of the agent-artist; and finally, in the end itself, the product, which ruled over all the other causes in the actual making. These were the four causes; material, formal, efficient, and final.

The recognition that the artist was imitating nature almost forced a reversal of the insight. The four causes also operate in nature so that their discovery and formulation make science. Art or technology thus becomes the midwife of science. If you want to understand something, make a similar object or artifact; then impute that artistic process of making to nature. We are not far from this in our current use of models in science.

There is no doubt that the Greeks used the analogy of art to penetrate nature and its secrets. Travelers brought back technical lore from Egypt, which they turned into geometry. This is apparently the origin of the Pythagorean development of number theory and geometry. The three-four-five triangle became the universal device for squaring the corners of buildings and for surveying lots of land property. It also led to the proof of the Pythagorean theorem in geometry.

This fragment of mathematics in its two aspects, applied and theoretical, precipitated a crisis in the Pythagorean society. The theorem proved too much—that any right triangle would have the sum of the squares of its legs equal to the square of the hypotenuse. In many right triangles this would mean that the hypotenuse was incommensurable with the legs. This would not have worried a builder, or an engineer. He could work with rough instruments and approximations. It would worry an incipient mathematician who had glimpsed the possibility of theoretical understanding. It is said that a member of the Pythagorean brotherhood who divulged the secret scandal about incommensurables was deliberately drowned at sea. The Pythagorean theorem had to be kept a professional secret until the problem of the diagonal of the square and the square root of two could be solved. Of course, the problem was later solved, supposedly by Eudoxus, who was a member of the Platonic Academy, and the solution appears in Euclid's *Elements* as highly sophisticated arithmetic and geometry. But the crisis in the Pythagorean society has been repeated many times in the history of technology and science. It is the archetype of all those strains that exist between the technologist and the scientist, in which professional secrets play such varied roles.

ORGANIZATION OF THE ARTS IN THE PAST

The arts organize themselves into crafts and guilds of artisans and technicians. They pass on the skills to their apprentices, they improve the arts, and they tend to have trade secrets. They also tend to generate and maintain theories that add understanding to skill. The so-called Hippocratic writings can be read with greater insight and penetration if they are understood as either exoteric or esoteric attempts to come to terms with two aspects of medicine—the arts of diagnosis, prognosis, and therapy, on one hand, and the sciences of anatomy and physiology, on the other. Sometimes the writer is persuading prospective patients of the competence of the physician. Sometimes he is trying to persuade his professional colleagues of the truth of his theories. Galen later struggles through, with the help of Plato and Aristotle, to the establishment of theoretical medicine and the self-recognition of the profession. Primitive as Galenic medicine may seem at present, and corrupt as it may have been at certain stages, it was the only medicine practiced for fifteen hundred years. It set the standards for its own profession and for the other professions of law, theology, and teaching up to our time, when it seems that any sense of profession, except its economic aspects of monopoly, is evanescent.

The Pythagorean society, as far as we know it, seems to be the prototype of what professions came to be. Its chief theoretical holdings seem to have been mathematical at a time when mathematics almost alone led the pursuit of theoretical knowledge. The word *mathematics* originally meant learning and things learned. The society was a novel kind of cult that generated and transmitted learning. This function was chiefly performed by the esoteric part of the brotherhood. It taught a somewhat vulgarized version of its knowledge to the exoteric members of the society that seemed to have made up the citizenry of a city, Crotona. The vulgarized learning was ethical and political in nature. The society was responsible for what it decided to investigate and what it decided to teach. It added to its membership and transmitted its learning from one generation to another. It is quite clear that the Hippocratic oath for medicine formalizes an imitation and adaptation of the Pythagorean learning to a more specialized body of learning. In both cases, there was a tendency to unify a body of knowledge and to respect theory as magisterial and architectonic for a self-governing community of scholars, teachers, and practitioners of an art or body of arts. The secrecy of the cult is a sign at once of the lack and the need for some formal institutional structure that the social environment of the time did not supply or recognize.

Connected with the development of certain arts into professions by the development of appropriate bodies of theoretical knowledge is a medieval distinction between the kinds of arts that was not emphasized explicitly by the Greeks. Certain arts that had reached a professional status were practiced on human beings, who also had artistic capacities. In these human subjects of the arts, there were primary natural and secondary natural processes that if left to themselves might accomplish their ends, but if aided by the professional would accomplish their ends more easily and more fully. Medicine and teaching were the frequently discussed examples of such arts. They were called cooperative arts because they were understood to be cooperating with rational natures.

But the term *cooperative* suggests that there might be another kind of distinction among the arts: those that can be practiced by the individual without needing aid, and those that cannot be practiced without the cooperation of other artists. Building or architecture is a borderline case, since presumably single men have often built their own houses and barns. But there are building operations that are unlikely to be undertaken and completed without the collaboration of many artists, such as the building of temples like the Parthenon or the cathedrals, which in many cases occupied several generations of many men. The brotherhood of free masonry was a society with secrets and standards of skill that recognized this kind of organized or collective art as its responsibility. Similarly, the building of harbors, aqueducts, and roads call for the orderly organization of many men and many arts.

There have been many kinds of organization that have met the need for order in the divisions of labor. Typically, the Romans allocated this organizing function to the army for their greater public works, as the Greeks and Egyptians had trained and managed slaves. Self-governing guilds have often passed through their technological periods on their way from religious cults to polities. We tend to forget this ubiquitousness of organization in the arts since Adam Smith established the science of economics on the thesis that the market both dictates the division of labor and gives a semblance of organization to it. We forget that he also was giving the first description of the organized factory. Although he warned against the organization of the arts by the corporation, he actually laid the ground for its modern predominance. The market now appears to be a rather long, lively, and fruitful interim of disorganization of the much longer continuum of highly organized technology.

PRESENT ORGANIZATION OF THE ARTS

I know no competent discussion of the question that this series of organizations of the arts seems to pose. There is the often quoted maxim of Marx and Engels that the means of production determine social and even cultural forms. Neither they nor anybody else has worked out the dialectical or other details of such determination. The question I am posing is somewhat simpler: what are the forms of organization that the arts demand for themselves? The Egyptians seem to say a slave system; the Greeks at one stage say a polity; the Romans say an army; the Middle Ages and many other ages say guilds; the eighteenth and nineteenth centuries seem to say the market; we seem to be saying now that the corporation is the answer. These seem to be little more than historical correlations. They do not answer the question that is now inescapable. We are very far and rapidly moving further away from the individual craftsman who needs only to pay attention to his own art. The present organization of the arts, what we call our technological system, has passed beyond the powers of any of the preceding forms of organization. How shall we bring it into order and effective service to the human community?

Bright-eyed observers tell us that the answer is already given and that we are more than halfway accepting it in practice. The human arts will be completely built into automatic machines. Human beings are in principle in the position of the Pharaohs, freed from labor. Technology and art, which can no longer be turned over to slaves, can be given to machines. Peter Drucker tells us that we unknowingly have trained ourselves to behave so much like machines that the substitutions of machines for men is easy. During the final stages of automation, we shall have to increase our engineering skills and scientific knowledge in order to finish the job in style and keep the apparatus in condition, but our main business will be those activities that free men have traditionally called leisure. Whether this be good prediction or prescription or not, we need to know a little more about how and why the possibility of automation confronts us.

The industrial revolution has had many dimensions and causes. On the technological level, the substitution of machines for tools seems to have been the essential change. The revolution has been the progressive passage from manufacture to "machino-facture." This process can be understood as the extension and penetration of the principle of the division of labor into technics. As labor was broken down into elementary crafts and integrated by exchange in the market, so complex operations in a given craft were broken down and reassembled—sometimes with mechanical operations substituted for manual operations, sometimes with the multiplication and integration of many more operations than the original craftsman could manage. Usually, this organization of operations was connected with the new prime movers—steam and gas engines, motors and generators—to supply the greater demand for energy. The factory was the progressive institution that could push the analysis of the jobs and organize both men and machines into larger patterns of organized operations.

Two parallel transformations can be seen in this factory system. The concatenation of machines and the use of the new prime movers progressively removed the human agent-artist from the linkages between the machines. The products of the separate arts or crafts were no longer the ends of the operations, but rather materials for stages in the overall production process. To be sure, there was an integrated end product, but the many intermediate ends became mere means.

The consequent or parallel development would be what Europeans call rationalization, the formulation of the rules that control the productive process. In the crafts, a great deal could be left to unverbalized and unmeasured skills. After fine analysis of jobs, their reintegration needs both elaborate verbal and mathematical expression, not merely to pass on the crafts from one generation to another, as in the past, but now for the coordination and management of the going technical process. This amounts to an emphatic return to the original ancient meaning of *technologia,* the giving of rules to the arts. It also connects with the development of the new techniques in analytical mathematics or algebra.

The invention and establishment of algebra as the art of mathematical analysis blots out many of the distinctions that older mathematics had maintained. For instance, arithmetic and geometry are no longer distinct. So, when the factory is rationalized, it is hard to maintain any distinction between men and machines. They both are values in equations of efficiency. This suggests two alternative possibilities that have worried us for a long time. Shall machines be taught to think, as computers do; or shall men become robots? Automation offers its solution of the dilemma. It will teach machines to think and also to do the work, so that emancipated man may occupy himself with the liberal arts, politics, the fine arts, and the divine arts—until such time as men wish to automate these arts as well and free themselves for still higher existence.

WHAT OF THE FUTURE?

We are here on the edge of something eerie and not a little puzzling to the pragmatic mind. Let's see if we can establish our position, as the navigator says, and maybe plot a course or two. The kind of abstraction that makes us see automation as an all-encompassing net is like the thinking that the Pythagoreans did when they first happened upon the tricks of measurement. The story goes that they did this with the monochord, a string that vibrated in a musical tone according to its length—the shorter the length, the higher the tone, and the lengths could be expressed in whole numbers or integers. The Pythagorean mind quickly generalized, thinking of many things that could be reduced to numbers, and quickly concluded in a kind of arithmetical astrology that all things are numbers or shadows of numbers. It is hard for even a modern pragmatic mind to deny what is after all the basis for the great successes of mathematical physics. The Pythagoreans

identified this process of measurement with music, and in celebration of their discovery made poetry about the music of the
spheres, not failing to continue their development of the science
of mathematics even to our day.

Plato took the Pythagorean theme as commonplace, and went
on to develop a theory of ideas that had the same trick of abstraction and hypostasis in it, but included along with numbers many
other kinds of ideas. It is a childish kind of Platonist that turns the
trick into metaphysics, as Plato says in the great confrontation of
the young Socrates with the venerable Parmenides. But Plato
recognized the moment in the long life of dialectic as important
and even essential to the intellectual enterprise. The theory of
ideas, reformulated as the logos doctrine, has had as long a life as
the Pythagorean doctrine. Its development has been somewhat
more versatile, serving law as natural law, serving theology as a
person of the Trinity, supplying common sense with its root in
reason.

As I suggested earlier, Plato might with his skill in abstraction
and hypostasis have "found" a system of the arts, a set of rules for
the arts, that would have reflected as in a mirror the firmament of
his ideas, the ideas of his theory of ideas. There is a suspicion in
his allegory of the cave that there was a level of artificial objects
that made a kind of logistic pattern midway between the shadows
on the wall and the ideal stars in the heavenly firmament. If he
had been faced with the panoply of artificial technical operations,
processes, and products among which we live, he surely would
have been led to construct something like the technical phenomenon that we find in Jacques Ellul's *La Technique*.

There is a great difference between Anglo-American and con-
tinental European thought about technology. The German and
French philosophical traditions are more hospitable to many-
storied imagination and speculation. Whatever we may think of
Hegel and Marx as artificers of ideologies, their speculative skill
and boldness and their recognition of levels of being and action
are not to be ignored or condemned. So French thought has
always had a clear strong line of analytical reasoning, established
and controlled by the Cartesian discovery or invention of algebra
or analytic geometry. Descartes generalized his discovery and

hypostatized it in his own style. He called it the Great Art, *Ars Magna,* and thought of it as the universal method for the intellectual enterprise. He saw algebra, or analytic mathematics, as the master architectonic of all the arts.

The essential power of all these abstractions and hypostases resides in their objective universality. They give clarity and logical mobility to speculation or theory. This kind of thinking gave us the great hypothetical worlds of modern physics: the systems of the worlds of gravitation, heat, and electricity within which our more empirical investigations still explore. So the idea of technology or of the technical phenomenon of Ellul offers us the schema for a logistic of the arts, a genuine theory of technology.

Suppose we accept some such abstraction, hypostatization, and universalizing of technology. What shall we make of it intellectually and practically? There seem to be three possibilities, with some variation in each of the three. We may accept the technical logistic as a system of determinism, a kind of artificial fate that we have brought upon ourselves or in which we have been trapped. A superficial reading of Ellul tempts one to this conclusion. But Ellul himself warns us that this is not his intention, unrelenting as his method may seem.

We may see it as a system that has developed piecemeal, without our intention except with regard to its slowly developing parts. A key to this view seems to be hidden in Ellul's many comments that the system has reduced all things, including our ends and purposes, to means. In other language, this means that we have developed an unlimited, autonomous, universal system of exploitation. Both the things in nature and in human nature come under the sweep of unrelenting exploitation. We have been pious in the later stages about exempting men from the exploitation; they must be conceived as ends in themselves. But the only assurance that this is still respected is that we have kept free contracts and the democratic processes. The irony of this may be that we have supposed that men themselves will not knowingly submit to exploitation. There is much evidence to the contrary. We may have at least temporarily been enchanted to submit our bodies and souls to the contingent processes of self-reduction to means. This comes close to my understanding of the alarm that Ellul is sounding. He is trying to wake the prisoners in Plato's cave and incite them to throw off the chains of their empirical, piecemeal thinking about themselves.

If this is a good guess, the wide-awake conclusion might be that we should accept the logistic clarities and necessities in the technical phenomenon and do a thorough job of searching out the articulations in it, of looking to the shape of the integrated system, with a view to remaking by disassembly and reassembly the most familiar and least understood phenomena of our time.

It may be recalled that this abstraction of technics from the arts, the rules from the actual makings, leaves the agent-artist and his ends out. For the sake of organization, they are assimilated as merely means. Thus we are left with an apparent automaton, an almost integrated and automated technical system. But it is merely a stage in development and dialectical understanding. If we are to deal with it competently, we must find some way of bringing back human artists and human ends into the powerful order that the technological system presents to our amazed and puzzled view. My suggestion is that we trace the human role that the system involves and detect where we have surrendered our judgments and our wills. If we can find these points of default, we may be able to recover our truly scientific understandings, our objective knowledge of our ends and the ends of nature, and our individual and common wills. This might give us back our reverence and love of nature, beyond our shrewd ingenuities in exploiting it.

11

THE PERMANENT
POSSIBILITY
OF REVOLUTION

IT SOMETIMES seems at the Center that we are always
involved in solving paradoxes. There is the paradox
about war that we share with the whole world: war has become
impossible as a workable political policy; all political leaders,
except possibly Mao, affirm this as a true proposition; but they all
prepare to wage war. Closely connected with this paradox there
is another that seldom reaches the clarity of statement that a true
paradox requires. This one concerns revolution.

Since the first world war, at the end of which the great revolution of our time happened, it has been said by self-styled practical
men that revolution is impossible. The reason given at first was
that machine guns in the hands of the government in power
would mow down the rebels. This was said and verified during
the war in connection with an attempt to overthrow the German
government. But the Russian Revolution did take place, and there
followed several others. Still the proposition continued to be
affirmed throughout the interwar period, when revolutions and
counterrevolutions became commonplace. It seemed that the
rebels as well as the governments in power could operate machine
guns. It would certainly be naïve now to suppose that nuclear
weapons will always be in the hands of the authorities.

But, of course, the association of revolutions with weapons and
sudden death is naïve. Very sophisticated writers such as Rebecca

From *Center Diary*: 17, March–April 1967.

West and Hannah Arendt restate the proposition that revolutions
are impossible with quite different meanings and reasons. At the
minimum, they are saying that revolutions never achieve their
aims. At some point in the process, the means of revolution get
out of control and the ends are lost, distorted, or replaced by
alien purposes. Therefore, all revolutions are invitations to illusion
and self-deception. But this again is a naïve view of revolutions.
It comes from the assumption that revolution is caused by hunger
among the poor, so that if in its course there is general famine and
poverty in the whole society, the revolution has failed. This view
of revolutions presupposes that the end of revolution is affluence.
This is not the account that most genuine revolutionaries would
give of their motives and behavior. This might be called the
radical economic interpretation of revolution. It may be true that
all revolutions have an economic phase or dimension, but it does
not touch the basic notion of revolution as a political process.

Rebecca West and Hannah Arendt actually are not indulging in
this kind of naïveté; they are saying something closer to Edmund
Burke's critique of revolutions: the basis of political union in a
community is so deep and mysterious in history that anything
like a revolution for an idea or for a new order is childish and
irresponsible. The destruction of law and order, no matter how
corrupt these may have become, necessarily entails so much
sacrifice of elementary decency and morality, so much corruption
of human character and sanity, that the sources from which a
new order may be generated no longer exist. All revolutions that
are genuine reach a point of no return. Revolutions are fatal
diseases in any society. To make the paradox unmistakably clear,
revolutions cannot be revolutions. They do not revolve; they ex-
plode and dissipate. The results of revolutions are dissolutions or
retrogressions of communities. The French and Russian revolutions are vast quarries of ruins for the historian to work as evidence for this hypothesis.

For current academic historians, one or another or all of these
views lead to a paradoxical moral hidden in the apparently objective statement that revolutions are impossible. The sociologist
and the political scientist tend to concur in the judgment, and
even such a catholic-minded historian as Toynbee goes on to
infer that attempts at revolution are signs of irreversible break-

down and disintegration in civilizations. The paradox, of course, lies in the discrepancy between the general statement and the events of current history.

The students and the youn,ʒer faculty members in American colleges and universities are ɔeginning to suffer from the paradox. They read the day's news in which revolution seems the familiar and dominating theme. They also read that in two-thirds of the world students play major roles in revolutionary movements. Then they raise the question about the United States and themselves, Have we lost the capacity and the will to revolt? Have we lost the common human basis for understanding and dealing with revolution in the rest of the world? All of us face the paradox in its undisguised nakedness when the President and the State Department announce alliances for progress that obviously imply the revolutions that we fear most acutely because they are impossible.

The paradox that we are witnessing many impossible revolutions can apparently be solved simply by saying that they are all incompetent, unsuccessful, and evil; but I would like to suggest that the makers of the paradox and of the apparent solution are superficial and irresponsible. They fail to discern the common principle that underlies both revolutions and politics in general. If we have lost the rationale of revolutions, we have also lost the reasons that support any genuine political life. Stated simply, perhaps too simply for quick comprehension, the principle is that every human being has a responsibility for injustice anywhere in the community. Governments, that is, the laws and the institutions that the laws establish, are the proper political means for discharging that responsibility. But, no matter how well conceived and founded, governments may gradually or suddenly, depending on the rates of change in the community, become functionless, overloaded, or positive hindrances to the processes of justice. The ordinary processes of government—making and repealing laws, administrating, adjudicating—are elastic and capable of adjusting themselves to the course of history; but they may also become rigid and cumbersome when the issues are heavy and when the rate of change is high, as in the British, French, and American revolutions of the seventeenth and eighteenth centuries.

In such times, the will to maintain the legalistic details of

custom and tradition and the consequent failure to adjust and
invent may lead to the rapid accumulation of injustices. The will
to create laws and institutions is replaced by the habit of domina-
tion on the part of the beleaguered authorities. Reason gives way
to force, and legality takes on the sinister meaning of the phrase
law and order. It is in such circumstances that the individual, or
some fraction of the public, rediscovers not only the right but
the duty of revolution, and is moved to grasp the means at hand
and to invent new means for discharging the basic responsibility
for restoring justice. This amounts to the recognition that the
permanent possibility of revolution is a necessary condition of
effective responsible government.

This view of government and revolution suggests that we ought
to be more careful in our time in the use of the term *revolution*.
On one hand, we tend to extend its meaning to such things as the
slow development of technology, as in the industrial revolution,
where the terms *development* or *evolution* would be more
accurate. On the other hand, we identify revolution with any
violent attempt to overthrow the government. It is true that
certain stages of revolutions are marked by slow and gradual
change, and it is also true that other stages may call for sudden
and violent change, but we miss the essential nature of revolution
if our attention to the contingent details frightens and blinds us
to the political causes that make revolutions possible and necessary. The occasional cause of revolutions may be hunger and
other acute kinds of privation, but such causes will not be
sufficient if the sense of injustice attending these evils is ignored
or the purpose to restore justice is forgotten. It is the neglect of
such considerations that has led the last generation of economists,
political scientists, and in general the behavioral scientists to deny
the possibility of revolution. Many of them explicitly say that they
do not know what justice means.

But if injustice is the occasional cause and justice is the final
cause or end of revolution, an understanding of revolution will
require consideration of some other features of past and current
revolutions. In the past, justice has had a context of scientific,
moral, and religious ideas, and these have often figured large in

the circumstances and rationales of revolutions. Preceding, accompanying, and following the Glorious Revolution in England in the seventeenth century, the writings of Francis Bacon, Thomas Hobbes, and John Locke ransacked theological and moral thought in search of new formulations of the ideas of justice and freedom that would fit the emerging society based on science and technology. The French philosophers of the eighteenth century engaged in a massive encyclopedic effort to identify injustice and project a new justice for the French Revolution, and the revolution itself followed a dialectical pattern of thought that has become a paradigm for all revolutions since that time. Our own Tom Paine and Benjamin Franklin contributed to the philosophy and rhetoric of both the French and the American revolutions. In all these revolutions there were also heroes, martyrs, and messianic figures who dramatized and personified the as-yet unformulated ideas of a new age.

Similar ideas and similar characters appear in the current revolutions of our time as ideologies and charismatic persons. These signs and symbols of revolution indicate that justice is a many-splendored thing and that its recovery involves many dimensions of human life and thought. Let him who enters on the revolutionary path never assume that he is merely replacing a mechanical part or merely substituting one constitution for another. Let the critics of revolutions not make similar assumptions. The reference of human affairs to the notion of justice is no simple matter; revolutions, like the great tragedies, are convulsions of human learning.

For the protagonists and the passive victims of a revolutionary time, revolutions are dark, mysterious, and threatening events. Many of their splendors are merely false appearances of light and preludes to disillusionment. So were the revolutions that stemmed from the first world war. Woodrow Wilson, who sensed the revolutionary aspect of the war, first understood the processes to which he contributed in the terms of the French and American revolutions, and he was not mistaken in his first perceptions of the European developments. But he was horrified at the deeper consequences that flowed from these, and was a tragic hero and martyr in the end. Lenin, Wilson's opposite number in many respects, was also a hero and martyr, but his identification of the accumulated injustices of the industrial revolution and his proposal of new institutions for the recovery of justice have set the style and rationale for the typical revolutions of our time. The deep irony of the events for him was that these revolutions, even in his own country, have taken place in comparatively nonindustrial countries. The great Russian Revolution, so impressive to us in its present establishment, has actually become the revolution of rising expectations for emerging nations. There are very few dictatorships of the proletariat, and very little true socialism or communism, but there are many charismatic leaders, teachers, and seekers for new forms of justice for people on the march toward full industrialism. I think that we Americans are at our best, most ourselves, when we join this revolution of rising expectations, and see our own revolution stuck in the oligarchic complacencies of our corporations, labor unions, bureaus, and other pluralisms of so-called voluntary associations. We may yet join the Negro in realizing for ourselves the full functioning of our Constitution. There are signs that this is already taking place when college students from all over the country set out expecting that they will go to jail or knowing that they may die.

The second world war has shown to an already troubled and conscience-stricken world how much unfinished business there is in the category of establishing justice. Some of the injustices have been smoldering for centuries in the old kingdoms and dynasties; others have accumulated in the industrial revolution and the colonial systems that succumbed to its apparently inexorable exploitation; still others have arisen from the displacements and migrations caused by the war itself. Combinations of Russian and American ideologies have brooded over and drawn out into explicit form deep local customs and wisdoms. In some cases, four, five, and six accumulated legal systems accentuate the local struggles and complicate the search for the new justice. Individuals and whole cultures are caught, crushed, and ground fine by the revolutionary mills of the gods. We who view these wonders at a distance have no trouble in finding reasons for thinking that such processes can bring no good and possibly immeasurable evil, even to us.

We do not even wish to recall that genuine revolutions would not have happened unless the status quo ante had not been worse than the present alternative. We are irritated and horrified when revolutions seem to lose their ways, change their leaders, and succumb to demagogues. We should perhaps remember that our revolution was singularly fortunate in its paternity; the Founding Fathers were aristocrats and gentlemen who fought duels when they disagreed or lost their way, as some of them did.

We bid fair, like it or not, to learn a great deal from our participation in these current revolutions, vicarious and distant as our part may be. We shall learn most when we join them by raising our own expectations of a freer, juster world; our affluence and our stability should enable us to bring more sophistication and reason to bear in working out the solutions to the common problems that the world revolution sets for us. The heritage of the American Revolution in the American Constitution promises great contributions to the revolutionary learning in the emerging nations. But we must make a new beginning by defining again for ourselves those parts of our Constitution that have become corrupt and stultifying in our own political behavior. A good beginning might be made by reading the prophetic writings of John C. Calhoun, who very early saw the fateful possibility of neglect and misuse of our political system. His view of the Constitution will help to put the problem of revolution, even world revolution, in a new light.

I have already commented briefly on the quick association that we make between revolution and violence. Perhaps it would be better to see this connection in the wider context of the classic mutual involvement of revolution and war. Thucydides made the great study of this involvement in his history of the Peloponnesian War, which so many statesmen and generals have studied in the last two generations. If we and the Greeks are right in seeing almost a necessary connection between revolution and war, and we now see that war is impossible as a political process, then there is a new reinforcement to the proposition with which this paper started, that revolution is impossible. If I am right in asserting that the permanent possibility of revolution is a necessary condition of sound politics, I shall have to show how revolutions can be disassociated from war, and I shall need Calhoun's help.

Calhoun makes a sharp distinction between two political processes, constitutional and governmental. Constitutions are established by unanimous consent, by what he calls the concurrent majority, which in principle is unanimous. The ordinary transactions of government, law-making and administration, proceed on the basis of the numerical majority. Calhoun says that even in his time, just before the Civil War, the process of constitution-making and amendment was frustrated and almost stalled. Numerical majorities generated by deals and power drives were isolating and suppressing minorities. In order to call this to public attention, he proposed that minorities whose interests, vital to the nation as well as to themselves, were being neglected or ignored should exercise what he called their constitutional rights by vetoing, negating, and nullifying the laws made by the numerical majority. He proposed that in these cases of irrepressible conflicts there should be an appeal to the constitutional process of the concurrent or unanimous majority. Nullification should be replaced by some formal measure for calling the constitutional process into play. His prophetic warning was that if this need was ignored in connection with tariffs and the imminent emancipation of the slaves, there would be not only civil war but the stultification and brutalizing of the political process in this country. We did have a civil war, and we now have a degradation of constitutional government. The name of Calhoun has for a long time been associated with nullification, interposition, the filibuster, and states' rights. These are the barest remnants of what he was proposing, but they could be reminders of unfinished constitutional business.

Thrown into the context of the twentieth century, Calhoun can be understood to have been proposing a formal procedure for tolerating and dealing with revolution without violence or civil war. Stated generally and needing much inventive implementation, his proposal was for a permanent constitutional convention to deal reasonably, deliberatively, and effectively with injustice, responsibility for which must be discharged. Calhoun did not work out the detailed procedure for the permanent constitutional convention, but he was obviously referring to the clause of the Constitution that provides for such conventions as alternatives to the more customary procedure for amending the Constitution. Article V of the Constitution reads in part as follows:

> The Congress, whenever two-thirds of both Houses shall deem it necessary, shall propose Amendments to this Constitution, or, *on the application of the Legislatures of two-thirds of the States, shall call a Convention for proposing amendments,* which, in either case, shall be valid to all Intents and Purposes, as part of this Constitution, when ratified by the Legislatures of three-fourths of the several States, *or by Conventions in three-fourths thereof,* as the one or the other Mode of Ratification may be proposed by the Congress . . .

It will be noted that the present amendments of the Constitution have been proposed by the Congress and ratified by the state legislatures; we have never actually used the procedure of proposal by a national convention and ratification by conventions except in the case of the first ten amendments that comprise the Bill of Rights, and even then the national convention was not used.

There have been several impressive attempts to call national conventions: once for the Bill of Rights, once for the tariff issue that led to nullification by the state of South Carolina, once for the issues that led to the Civil War—this one endorsed by Lincoln—and then the recent attempts to call a convention to enable the entry of the United States into a proposed world government. None of these attempts succeeded because the required endorsement by two-thirds of the states was not forthcoming. Amendment by Congress and the legislatures entangles great issues with the wheeling and dealing of power politics and the corrupt ways we have of generating majorities. A national convention to consider great matters of constitutional importance would not only have to decide by a three-quarters majority but it would also generate a great movement of popular education through public debate and thus reach deeper levels of consent than our elections.

The proposal for a permanent constitutional convention stems authentically from our eighteenth-century Constitution. It is therefore interesting as a projection of eighteenth-century thought. But it interests me for another reason closer to the theme of this paper. If we are to extend our public intelligence to comprehend, tolerate, and use both the domestic and foreign incipient revolutions of our time, we would do well to conceive of our task in terms of membership in a permanent constitutional convention, first on a national scale and then later on a world scale. If we are to deal with revolutions and wars responsibly, we would do well not to suppress their causes by police or military force. This is no longer a matter of nineteenth-century liberal sentiments of decency and idealism; it is, strictly speaking, a matter of life and death for any government.

As parliamentary government, with its systems of representation, deliberation, and voting, comprehended incipient revolutions of the eighteenth century and turned into what we now call democratic self-government, so we must provide constitutional conventions that will turn current causes of war and revolution into institutions and laws. We should extend the due processes of law to the deeper processes of justice that revolutions present to communities that exist because they respect justice, peace, freedom, and order.

12

ON MARTIN BUBER

|||||||||||||||||||||||||||||||||||||||||||||||||||||||||||||||||||||||||||||||||||

T HERE is a saying among lawyers that hard cases
make bad laws. If this is true, we ought now to be
seeing some bad laws in the making. But we may also expect to
see some hard thinking, some critical thinking, that will make
good jurisprudence. Some of this will be reported from court
opinions, some in law journals, and some in politics leading to
legislation. The individual citizen may feel all this in his personal affairs. He may be forced to face hard decisions. And all
this may lead to the improvement of politics in general.

For anyone who reads a good newspaper, most of these motions
in public affairs can be verified daily. Our own Supreme Court
has been dealing with hard cases that have made laws or changes
in laws that at least some think bad. There is heated controversy
about these opinions of the court, and there are moves to correct
them by legislation. The citizens complain about a thing called
alienation, which means that they are finding effective common
decisions difficult. Some recognize the alienation and try to do
something about it, and this means political action of some kind,
although not yet necessarily good politics. And these developments are happening not only in this country but all over the
world. In some places they have the appearance of rebellion and
revolution.

And so we are hearing a rising controversy, the pleadings and
debates, the briefs of the friends of the courts and the friends of
the legislators—small and great debates, private and public—and
finally the sit-ins and teach-ins. Part of this mutual persuasion

From "Civil Disobedience," An Occasional Paper Published by the Center
for the Study of Democratic Institutions, 1966.

goes to the aid of the individual who has to vote and suffers the
pain of indecision; part of it is concerned about the ancient
question, What is law? This is, of course, the central question of
jurisprudence, or the philosophy of law. For many Americans it
is a new question, unfamiliar because neither our lawyers nor our
philosophers have paid attention to it before.

There have been exceptions to this academic default. We have
lone figures who represent the European schools of jurisprudence.
There are those who say with the positivists that law is the
command of the sovereign enforced by the state, which holds a
monopoly of force. There are those who say that law is the instrument of public policy that arises from conflicts of interest and
power in society. The legislator, the judge, and the administrator
are the decision-makers, and their decisions make law. Sometimes
these decision-makers do more than react to pressures and
interests; in the style of Rousseau's legislator, they see through the
welter of conflict and divine the popular will, the general will.
They persuade because they discover and show to the people
what the people really will, rather than what they blindly think
they will.

There are those who take seriously the theory that law-makers
discover rather than make law, and find that genuine law is what
the people ought to want. Their definition of law is that a law is
a rule of reason directed to the common good and promulgated
by the proper authority. In a democratic regime this means that
the authority or authorities are the representatives of the people,
elected or appointed to practice their deliberations for the explicit
end of discovering the specific requirements of justice, peace,
freedom, and order in the current circumstances. The consent of
the governed in this case is based on the capacity of the people
to learn the real good that is hidden in the confusing apparent
goods of their immediate experience.

Fragmentary echoes of these traditional schools of jurisprudence are heard in the current discussion. Because these echoes
are thin splinters from the bodies of doctrine from which they
come, they more often than not further confuse the discussion.
Some of this confusion is moderated by the new style of the
ordinary common man, who has learned to talk again directly

about justice. It is remarkable to hear this new voice circumventing the sophistication of the learned and professional schools, which have found justice too abstract and empty for them to honor.

No doubt the mills of the schools will grind out extensions and new meanings of their doctrines, but they grind slowly and exceeding fine. It therefore may be proper to strike a fresh note, borrowed from a modern school of philosophy that has not yet paid attention to law. It comes from Martin Buber, who is known for penetrating insights rather than a system of thought. The insights come chiefly from his reading of the Bible and his experience of life in the last two generations. He has been one of several who have made the term *dialogue* a password between men of goodwill.

Buber set out to show how the Old Testament, the Torah, could be read as a continuous and continuing dialogue between the people and God. It is through this dialogue that the Jews become the chosen people, a nation, a polity, the people of the law. But this is not to say that the theocratic principle was being imposed by a tyrannical God; the Jews always insisted on talking back to God, and the backtalk was not merely verbal. It was a dialogue between real persons, free persons, whose conduct involved their whole persons and whose learning involved defiance and submissiveness on one side and punishment and mercy on the other. It also involved patriarchs, judges, kings, and prophets as founders, leaders, spokesmen, and protagonists in a grand drama. Buber's primary interest is always religious; consequently there are commands issued with thunder and lightning, but there are often responses like earthquakes. It would be a comic reduction of Buber to say that the Torah is a record of centuries of litigation, but it would not be far from accurate to say that the Torah is the demonstration in dramatic form of the doctrine that law is a teacher. This is, as a matter of fact, the fundamental meaning of the word *Torah.*

But the secret of this dialogical teaching by litigation is that by long habit with the Jews, laws are not dogmas; they are questions to be pursued. They may be partial answers to previous questions, but they always bristle with new questions, questions asked of individual citizens or of groups of people, sometimes of the whole people. One of the high points in the Torah came on Mount Sinai, when Moses went up the mountain to talk with God, perhaps to negotiate with God about a covenant. The first time he came back with a table of commandments he found that the people had already repudiated the whole project, and he had to go back and renegotiate. The later episode, when the people asked the judge Samuel for a king, resulted in a three-way negotiation in which God had to moderate Samuel's refusal to accede to the people's demands. Samuel's part in the negotiation was the dire prediction of what would happen to the people under kings, and when it came true, the prophets arose to talk back to the kings, as well as to God. And so when the Jews go into exile and finally into dispersion, the rabbis develop the endless dialogues of the Talmud and the Mishnah, all about the law.

But what does it mean to say that laws are questions? In grammatical terms, laws are obviously imperative sentences; they are, in positivistic terms, commands issued by an authority to be obeyed by subjects on pain of punishment. But if the subjects are free persons who can object, talk back, and disobey, there is at least a moment when the law is a question, Shall I kill, shall I steal, etc. If the moment is extended, there will be an argument with many more questions, questions about the jurisdiction of the law, about the meanings of killings, stealing, lying, and adultery, about the purposes of the law and the common good. These are familiar questions in the courts and, mutatis mutandis, for the legislature and the executive. In fact, whenever the law is in operation, it is itself a question and is up for questioning.

This insight, of course, is not wholly new in Buber. It is familiar in Plato's *Dialogues*, where Socrates is its protagonist. It was fully lived out in Gandhi's career in law and politics. But it seems that Buber has given it its fullest development and range of application. The dialogue for him involves the full range of human action and it reaches to the depth of human freedom. Whenever it is introduced into the realm of jurisprudence, it redefines law and gives it a significance that cuts across and enlivens all the conventional teachings of jurisprudence.

Even when the dialogue is not invoked as the proper context of law, it is necessary and proper to conceive a law as a question. It is a general or universal rule of reason formulated and authorized for the government of intelligent and free individual human beings. This means that it will necessarily have alternative interpretations in application; judgment and decision concerning the case will require definitions of terms, hypothetical middle terms, and observations of time, peace, and circumstance. All these are commonplaces of the courts, but they are also tools that the citizen uses in his daily practical reasonings. They are the means or organs of his consent, and without this the law is arbitrary and blind.

Considerations such as these would seem to be the true premises for the positive as against the negative reading of the First Amendment. Free speech, press, assembly, and petition are more often than not thought to be privileges, rights that are claimed for and by the individual, immunities from public law. But important as these are for the individual, they are more important for public order and freedom. They are the routes by which the laws are learned and understood, by which they become imprinted in the habits and hearts of the citizenry. They are the means by which the laws are continually improved and adjusted to change. They provide the receptacle of deliberation within which the law lives. If the law asks questions of the people, the people respond by questioning the laws as well as their own hearts.

The current struggles for civil rights and for peace are heavily laden with questioning and questioned laws. Law-making, law-administration, and law-interpretation are extending the meaning of the rights of the First Amendment from literal speech and writing to the practical dialogue in which action can speak louder and more effectively than words. It is as if the elements of speech, press, assembly, and petition are being composed in living dramas, and these dramas are seeking legitimacy. Current history, as with the Greeks, is being written in tragic and comic styles. But this is not to say that all the world is a stage, but rather, as the saying goes, that politics has taken on dramatic form and moved to the streets. We are learning law by acting out justice and injustice in the streets, and the conflict of laws is reaching its full expression in living dramatic conflict. The authorities are saying that protests are justified, but not when they break the laws, and the answer is coming in terms of civil disobedience as the dramatic means of making laws, and making them just. We say that these legal-illegal dramas are the people waking up, and this gives rise to new politics; and, it can be added, this is the revival of law, not only the new laws that are being made, but the whole body of law achieving a new meaning and life.

But this brings us to the crucial paradox of this kind of juris-prudence. If all laws are questions and generators of questions, is the doctrine not bringing all law into question? Is it not an invitation to anarchy? That could be the risk. Law as the com-mand of the sovereign, be he king or people; law as the resolution of conflicts or the rational formulation of social policy; law as the rule of reason directed to the common good; civil law as the dis-covery of natural law—all of these traditional doctrines are brought into question. And it could be that each or all of them together have no answer to the question. If this is so, the whole political adventure of mankind is rendered futile. There are fringes of existential philosophy that are saying that this is the case, and they are pointing to the whole scene of a revolutionary world as evidence. The dialogical drama at this point becomes Job-like, as Buber does not hesitate to point out.

But this is to forget that most political orders and bodies of law have been cradled and born in revolutions, and that they are kept alive and responsible by the permanent possibility of revolu-tion. Governments derive their just powers from the consent of the governed; it is often forgotten that the word *consent* contains within it the meanings of both *assent* and *dissent*. When this is forgotten, law becomes the arbitrary, absurd machine that no man can either obey or tolerate. If the law loses its power to persuade reasonably, it is no law.

The power to persuade is correlative with the power to question, and so the law exists in the dialogue. This is the more adequate statement of the relation between the command of the sovereign and the obedience of free citizens. The command of the sovereign that is accompanied by overwhelming force is a kind of persuasion, but it achieves only the superficial appearance of obedience. It engages only a small part of a human being, and turns the rest of him into defiance or lethargy. It makes him a thing, and a heavy unmanageable thing, such as we see eloquently dramatized when the police load bodies into paddy wagons or trucks in our current demonstrations. The command that allows itself to be examined and questioned while it is being formulated, that announces itself as reasonable and argues the case that falls under it, that continues due deliberation while it is being enforced, gains the whole human being and enlists him in the common search for justice. A good law not only is a question, but it keeps the big question—the question of justice—open. When justice is sought, then the rest of the common good, peace, order, and freedom, are added to it.

Martin Buber states all this in a wider context. The dialogue of question and answer takes place only between persons who confront each other as I and Thou. These are preserved and maintained as whole human beings as long as the dialogue continues. When the dialogue stops, the I's and Thou's become It's, and they are subject to manipulation, coercion, and exploitation. The law itself becomes an instrument of such management. This is what happens when associations, corporations, political parties, and governments seek power, and because they seek only power, necessarily fail. Those who are willing to sacrifice the dialogue for the greater good suffer the great disillusionment. They heroically surrender themselves to the collective cause, and by that very act become useless to themselves and to others. Furthermore, they lose the good of the intellect, truth is eclipsed. They enter the modern hell of ennui, anomie, alienation, and all the other fashionably named senses of unreality.

It may be pretentious to see the dialogue as a new doctrine of jurisprudence. Perhaps it is better to call it simply wisdom.

13
REDISCOVERING NATURAL LAW

ACCIDENTALLY ON PURPOSE

The Universe is but the Thing of things,
The things but balls all going round in rings,
Some of them mighty huge, some mighty tiny,
All of them radiant and mighty shiny.

They mean to tell us all was rolling blind
Till accidentally it hit on mind
In an albino monkey in a jungle
And even then it had to grope and bungle

Till Darwin came to earth upon a year
To show the evolution how to steer.
They mean to tell us, though, the Omnibus
Had no real purpose till it got to us.

Don't you believe it. At the very worst
It must have had the purpose from the first
To produce purpose as the fitter bred:
We were just purpose coming to a head.

Whose purpose was it? His or Hers or Its?
Let's leave that to the scientific wits.
Grant me intention, purpose, and design—
That's near enough for me to the Divine.

And yet for all this help of head and brain
How happily instinctive we remain,
Our best guide upward further to the light,
Passionate preference such as love at sight.

Robert Frost

A CRISIS in human law is the occasion for the discovery of jurisprudence. So it has been in the past; so it is at present. It is true that there have been minor crises in the life of the Supreme Court that have not led to the search for juristic reasons, as there have been political crises that have found only political solutions. In fact, the case can be made that the American government has had a happy career without need of philosophical help. This is partly because a great deal of jurisprudence was precipitated and built into the American Constitution, and because our politics has lived and flourished on its previously funded capital of wisdom. But there are signs that the present crisis in our Supreme Court and in our politics will not issue in a clarifying judgment without recourse to deeper reasonings than we have ever tried before. That is the reason that strange echoes of the great tradition of natural law are coming from the most unexpected sources.

I would like to strengthen the resonance and extend the range of these echoes by recalling the other occasions when natural law has been discovered and rediscovered in the past.

THE GREEKS

Plato's *Dialogues* can be read as the sustained effort to meet the crisis in Greek law when it was realized that the Peloponnesian War had been a self-inflicted wound on the city-state, not only

Originally published in January 1962 as a Report to the Center for the Study of Democratic Institutions.

upon Athens but upon all city-states. Plato saw the crisis epitomized in the trial of Socrates, and his record of the case, the *Apology*, became the basic text upon which all the other dialogues are extended commentaries. The many modern technical reviews of the procedure of the court that tried Socrates do not begin to compare with Plato's substantive criticism. Some of his dialogues reach into the depths of moral philosophy, some lay the foundations of political theory even to our time, still others probe the possibility of finding true science in the tangle of human opinion and observation, and they all culminate in the attempt to write a constitution founded in natural law. This reading of Plato is admittedly ex post facto, that is, seeing many complex consequences in the original; it has always been difficult to read Plato in any other way.

The Greeks were puzzled, even before Plato, by what man had made out of nature and by what he had done to himself in the process. The puzzlement had continued into the endless arguments of the Sophists about nature and convention. The arguments had continued through Plato to Aristotle's conclusion in the *Politics* that the state had been founded to meet the minimal necessities of life, but it had gone on to order artifice and convention in the good life. Plato's version had been given at greater length and detail in the *Republic*. The minimal state had arranged for the division of labor and the exchange of vital necessities. But the resulting greed and luxury had led to trade and war, which in turn infused honest labor and enjoyment with fraud, flattery, and sophistry. The arts serving natural ends had been inverted so that the ends were subordinate to the means; for instance, the exchange of goods served the arts of moneymaking. As a consequence, vice took the place of virtue, and it was impossible in politics to tell the difference between justice and injustice. It was possible for Plato to put the strongest argument in the mouths of a series of vivid characters, such as Thrasymachus, that justice was the interest of the stronger. These were the strong characters supported by a "fevered state," a pathological polity. This account of the confusion of the arts is given in the style of fiction as a part of a utopian construction. But it is by all contemporary historical confirmation a vivid, accurate description of life in post-war Athens, and in the other Greek cities. It is not unfamiliar to us, and our nation-states.

Plato's prescription for purging the arts is to seek their roots in nature by tracing them back through the opinions and practical beliefs that they generate to their underlying sciences. He begins by showing the structure of means, ends, and skills in any art, and then goes on to show how one art serves another; for instance, how the art of flute-making serves the art of flute-playing. The genteel literary reading of the dialogues often attributes the frequency of the homely art theme to the earthy human qualities of Socrates's character, but the framework proposed here would make Plato the researcher in Greek technology. He is concerned to get the whole technology in a single view, and it results in the end in seeing politics, the art of government, as the master art that as end gives order to all the other arts; hence also to the classes and virtues of men.

This technology, or system of the arts, is developed, analyzed, and articulated in many places in the *Dialogues,* but most impressively in the *Gorgias,* Book I of the *Republic,* and in the *Sophist.* It is always closely associated with the running discussion of the tyrant. I think we can see why this association is made if we imagine a similar attention to our own modern technology. If we look at all of our occupations as elementary units of a unified, highly organized industrial system, we are struck with the possibility that some dictatorial managerial bureaucracy could take over and with scientific and engineering know-how could exploit the system for almost any arbitrary purpose. It is a system of power asking for an efficient use. In fact, we are today watching with some worry a whole society or civilization devoted to just this end. In this mood we think we are wrong in attributing the diabolic force of such systems to evil men alone; the tyrannical essence of the Fascist or Communist regime belongs to the technological system as much as to the characters selected to manage it, and the rationalization of the arts that it entails is part of the secret of the satanic spectacle. It is also significant that the engineering of human beings, since they at least retain some of their rationality, involves the manufacture of an ideology to keep up morale.

❋   ❋   ❋

The sophist was for Plato the prototype of the tyrant. With his sophisticated expertise, his claim of omniscience, his obvious hunger for power, and his hard salesmanship, he imitates and caricatures government. Our contemporary impulse is to expose and oust the tyranny and to try to democratize the system; we even fight world wars to accomplish this end. But Plato had apparently seen many vacillations between tyranny and democracy. *Demos* can also be a tyrant and will be tyrannical almost inevitably if it merely represents and organizes the will to power. Therefore, Plato in the *Sophist*, where the technical system was most completely and rationally seen, turns to a metaphysical search for the cure of the constitutional ills of technology. The search takes the form of asking for the difference between the sophist who is the technician and the statesman who must be a philosopher. Without this there is no dependable way to tell the difference between the technical rules and the political laws, between tyrannical and legitimate government. At the end of the *Sophist* there is a dark saying that the sophist technician is, like Oedipus, a patricide and a regicide: art has usurped the regulative function of knowledge or science.

There is a likely story often told in histories of science concerning the birth of Greek science. It begins by noting that the Greeks at first believed that the arts were gifts of the gods to human beings. Prometheus, Apollo, Hephaestus, Athena, Asclepius, Hermes, Aphrodite, and others taught men not only their skills but also the ends for which they were to be used. Having once delivered the doctrine and the practice, the gods continually presided over the further transmission of the arts by training and apprenticeship under human auspices. At some time, probably at the beginning of the Greek industrial revolution from subsistence to commerical agriculture, the tutelage of the gods fell into the background because somebody discovered that any free mind could initiate an art and carry it on by imitating nature. Perhaps this was celebrated in the story of Pandora's box.

But Epimetheus, Pandora's husband, made another discovery: that artistry could be detected in and extracted from nature. Nature itself was a great artist that delivered not only tricks and skills but also insights into precious secrets. Sometimes the model

Artist was detected behind and above nature, sometimes it was recognized in nature itself. Thus Plato's *Demiurgos* and Galen's Nature, perhaps also the Delphic oracle, took the places of the divine inventors of the earlier period. The modern philosophical anthropologists would like to say that the Greeks first projected their arts into the Titanic and Olympian hierarchies and then shortened and simplified the projection into Nature.

A kind of sophisticated version of these myths can be seen in the vital center of Plato's *Republic*, the figure of the divided line and the allegory of the cave. The education of the philosopher-kings is a recapitulation of the mythical origin of science. Common language had attributed a kind of wisdom to the artist in recognition of his skill. This is recognized and called knowledge of the visible world in the two lower sections of Plato's divided line. Observation and practice with mirrors and instruments, which imitate nature, yield a coordination of observations that is proper to the clever artist or artisan. A kind of right opinion, born of the self-persuasion of successful practice, tempers and refines the skill and wisdom of the common man. This is the source from which modern empirical science stems. It should be recalled that it was to these men that Socrates went in his divinely assigned search for the wisest man in Hellas. If Socrates had been the sophist that Aristophanes accuses him of being, he might have educed from his survey of the arts and the artists the great composite artist that Timaeus constructs and calls the *Demiurgos*.

But obviously this is not what happened. Socrates found the artist or the technician the archetype of the foolish man; he is the man who thinks he knows when he does not know, the man who doesn't know that he does not know, the man who has no suspicion of what he does not know. And these artists may be anything from shepherds and poets to politicians; all of them are potential tyrants. These men are the prisoners in the depths of the cave who are fascinated and enslaved by the shadows that they have learned to trace and correlate and predict, even to write poems and make speeches about. Socrates had been shocked at his discovery of the learned ignorance of his fellow Athenians, and he was able to convey that shock to them. He did this through his questioning of them, but he also did it by his behavior, perhaps most effectively by his trial and death, when he defied and also obeyed the laws.

The shock marks the passage from the visible to the intelligible world in the divided line and in the cave. The shock blinds and paralyzes its victims in the visible world, and then awakes and revives them in the invisible world. The Platonic account of this shock portrays Socrates as a comic Oedipus who blinds himself in order to see. The cumulative failures of empirical observation and practice come to the crucial point of conversion and to the recognition of hypotheses and principles, the beings of the invisible world that constitute science.

For Plato the mysterious bridge from the empirical to the rational world had been provided by Pythagorean mathematics. The word *mathematics* suggests the function that it plays: it means learning. Apparently the great occasion for Pythagorean learning had been measurement of musical tones by the straight line and the numbers in the monochord, a string taken from a lyre. The tones and intervals of the musical modes, the musical appearances, were "saved" by the corresponding order of the numbers and their ratios. The same kind of correlation could be made in other material and instruments, and this led to a kind of frenzy of measurement that, carried out in the discipline of the Pythagorean order, led to the general conclusion that there were numbers in everything and that even celestial bodies played musical themes. Plato is saying that the Pythagoreans had been the mystagogues who had freed the Greek prisoners and had shown them the realities that cast the shadows on the wall of the cave. He is also saying that if the corruption of the city-state is ever to be cured, the philosopher-kings must first have become Pythagoreans and learned the sciences that will disentangle and order the arts.

But although mathematics is necessary, it is not enough. Wonderful and sweeping as it is, it is only the beginning of learning, a bridge of asses, so to speak. It substitutes objects of thought for objects of sense, but in doing this it leads on by its methods to a fourth division of the line, to objects of thought that are not mathematical. The *Dialogues* themselves are the best example of this pedagogical function. Most of the arguments in the *Dialogues* are mathematical in method or in form, but mathematical subject matters are only used for illustration, and as illustrations they seem to be only paradigms of weightier matters. Not much is said about these weightier matters as the fourth division of the divided line is discussed in connection with the final stage of the education of the philosopher-king. The presumption is that the actual discussion of the whole of the *Republic* as well as the other dialogues exemplifies the subject matters, the human virtues, the nature of the city or state, the laws. But the method is clear. It is to take the hypotheses and principles that the mathematical sciences have discerned in the arts, to treat them as forms and essences in themselves, and to explore their connections; starting with ideas to move through ideas to ideas under the great categories, being and non-being, same and other, one and many, good and evil. This is the dialectical method, discovered in the practice of Socratic questioning of the artists, now applied with systematic rigor exemplified in the later dialogues on the level of higher education. There is the upward dialectic that moves away from the empirical and pragmatic to the elements, causes, and principles; and there is the downward dialectic that moves from principles back through hypotheses to concrete affairs. The products of this method were to be the sciences that Aristotle founded.

The thesis that I have been following in this interpretation of the Platonic *Dialogues* is that Plato saw an epitome of the legal and political crisis of the city-state in the trial and death of Socrates. The indictment brought against Socrates was initiated by a poet and a politician, two representatives of the Athenian arts: one a practicing artist, and the other a self-styled master and censor of the arts. The theme of Plato's lifelong critique of sophistry and tyranny is struck in Socrates's counterindictment and cross-questioning. The sophists are operators in opinion and power and are not concerned with wisdom and truth. Furthermore, they have no concern for the virtues of men or the common good of the state. From this scene Plato sets out to find the truth in science and the good of the state. He has Socrates accompany him as far as the *Republic*, where the arts are purged and clarified, science is established as the basis of education, and dialectic is recognized as the basic political process by which laws are made.

Then Plato goes on as the Stranger through the later dialogues to the *Laws,* where he joins the Cretans in drafting a constitution.

There is no doctrinal answer to the quest, and, if we can trust the thirteenth Epistle, the default in this respect is not accidental. Plato used doctrines, even what we would call sciences, as hypotheses and starting points. He tells Dion, the Syracusan tyrant whom he tutored, that any written exposition of his teaching would be an imposture. The *Dialogues* practice what they preach, a relentless dialectical exposure of ideas masquerading in dogmas and opinions. This dialectical art was what was needed to cure the corrupt state of its ills, and it was the perpetual assignment made to the philosopher-kings who were members of the Nocturnal Council. The endless mutual persuasions in any community could result in good laws if the formal processes of government provided insights for the citizens and magistrates alike. Sciences might and would result from insights, but they are byproducts, and dangerous ones at that, if they are not continually revived by criticism, revision, and relearning.

Drastic as this teaching is, and unduly skeptical as it often is in practice, as Plato remarks in warning that untempered youthful minds will misuse it, it yields, in the case of the dialogues, communicable insights. The human arts if left to themselves degenerate into a fatal confusion of sophistry and tyranny. In order to maintain their proper order and health they must be examined and reexamined for the essential knowledge that they contain and conceal. This knowledge will reveal forms, essences, and natures in which concrete affairs participate and through which concrete affairs are intelligible. Furthermore, these forms and natures are the discernible purposes of things; they must therefore be understood under the aspect of the good. These are the reported insights of Plato, which are to be found in many doctrines and sciences that the insights have generated.

It is one of the melancholy facts of history that the Greek city-state did not recover from its fatal corruption by the Peloponnesian War; that the great intellectual effort to meet the crisis, initiated by Plato and completed by Aristotle, was too late. That the effort was not too little is evidenced in the thousand-year life of the Academy, and perhaps more immediately in the planting of city-states throughout the Near and Far East by Alexander, who was Aristotle's pupil. It is in these institutions and in the Roman Empire that came heir to them that the thought bore fruit. But even with these evidences it may seem strained and overdone to read the *Dialogues* as researches in natural law. Neither Plato nor Aristotle commonly uses the phrase *natural law*. It is only in the practical and theoretical men whom they influenced that the idea of natural law comes to separate and clear formulation, and only after their thought undergoes a kind of degradation and rebirth in the minds of the Stoics during a time of troubles more extensive and acute than the period of the early decline of the city-state.

The Stoics were for the most part men of practical affairs. For them the Socrates portrayed in the *Dialogues* was a hero, and they made a doctrine out of his thought. Practical human affairs could be disentangled and straightened out by the use of reason, and for the most part reason in the dialectical style. Ethics, the science of human action, was founded on physics, the science of nature, and on logic, the rules for reasoning. The emphasis on the dialectical use of reason made their physics into a cosmology rather than the empirical discipline that it is today. The great motions of the universe conformed to laws, the laws of nature, that were discoverable by reasoning or logic, or to the movements of thought among the pure forms and essences that Plato sought. For the Stoics, what Plato had described as the "community of ideas," which was only the notion of the interpenetration or mutual implication of ideas, became the *Logos,* the perhaps infinite total of all the ideas that govern the universe, or the cosmopolis. This notion is not utterly foreign to Plato's and Aristotle's thought, but it just would not have occurred to them. It would be almost inevitable to a Roman whose practical problems would drive him to a reading of the Greek philosophers.

THE ROMANS

I do not know how the seeds of law were sown in the early Roman republic, but it is quite clear even before the republic that the characteristic Greek suspicion and hatred of tyrants was operative. The Romans were determined that they would live under a government of laws, not of men. Such a commitment did not lead to an easy political life, but there is no more enlightening theme for the interpretation of Roman history than the essential devotion of the Romans to essentially legal politics, even under the emperors. It follows from this commitment, active and practical though it may be, that the intellectual history of the Romans will concern itself with the distinction between good and bad laws. For them the laws, which at least intellectually seemed to be the solution of the problem of convention and nature for the Greeks, take the problematic place of the arts. The right ordering of the laws takes the place of the right ordering of the arts.

By trial and error and political conflict they worked themselves through the different kinds of states that Plato and Aristotle had predicted; they passed through monarchy, oligarchy, democracy, and tyranny and the various forms of law that are generated by them. The practices of the courts, the senate, and the tribunes and prefects invented, refined, and revised the legal corpus. Wars destroyed and renewed legal habits and understandings. The people, from tribune and emperor to slaves, increasingly became a political and a legal people. Many of the educated officials got their education from the Platonic Academy, and the vicissitudes of academic dialectic were felt and propagated throughout the Roman body politic. Repercussions from Alexandrian thinking and from the political experience of the Alexandrian city-states of the East kept the more doctrinal and scientific teachings of Aristotle alive, particularly when defense, pirating, or conquest forced changes in domestic politics.

Perhaps the great time of legal crisis came when the republic became the empire. Great affairs, commercial and military, forced revolutions, but the crucial events were met and dealt with by minds thoroughly tempered by formal legal training and by tough political experience. Cicero is only the best-known of these men because his writings have survived, but there were others who would have called themselves Stoics, some who called themselves Epicureans, and there were poets who celebrated the great events. Plutarch's *Lives* and even Shakespeare's *Julius Caesar* dramatize the intellectual character of these philosopher-kings. Plutarch makes it clear that they were imitators of the Greeks intellectually and often corrupt fumblers in practice, but they are nonetheless authentic participants in Greek thought and action. They knew what it was to search for the reasons of their laws and their politics; they belong to the Hellenic world.

Virgil's *Aeneid* is an expression de profundis of the common Greek and Roman experience of politics. Its main structure and theme have been compared with Plato's *Statesman*. Whether Virgil had read the dialogue or not makes little difference; it would almost be better testimony if he had not read it. Plato raises the phenomenon of revolution to the status of a principle of history. Politics begins in divine government, governments of gods, not of men. Divine justice, peace, and freedom flow through channels of law throughout the community. Then, as men learn from these laws, they find themselves able to run their own common affairs; they amend the laws to meet the vicissitudes of history. As time goes on, they make new constitutions and get fresh starts out of their crises. But each new start pegs affairs on a lower level until there is the near-chaos of tyrannical democracy. Plato pictures this as the running down of a celestial clock, a kind of political entropy. But at the low point the gods again take the pilot's wheel and wind things up again. They do this through pious men. This is the principle of revolution, also the mystery of conversion, through calamity and catastrophe, in political tragedy.

The great narrative theme of the *Aeneid* recapitulates the revolutionary pattern. Pious Aeneas, carrying his even more pious father, Anchises, on his shoulders, leaves the flaming ruins of Troy. He becomes more and more like the wily Odysseus, even following the same course in the Mediterranean, falling under the charms of Dido and her imperial power, until he recalls or discovers his mission to Latium, where he repels his enemies and founds the city of Rome under divine auspices. But Virgil is celebrating another revolution, the ignominious end of the Roman republic and the establishment of the empire under the divine Augustus. Perhaps the most impressive sign of Virgil's prophetic and magical power, for which he was famous for a thousand

years and more, comes from his insinuation that the authority of
law depended upon the magic of deified emperors.

Whatever the nature of the powers here invoked, the poetic
facts are a monument to the depths of the crisis and the intellectual and imaginative efforts to surmount it. Many revolutions
have made the same or similar appeals to divine law and government, though not all of them have founded thousand-year Reichs
or empires.

But the lawyers and statesmen of Rome were more skeptical
than Virgil. They did not trust the responsibility for their affairs
to the gods; even some of the emperors suffered formal deifica-
tion with reluctance and fear. In a more workmanlike way they
paid attention to the laws, to the senate and the people, who
made the laws and lived under them. But they never doubted
the necessity to seek the reasons for their laws; they asked their
questions of nature rather than of the gods.

It was the burdens of the empire that brought the Stoics, who
had survived the corruption of the republic, into their own. Pride
of wealth and power had transformed defensive wars into wars
of conquest, or pacifications of the barbarians, as they were often
called. The emperors, the army, and the senate came heir to responsibility for the security and order of many alien and diverse
peoples. No matter how barbarous and uncivilized these people
were, the Romans quickly learned that they had their own legal
orders. (All Gaul is divided into three parts, each with its
language, institutions, and laws.) The great debate in Julius
Caesar's mind had been whether the pacified peoples should
become citizens of Rome and come directly under the laws of
Rome or whether Roman governors should sponsor autonomous
provincial law administered by local magistrates. The debate,
which continued throughout the empire, became the great political dialectic about the nature of law.

The Stoics continually made the saving distinctions. There were
laws specific to a local community, civil laws, whose roots might
reach far back into unique folkways and folk lore, the *mores*. But
among these laws and between communities, comparisons revealed a matrix of common laws, both customary and statutory,

diverse in origin but identical in purpose and practice, laws of people, *ius gentium.* They revealed a body of principle upon which judges and administrators drew for reasons when they had to decide hard cases. Here the Stoic legalist saw through the artificial and conventional positive law and rediscovered what the Greeks had meant by nature. But in Stoic doctrine the principle available to reason would be selected segments of the *Logos,* which was the principle governing nature. Hence, they were called the natural law, *ius naturale.* For a judge or a prefect the Stoic slogan, return to nature, had a specific meaning; it meant return to natural law.

The distinctions between civil law, *ius gentium,* and *ius naturale* helped in the necessary task of adjusting, sorting, and codifying the bodies of law in the empire. From this process there were derived political and institutional arrangements, often invented ad hoc, to deal with that oldest of all political problems, the one and the many. But the problems that these new politics brought to light forced the more philosophical minds to a new venture in speculation. The problems of the city-state spread to the country or the region, and there seemed no end to the addition and expansion of jurisdiction. *Urbs* led to *orbis,* as in the ancient days city had led to sky. The great community was the cosmos. As civil law and the *ius gentium* dealt with the parts, so the *ius naturale* dealt with the cosmos, and Zeus, or Jupiter, was resurrected as the Great King. This has more poetry and rhetoric than it has of logic, but for a Roman it had vital reality. Both emperor and slave were helped to identify their stations and their duties in a world that rode uneasily on the surface of a chaos. The emperor was apotheosized as well as deified, and the slave, like Epictetus, could claim the dignity of cosmopolitan citizenship. Law, neither before nor since, has had such penetrative power.

The historic consequences of the pervasion, permeation, and penetration of this great community by law have been and still are immeasurable. That a small community could commit itself so effectively to legality, that, as it grew, it could, albeit with setbacks, invent and refine its laws to keep pace with power and dominion over ever-increasing populations and last for a thousand years—this in itself is incredible. But that the principles and the spirit, not to mention the concrete institutions and literally the same civil laws, should have expanded and permeated the civilizations of both East and West to our time, so that it is still an unfinished story—this, as history runs, is unparalleled.

It would be foolhardy to seek one cause, or any finite number of causes, to explain so much. But it would be equally foolhardy to ignore the great themes in it. The United States at its founding and also today is not ignoring some of these themes. The Roman noms de plume used by the authors of the Federalist Papers remind us that the founding fathers continually patterned their public characters on their Roman opposite numbers. We today are struggling to come to terms with the problems of our expanded power over many peoples both domestic and foreign, and we try to draw the boundaries between us and the new barbarian. The liberties under law of the American citizen are not only a slogan to be sold but a model to be loved, hated, feared, and emulated around the world. We and all the other peoples in the world are driven to think cosmopolis.

Part of the difficulty of our time is to find the boundaries of our legitimate jurisdiction, and to measure the extent of our influence and power that far outruns boundaries. There are too many people taxed by our acts without representation. Our laws reach to matters for which we do not want to take responsibility, and we have to take responsibility for matters not touched by our laws. In literal terms, we continually violate our own legitimacy. The Romans of almost any period would have been sympathetic and could with their own hindsight offer us advice. They would be familiar with the rough dynamics of legality.

If we had such a Roman delegation to consult, there would be many matters up for debate. We would undoubtedly want to tell them about their political mistakes, ask them why they did not invent better instruments of representation, why they did not federalize their empire as it grew. It would be ironic if we would want to scold them for allowing the military and the civil to become dangerously confused. They could probably tell us something about the depths of these problems that we have not plumbed.

But the most lively argument would come from a common consideration of our theory and practice of law. The delegates from the later empire would undoubtedly want to recommend the codification of our laws. We would at first demur and remind them that the codifications of their laws were early signs of death of their community; but they might in turn ask us which kind of death we prefer, swift and complete and chaotic, or slow and reasonable after a long and fruitful autumn of political service to the world. After these sobering exchanges, we might be glad to weigh the costs of codification and listen to the methods and the probable discoveries that we might make. If we listened, we would be engaged in a better conversation about natural law than we pursue at present.

Pluralism is the present style in which we pose our problems to ourselves. We rather like our present illegitimacy with respect to our voluntary associations, but recently we have found it necessary to legitimize or find protections for others of our illegitimacies, and we draw our authority for doing this from the Bill of Rights. The Romans, accepting our terms, would suggest that we explore the possibilities in legal pluralism. An empire is a great school in the art of dealing with groups, minorities, and nations, whether they be inside or outside the jurisdictional boundaries. The Romans very early learned to recognize and honor the "languages, institutions, and laws" of the peoples that for one reason or another came under their aegis. They neither assimilated these heterogeneous legalities, nor did they excommunicate and ghettoize them. They undertook to enforce the living law of the group, even though this often raised serious threats to the integrities and viabilities of both the larger and the smaller communities. The discovery of common laws came to be expected, and, as they were found, they were added to the corpus of *ius gentium*. When the conflict of laws passed the bounds of literal adjudication, there was appeal to the unwritten laws of the cosmos, which were still assumed to be reasonable. The Western world has long lived under the mysterious radiations from one of the great cases that involved a Roman court and the Jewish Sanhedrin in Jerusalem. This involved not only a conflict of local and imperial laws but also an appeal through *ius gentium* and natural law to what had always been ambiguously known in the Hellenic world as divine law. What is remarkable is that this case could not have happened if there had not been an unshakable commitment to legality on the part of both communities.

In one respect the Romans governed the local communities more directly than we do in the United States: they did not recognize the so-called independent sovereignty of these subcommunities as we do our states. They sent out proconsuls, administrators, and judges to apply the laws of the senate and the Roman people. But in another respect they governed them less in that they recognized, respected, and even enforced the indigenous laws of the locality. They did not ensure to each political division a republican form of government. On the contrary, they encouraged the prior diversities in forms of government and maintained them.

The problems that this policy uncovered were lessened and moderated by the simultaneous discovery that separate peoples have some common laws, and this led to the search for the common principles behind all civil laws, and these common principles were often honored in the dealings between the empire and the surrounding barbarian peoples. Thus, the levels of plurality and unity in the empire were distinguished and correlated with the distinctions in kinds of law. The differences and similarities with our federal pattern of plurality and union are instructive. We tend to see in any empire something we now call monolithism, a heavy, enforced, coercive power. But at least in one respect the Roman laws allowed and supported more freedom, the freedom to diversify governmental and legal forms to fit local languages, institutions, and indigenous laws. The Romans thought it was in the interest of the empire to do this. Their theory of natural law enabled them to recognize and establish the diversity that resulted.

It might have been better if we had imitated this pattern in our federal Constitution, allowing the states to choose different forms of government, and it might be a good thing now if we amended the Constitution to allow it. One advantage could have been and could still be that we would feel freer to extend law to many faltering voluntary associations without the fear that we will smother their liberties. We always have extended enforcement to private contracts; why should we not enforce as well as grant charters to corporations, schools, universities, churches, unions, which now are left to themselves to seek their legitimacies? We have enough experience to understand the principles of legal pluralism, enough also to extend it where it is needed.

But Roman law has, particularly for the Anglo-Saxon world, which does not know natural law, become identified with legalism and legal fanaticism. With regard to legalism, we are told that laws are very special instruments, that society is more than government, and there is danger of dead and unresponsive formalism in submitting social problems to legal solutions. Then there is the opposite and perhaps greater danger of legal fanaticism, which consists in imposing arbitrary legal rules on every last item and hidden corner of society. Both of these become formidable if the coercive auxiliaries of law are allowed to take the foreground, and the army or the military is allowed to back them up, as much of Roman history seems to show was the case. Because of our own recent history, we too easily associate and identify these legal diseases with one or another dictatorial totalitarianism. But the so-called totalitarian phenomenon is a quite different disease. It arises from another Roman invention, the dictatorship, whereby laws are suspended so that the power of the government can be temporarily concentrated in one person to meet an emergency. If the temporary dictatorships became permanent by stealth or by default, the result was tyranny, government without law or by the misuse of law. Formal and fanatical legalism gone to extremes may do enough damage to destroy itself, but the growth of law in itself does not lead to tyranny. The carefully framed institution of dictatorship shows that the Romans understood very well the difference between government by law and government by men.

Two treatises of Cicero, *De Legibus* and *De Officiis*, show the effect of paying attention to the principles of natural law in the discriminations between the kinds of law and the diverse connections they have with the structural parts of government. Too often in our sloppy ways of thinking democratically, we look upon election and appointment as the conferring of power on a representative. We picture an official as an engineer with his hands on the throttles of power. For a Roman this would have been only a secondary attribute of office. The primary attribute would have been authority and responsibility under law. These graded authorities, responsibilities, and only consequently powers were the main articulations of government. They are valid and effective only if they cut society where the natural functions and joints exist and operate. Ultimately, the specifications of office must correspond to the natural powers and faculties of individual men. The form of the state must correspond to the powers of men, as Plato had correlated them in his *Republic*. The Stoic found it easy to correlate these parts and functions with the parts and powers of the cosmopolis. The city or nation exists suspended between man, the microcosm, and the great community, the macrocosm. Nature through law penetrates and pervades all.

This is not to say that Roman law was enabled to meet all of its problems; Rome, after all, did decline and fall. Whether Gibbon is right or wrong about the primary and secondary causes of the fall, there were internal conditions continually generated by events that did not find their legitimacies. The Roman citizen, the family, the corporation, the army—these were tough and almost indestructible institutions; but there was that almost institutionalized residue known as the proletariat, part slave and part free, that had no status, no legitimacy, no part, in the empire. That this unconquered, unpacified, unpoliticized power finally disrupted the whole legal structure is evidence of the essential place of law in a community. That the failure of law to penetrate this power was fatal is negative corroborative evidence that law was the essence of the life of the empire. It is probably true that there will be in any society a residue of rootless, unorganized, and legally unassimilated proletarians. It may be hubristic for any community to try to absorb the residue, as modern socialisms do, but the persistence of the problem probably should not yet allow us to condemn all attempts to solve it as totalitarian.

THE CHURCH

Gibbon attributes the fall of the Roman empire to barbarians without and religion within the great community. Toynbee's transformation of this formula into the generalized theme of the emergence of a religious community from the ruins of a civilization—that is, from a community that has been politicized and legalized—can be seen in still a third proposition. In order to integrate and maintain a system of civil law, the Romans had to appeal to a higher law, the natural law; but in the final crisis there was an appeal to a still higher law, divine law. This was not a new theme in Hellenic thought and experience. It is the essential theme of Greek tragedy. After human reason has been fully invested in a human enterprise, and every last glimmer of light has been collected and focused in the issues, there is a catastrophe and then a theophany. With hindsight, this is the injection by the playwright of a deus ex machina; for the victim of catastrophe, theophany is the recognition of a revelation. The Greek historians Thucydides and Herodotus saw events this way, law as the human reason of the community, full of hubris and leading inevitably to nemesis, and visited finally by divinity. The Romans were less able to use the tragic lens on themselves, but perhaps for that reason were, as a people, able to play the tragic role. If this is at all valid as a historic vision, Christianity is the climactic theophany for the series of tragic episodes in Hellenic civilization. It is the vision granted to a world disciplined and purged by a devotion to law. It allows us to see law, as it were, from above.

Of course, this is only another way of saying that Christianity was messianic. As Jewish law came to have a messianic implication, so also Roman law, even at the time of Christ, reached for salvation. Both Isaiah and Virgil, not to mention Plato, are recognized as prophets of a religious community. By the time of Constantine, church councils were quasi-constitutional conventions. From then till now, theology is continually thrashed out by dialectical methods as opinions of a supreme court. The church is a theocracy.

The church expanded throughout the empire, first as a pro-

letarian organization whose sufferings and protests enriched the
gospels and the sacraments, then as an illegal community strong
enough to court and accept persecution, finally as a polity well-
enough organized to receive the responsibilities of a faltering
regime and extend its own genius to the barbarian world. It was
even more penetrative and assimilative than Roman law had been
in receiving and "saving" local languages, institutions, and laws.
It was catholic, both in its universality and in its adaptability. It
soon adopted the distinctions between kinds and levels of law
from the Romans. There were local civil laws, there was the *ius
gentium*, the *ius naturale*, and finally the clear acceptance of
divine law, revealed, to be interpreted and adjudicated in labyrinths of local custom and hierarchies of jurisdiction.

Theology, whatever else its functions may be, was an arbitrator
of law. The *logos* had had a remarkable history. First discerned
and named by Heraclitus, then arithmetized by the Pythagoreans,
analyzed and elaborated by Plato, applied and distributed to the
sciences by Aristotle, it had identified itself in Alexandria with
two great structures, the Jewish Torah and Roman natural law.
The church lifted it to a higher eminence; it became the mind of
God and the exemplar of creation. It exemplified a general law
of logic—the higher the eminence, the greater the scope. The
Word became the Second Person of the Trinity. Plotinus and some
of the Stoics had anticipated some of this transcendence, but they
had not made it one of the mystical parts, a Person of the Deity.
As imminent, it was providence, the government of the world; but
the residue was still natural law, very much in the created world
and therefore accessible to human or natural reason.

To understand this hypostasis of the *logos*, it will help to
review some of the history of the dialectical process that led to it.
Plato thought he had discovered an infinite process in his upward
dialectic and therefore also in the downward dialectic, something
like the infinities that are found in the modern mathematical
continuum. It was possible to distinguish and to identify abstractions or ideas in the ascending series from particulars to the
great categories of being, one, same, good, etc. Between any two
members of the series there is a third to be found, and in both
mathematics and logic this yields an infinity; it results in a great

and refined power of calculation in mathematics and an unlimited power of speculation in logic and metaphysics. Also, Plato
accepted the findings of his dialectic, wherever it went, as
essences. The red in an apple, the life in a body, the justice in a
community, might be encountered as accidents or properties in
concrete individual things, but dialectic would show that they
were also essences in their own rights, redness, the soul, and
essential justice.

Aristotle found both Plato's infinities and also his hypostatization of essences indiscriminate and in the end, because of his
rigorous application of the principle of contradiction, unthinkable.
He found two kinds of substances in general: individual substances and God; all the rest are accidents of these substances in
one mode or another. Some accidents, such as mathematical
properties, can be treated as if they were substances, as quasi-
substances, but they are not actually independent. This basic
strategy made the founding of the Aristotelian sciences possible,
and makes the basic rift between Plato and Aristotle. Free Platonic
speculation continued as Neoplatonism and Stoicism, often playing
havoc with the formal Aristotelian sciences, and also suffering a
kind of blurred degradation in passing through the Latin language and the Roman legal mind. The results can be seen in
Cicero's writings.

But the dialectical recovery came in two minds: in Plotinus, a
pagan, and in Augustine, a Christian. Both were adepts in following the arguments wherever they led, to infinite series of essences.
Both were mystics, and relentless in their efforts to understand
what they saw by mystic vision and faith. They discovered and
accepted many of the same hypostatized essences, among them,
or rather as a summation of them, the *logos*. For Plotinus the
passage up and down this dialectical ladder was a continuous
journey demanded by his mystical vision; for Augustine, the
Christian, the access to the upper part of the ladder was a gift of
God's grace, a leap enabled by faith, hope, and charity within
the Christian revelation. In their practice of the dialectic art there
seems to be little difference. Both were guided by a divine
terminus, but their visions of this differed, and it was this difference that remained to be clarified by the disputations of the
schoolmen of the Middle Ages.

This difference was to become the distinction between nature and grace, in terms of human knowledge—what can be learned by the light of natural reason and what can be learned only by revelation. The revival of Aristotle helped to sharpen the argument, and the strategist of that argument was Albertus Magnus, the teacher of Thomas Aquinas. For him, Aristotle was the philosopher of nature, the mind that explored and exhausted the powers of reason for natural knowledge, physics, metaphysics, ethics, and politics. Albertus found Plato, Plotinus, Augustine, and the Augustinians the dialecticians who could probe the mysteries of the hypostases and emanations that enlightened reason found in God and the angelic hierarchy. Reason is common to the two realms, but it is put to different speculative uses and gets its medieval development from different sources. In Thomas Aquinas the line between nature and grace is sharply drawn and the consequences are precise.

To conclude this much oversimplified dialectical development, the *logos* that was understood as the essence of Roman natural law is here distinguished from it and clearly becomes divine law, the law of heaven, as it were, the exemplar of natural law. One is tempted here to recall Augustine's distinction between the city of God and the city of the world, and to say that the law of the city of God is *logos* as the law of the city of the world is natural law. Then one might go on to point out the historical consequence that the earthly church developed canon law from the *logos* as the worldly empires developed civil law from natural law. The consequence would then be the theological doctrine of the separation of church and state. But this sociological reduction, valid as it may be for understanding the civil problem of church and state, is a misunderstanding of the city of God. The earthly church, even if it were concretely catholic and universal, is only a small and distant province of the divine polity, and canon law belongs only to the local earthly community; canon law is the civil law of the city of God, as it were.

The most proper jurisdiction of divine law is heaven, where its first citizens are angels and sanctified souls. In the Thomistic doctrine the divine government rules over a perfect community in which the highest good, which is both common and individual, is immediately known and willed by intuitive intelligences. There are different degrees and modes of participation distributed according to perfect justice and love. God is the sovereign, but there is complete voluntary consent. This is the truly ideal republic in which learning and persuasion have been consummated, where the political problems of human government are already solved. It is that state toward which all human projections and strivings are directed. To use the Thomistic version of Platonic throught, the eternal law of divine government is the exemplar, "laid up in heaven," in which all human governments participate. The middle term through which the participation is mediated is natural law, as it is understood by human reason. Natural law is the human mode of understanding eternal law, or the *logos*.

The relation of divine or eternal law to natural law can be understood by analogy with the relation between the old law and the new law of the Bible. The Jewish community lived under the law of the Ten Commandments and Deuteronomy and also increasingly under the prophetic hope of a messiah. With the coming of the messiah there is a new legal dispensation that is sometimes in the Gospels called the fulfillment of the law, and sometimes in the Pauline epistles called the repeal of the law to make way for the Spirit, and again sometimes called the new law of love. The present epoch was first expected to be a thousand years of learning under the new law, a millennium at the end of which there would be the second coming of a Christ and the establishment of a divine government. The dialectical speculation of the Middle Ages did not deny the historical order, but added to it the nontemporal dialectical hierarchy of laws, positive laws of custom and statute, the *ius gentium*, the natural law, and the divine law. The dynamic strivings of history take place continually and simultaneously under these legal auspices. The levels of law provide an order of appeals from lower to higher cosmic tribunals.

THE MODERNS

So far, I have been calling on my own meager version of the common man's history of Greece, Rome, and the Middle Ages in order to educe from primarily philosophical texts the themes that converge and coalesce in the theory of natural law. These themes seem to emerge from crucial problems that the communities tried to solve. Thus Plato, and to a lesser degree Aristotle, saw the arts or technology of the Greeks suffering from perversion and confusion and causing a fever in the political community, which Plato took to be a sign of incurable disease. The *Dialogues* are the record of the search for and partial discovery of rational science, which might provide the basis for ordering the arts including government. There is not much doubt that Aristotle brought that task to a creditable accomplishment. Though there were other purposes of this work, both Plato and Aristotle hoped and believed that such science or sciences would inform the laws by which the arts could be ordered. Neither used the phrase *natural law* in a technical legal sense to describe or name the result, but they saw an idea and a function that has ever since been designated as natural law. Because of their insights the general notion that law is a medium of knowledge and an instrument of education for the human community becomes an essential part of any natural law doctrine.

The crisis in Rome is of another kind. It arose from a conflict among a great multiplicity of laws and political communities. The Romans were driven by this problem of pluralism to search for the common features of bodies of law in order to avail themselves of principles that would guide them in articulating diverse systems and arranging workable relations between them to serve a common good that was in principle universal or catholic. Local differences forced them to construct a hierarchy of the different kinds of law, the levels of which correspond to the areas of jurisdiction. They did not stop before they identified the jurisdiction of the highest principles, the principles of natural law, with the cosmos.

The medieval philosopher of law had to deal with a community that was in principle and in dogma even more comprehensive than the Roman Stoic cosmos. The Romans conceived the gods as rulers within the natural universe. The Ruler of the Christian world transcended the universe, and the majority of His subjects were outside nature. The dialectic by which the church interpreted the basic revelation of this supreme community was aided by grace of the theological virtues faith, hope, and charity. This makes it quite clear that natural law, whatever its transcendental derivations, is fully available to natural human reason. It is not, as often said, a matter of faith, religious commitment, or mysticism. It is a matter of knowledge if one chooses to use his natural intellectual powers in the modes of theoretical and practical reason. In fact, the seeds of natural law are embedded in every human reason, and some of its most genuine expressions come from the untutored and unsophisticated mind. If we could find some way of eliminating conventional and sophistical corruptions, we could say that the knowledge of natural law is moral common sense. Something like this elimination of corruption is in fact the aim of deliberation in legislation and due legal process in the courts. From the civil point of view, the Middle Ages are a time when law and politics squarely faced the fearsome problem of religion, the religion that Gibbon said caused the fall of the Roman empire; the outcome was the distinction between natural law and divine law. The distinction is the theoretical basis for the so-called practical agreement on the separation of church and state.

As we move on into the modern period from the thirteenth century when this clarification was achieved, we encounter a series of confusions. One of these comes about from the rise of the nation-state as a transplantation and extension of the Italian city-state north of the Alps. Monarchs, pressed by the problems of size and complication, acted like the early Roman emperors; they yielded to the temptation of quasi-deification. These attempts were not successful, but they left a ragged doctrine of the divine right of kings. They leaped over natural law to divine law to root their authority in heaven, and their art of governing or reigning suffered from hubris.

Similarly, in the attempts to rebel against tyranny in the seventeenth century, the new commonwealths sanctified themselves. The Levellers, the Covenanters, the Commoners of Cromwell, thought of themselves as founders of holy communities, often recapitulating the polities that can be found in the Old Testament and in the early Christian ghettoes. They took the proposition "Defiance to tyrants is obedience to God" as a constitutional principle. The conscientious withdrawal from a political community implied for them their single membership in a divine commonwealth. Most of these attempts to find the basis of political union led to short-lived polities.

But as revolutions ensued, and social contracts took the place of covenants with God, there grew up the artificial myths that parodied the biblical state of innocence. Hobbes, Locke, Rousseau, and Montesquieu substituted the state of nature for the state of innocence, and they derived individual natural rights from a variety of such "states." These accumulated and culminated in the doctrine of the rights of man of the French revolution, and the doctrines, each in its own way, led back to the puzzlement of the Greeks concerning what was natural and what was artificial and conventional in human society—consider Rousseau's prize essay on the question, Has the progress of the arts and sciences contributed more to the corruption or to the purification of morals?

These revolutionary apologies tried to return to nature, even in the Stoic sense, but it is quite clear in all of them that the nature to which they sought to return was no longer there. Something, in fact a great deal, had happened to it. Some of these things are still in stories we tell ourselves today. We see the new man of the Renaissance as a prisoner of another world released into the warm, rich, varied world of nature. He spends his time in observing and enjoying sights, sounds, smells, tastes, and feelings within himself. If he has intellectual skills, he tries to explain what he sees and hears by mathematics and experiment. He discovers for the first time what he calls the fine arts. He explores his imagination rather than his memory. He begins to invent rather than discover. As Galileo says, he reads the book of nature. He is a grammarian and an algebraist, perhaps a rhetorician, but hardly ever a dialectician or a logician. If he does venture into speculation, he thinks he has passed into the supernatural world of theology. The nature of the Greeks, the Romans, and the scholastics does not exist. The laws of nature that offer themselves for his enlightenment are mathematical and mechanical; they do not reveal their ends; they do not inform morals, to say nothing of justifying or correcting laws. The senses and the passions declare war on morals and reason, and they gradually take reason prisoner and put it to work on their side. Morals and final causes are left to poets, philosophers, and theologians, whose minds have been darkened by the dark ages and seduced by medievalism.

Nature itself is torn asunder by the battle; it is bifurcated. Part of it becomes the dark brutal motions of masses verified by measurements of primary qualities—solidity, shape, size, and motion—and part of it becomes motions of the psyche or spirit, a stream of consciousness in which float the secondary and tertiary qualities—sense, feeling, imagination, values, and the remnants of reason that still inhabit the intellectual "soul." There are still those, like Kant, who honor, even reverence, theoretical and practical reason. But even he puts a sign over the realm of science: Let nothing enter that is not informed by mathematics; and he defines nature as "all that comes under the categories of scientific understanding." Ends are regulative but not constitutive of nature; they are ideals of reason.

Finally, nature itself reappears as an ideal person, the only half-believed mythical goddess of the poets and the idealistic philosophers. She presides over the world that has not yet been admitted to science. Natural law is the unattainable ideal of the skeptical scientist or of the positivistic and realistic legalist who has lost his way in jurisprudence. This idealized and mythical apotheosis of nature has happened before, as when the Roman poet Lucretius dedicated his poem *De Rerum Natura* to Venus, the Mother of all things that came to be and passed away in the drift of the atoms. Needless to say, Venus reigned over natural process, but did not rule. Many of the present searches for a basis of jurisprudence in natural law are reconstituting this myth.

THE KNOWLEDGE OF NATURE

The way of speculation is now, as always, beset by threatening presences: on one side, religious dogma, and, on the other, empirical science. The effect so far is timidity in speculation. A part, the essential part, of natural law doctrine is speculative in both

senses of that troubled word. It must be theoretical in its insistence on dealing with the facts for what they can yield in the way
of knowledge, and it must dare to go beyond facts, to explore and
exhaust what the always meager data indicate in the way of
abstract knowledge. This is to say that we must recognize, trust,
and follow reason, wherever it leads.

In one sense there has never been a time when reason was more
cultivated and trusted than it is now, but this is true only when
reason gives itself to mathematics and when mathematics re-
nounces any claim to truth. Most of the other uses and levels of
reason are suspect. Both the academy and the public set severe
limits to the tolerance they will accord to what they call "too
much discursive abstract reasoning." Abstract reasoning from
hypothesis to data will pass, but the reasoning from one hypothesis to another or from hypotheses to principles is mere dialectic
and leads to forbidden absolutes. This proscription eliminates one
of Aristotle's intellectual skills or virtues, as well as the methods
of Plato's researches in the *Dialogues*. It hides the essences that
provide the clarity and structure that natural law once provided.

Another proscription of longer standing eliminates another more
important intellectual skill or virtue that Aristotle and Plato depended on—intellectual intuition—the power by which the mind
first seizes and contemplates an intellectual object. Kant, so far
as I know, was the first to explicitly deny the possibility of intellectual intuition. More accurately, he said that it might be
possible for God, but not for the human mind, which was
essentially discursive and analytic. John Stuart Mill illustrates in
his *Logic* the absence of intellectual intuition in modern scientific
method. He sets it as a kind of puzzle for his readers to explain
the fact that most of the great scientific hypotheses were established on the basis of single observations, thus raising doubts
about the efficacy of his own famous "methods," in which the
accumulation of many observations is necessary for verification.
The still-unending attempts to validate the scientific method show
that secondary inductions, those that pile up evidence and increase probability for hypotheses, follow Bacon's, Hume's, and
Mill's methods, but the primary inductions, which alone justify
the secondary efforts, are still a mystery.

Aristotle, in one of his more literary paragraphs, describes the primary induction, or what he calls the intuitive induction. He says that it is as if an army is in retreat, slipping out of control into disorder, and one man, a private, decides to turn about and take a stand to face the enemy. The others note his position and posture, turn about like him, and line up on him as pivot. This is what the single case does in the primary induction to "save the appearances" and establish the hypothesis. So the strategy of the intuitive induction may be used not only to find and verify a hypothesis but also to discover and establish a principle, which is the foundation of the science. The power of the mind that governs this strategy is the habit of intellectual intuition. The fact or the datum is the occasion, but not the source, of the insight. This is the intellectual power that Plato puts at the top of the divided line; it is also the power that is the source of Aristotle's great artistry in founding the sciences. It is that toward which the upward dialectic moves. It is the secret that the social scientist of today, lost among hypothetical values, cannot discover. It is not to be confused with hunches and emotional ecstasies, although these may contain insights needing clarification.

Trusting intellectual intuitions feels to us like betting on special experiences or falling for dogma, perhaps groping among possibilities, but, with sufficient critical strategy and dialectical discipline, it is merely recognizing what can and therefore must be thought.

I have paid this much attention to the lost powers of the intellect because these two, so-called discursive understanding and intellectual intuition, are particularly important if natural law exploration is to free itself from current epistemological tangles, most especially the tangle that is called value theory. In practical sciences, such as law, the principle is the end; it is the beginning of any reasoning about the means. It must be an original starting point, as the word *principle* strictly indicates. It cannot be deduced or induced; it is a first premise. It can be reached only by intellectual intuition. Otherwise, values, subjective, relative, and apparent goods, have to be substituted for ends, or goods, that are real and known.

But the uncriticized dogmas of religion and empirical science invade and disrupt the proper work of the intellect at points that are crucial to natural-law thinking. We are shocked, romantically moved, or amused when we read Virgil's demonstration of natural love as the pivotal insight around which the *Divine Comedy* moves; when we read of the loves of the magnets in Gilbert; when Kepler attaches "intelligences" to the orbits of the planets; or when Bacon or Leibniz allows events to perceive one another. We allow the latter-day theologian to warn us off these modes of thought by telling us that these are only poetic analogies inspired by far-off divine events. Or we allow the devotees of the scientific method to tell us that such thoughts are vestiges of primitive animism and superstition. Actually, these poetic and scientific makers of the modern intellectual world were thinking in a bold and highly rational style about ends and means. They were not indulging in what we call pathetic fallacies, the imputation of psychic powers to inanimate things. It is we who are the prisoners of the pathetic fallacy; we substitute occult powers for legitimate objects of rational processes.

The result of this is that we split the natural world into two parts: one that is drained of values, and one that is haunted by errant emotions and wishes. This split is the work of about one century of the late Renaissance. The so-called rationalists were world-splitters. There was the rational world within which efficient, sometimes only mechanical, causes worked; and there was the other world in which final causes persisted. Stones and atoms typified the former; men, the latter; and there was doubt about plants and animals. There were bold thinkers who could reduce the human world to the mechanical, and these still survive. But we are on the whole left with the moderate position in which purposes are restricted to the human world. The final causes, ends, and purposes of men, however rational they may be, must not be imputed to the natural world of science if we wish to maintain so-called objectivity.

The classical view stemming from Plato and Aristotle, and taken for granted until the late Renaissance, allowed reason to find final causes as well as efficient causes wherever it went. Long chains of reasoning in both modes comprehended nature, and ultimately the work of reason in one mode was not adequate unless it was supported by the other. Of course, there is another radical classical view, never lost in spite of the predominance of Aristotle and Plato: the view of the atomists from Leucippus and Democritus to Dalton and Newton. It is this singleminded view that has dominated the scientific method until fairly recently, when the double vision of the older view has returned to scientific respectability in the so-called principle of complementarity. It is this late and tentative revival of the full rationality that provides some of the theoretical background for the new concern about natural law.

For natural law, speculative freedom is necessary and vital. It is necessary to find some way of healing the rift that makes it necessary to warn students of one generation after another that they must not confuse the two meanings of natural law: the laws that the scientific method seeks, and the laws that underlie human law. The former are not commands of a rational creature, it is said, while the latter are. Nature is determined throughout by the laws of science, while human beings in their freedom can disobey human laws, even natural law. Both sides of the distinction are inaccurate, and the general warning is false. I shall try in the following pages to show why.

THE METAPHYSICS OF NATURAL LAW

Whenever and wherever ethical and legal theories have sought critical standards in natural law—in the case of the Greeks, in the case of the Romans, in the case of the medievals, even in the case of the moderns—they have sought validation for ends or values in some notion of the good, some general notion of the good that does not lie within the scope of the specific categories of their disciplines. There is that abrupt, surprising statement of Plato's at the early crisis in his search in the *Republic*: the good is the principle of all being (existence) and essence. This is a proposition in metaphysics, which is something beyond and after any science of nature, although not anywhere that is indicated in the modern term *supernatural*.

Plato and his imitator Augustine are remarkable for their addiction to dialogue and the height and speed of their ascent to metaphysics that the dialogue allows. They both are much more concerned about insight than about demonstration. Socrates or the *magister* in a dialogue begins with the ordinary judgments of his interlocutors. In expression of common sense or of conventional opinion the ordinary man makes many judgments of right and wrong, good and evil, honorable and dishonorable, fair and foul. The judgments of wrong, evil, dishonorable, and foul seem to be made with a good deal more emphasis and conviction than judgments of their opposites. The dialectician asks the reasons for these judgments, and he gets answers that reduce themselves to one hard term that comprehends a variety of synonyms. With good strategy the hard term turns out to be "evil," and it is usually asserted with a great deal of conviction. The turning point of the argument comes at this point when the questioner points out that the interlocutor must know what good is, as otherwise he would not know the evil.

The common man at this point may feel trapped or paralyzed. Either he must go on to find out what he knows but does not think he knows, or he must stop talking. If he consents to go on, he finds he is on a very high level of abstract discourse, passing from idea to idea and increasing in altitude. With dialectical persistence and patience, seemingly very ordinary ideas take on extraordinary power and meaning. So it is with the good, and so it is with the associated so-called transcendental predicates. This discovery by the common man that he has always been involved in metaphysics with being, good, true, one, same, etc., is dazzling. As Whitehead said of Plato himself, he is in the *Dialogues* a man continually dazzled by the brilliance of his own insights. This is the intellectual intuition at work.

An apocryphal story has it that Plato once delivered a lecture on the good, and that many attended at first, but that after several hours only Aristotle remained. It has always been interesting to guess what transpired between them on that occasion. The best guess is that Aristotle talked back and that Plato joined the common search, as Socrates always did when the pupil responded. They must then have discovered something like this: anything judged to be good has an essence or form, an answer to the question, What is it? But it also has something that can be distinguished from this, its being or existence, an answer to the question, Is it? A thing is good if and insofar as its existence fulfills its essence; it is evil or bad if and insofar as its existence fails to fulfill its essence. Aristotle may have on the spot begun what he certainly went on to do later; he varied the formula to fit the different essences and their relations to their existences. Thus, a thing has a matter that more or less perfectly fits and fills the form; it has a potentiality that more or less perfectly actualizes itself; it has a contingency or dependence on circumstances that may or may not allow it to exist. A man has a desire or a will that he may not be able to realize. A form itself may have a perfection because by itself it does not need anything added to support its being. This is the good in its many contexts and relationships. It is clear that the argument could go on for a long time, perhaps after the deaths of these two men, perhaps until now and beyond.

Our first encounter with the notion of objective good based on essence and existence throws us back into a tangle of sentimental associations. If good is built into everything as other properties and accidents are, we quickly infer that the aggregate of goods adds up to a summary providence in nature or in God that justifies an ultimate optimism, the optimism made famous by Leibniz and Voltaire of the best of all possible worlds. The inference is too quick and too easy; F. H. Bradley issued a warning when he said that this is the best of all possible worlds, but everything in it is a positive evil. The best world possible is none too good.

And there is another caveat. When we infer optimistically, we are usually thinking egocentrically or anthropocentrically. If there is a massive quantum of good in the world, we think it must be a good for us. We must recall that the distribution of the transcendental good is more equable. The last discovered sub-atomic particle, if it exists, has its measures of essence and existence, its own proper good and evil, as do stones, plants, and animals, with no reference to men.

But the argument goes on to show that evil is also very widely distributed. Wherever there is a failure of existence to fit and fulfill an essence, there is evil, and a radical built-in evil, the so-called evil of privation. Essences can be conceived as possibilities, and there are very, very many of them, perhaps an infinite number, as Leibniz said. One can think of space and time as the narrow conditions set for their existence. The universe at any given time and place may be poor indeed in realized goods; in fact, to our minds it seems to be mainly privation and evil. But the metaphysical summary or census of goods is not our problem at this point, perhaps not possible ever for our minds.

The world presents us not only with a distributed multiplicity of goods and evils but also with a vast pattern of coexisting goods and evils. For any one good to exist, there must be a context of other goods, and they must be articulated if they do not prove to be mutually annihilating. It was this vision that lay back of modern theories of evolution. If the essences are species, then there is a struggle for existence and survival depends upon mutual adaptation. One good is the condition for the existence of another good; in fact, many other goods. One good is the means to another good considered as end. This signifies that any good is a kind of teleological center around which there exists its means of existence; and, vice versa, any good is a means to the existence of other ends. We are used to seeing ourselves, each is used to seeing himself, as ends or end, to which the universe ministers. It is a humbling and beneficial exercise to realize that all other things could validly find the center in themselves. Each entity generates a kind of individual providence for itself. It may be fortunate that not too many providences are blessed with our kind of intelligence. We have a difficult enough task to find the common good of our societies. We wonder at present whether the society of the subatomic particles in plutonium and hydrogen has a common good that can be connected with ours.

This articulation of the world as means and ends with all of its one-many and many-one relations, its versatile interchangeabilities of ends and means, its ubiquitous evils, its aspect of struggle for existence, is the teleological universe, the world under the aspect of the good. But the system of final causes is no more complicated than the systems of efficient or mechanical causes. In fact, it was possible for Bergson to make a case for thinking of mechanical causes as merely the inversion of final causes. Both, he said, are results of highly rational objective thought, the ideal objective of all scientific investigation. Science itself is fragmentary, episodic, and progressive, and therefore does not prove or demonstrate the cosmic views, either mechanical determinism or teleological order. It takes them for granted, and judges its findings by how far it fails to reach the totalities. These views are presupposed similarly by any effort to find natural law.

THE SCIENCES IN NATURAL LAW

Some of the answers to the questions that the Greeks were asking in their search for a rational basis for law are given in this metaphysical doctrine, the theory of the good that arises from the discovery of essences and the problems of existence that the essences pose. But the difficulties in the upward dialectic that seeks the essences are repeated in reverse in the downward dialectic that elaborates the sciences of nature. Metaphysics supplies an apparently well-grounded set of principles. Under them, Aristotle was able to establish physics, the general science of nature, within which many ingenious and elegant hypotheses ordered things by material, formal, efficient, and final causes. The strategic lines in the structure were levels in a hierarchy of beings. As corresponding to these levels he identified seven substantial forms, or essences, upon which all the other properties or accidents depended.

There were the four elements: earth, water, air, and fire. These together made up inanimate nature. We still honor them in our doctrine of phases of energy: solids, liquids, gases, and heat. Then there were plants, animals, and men. There was even room within his spheres for a fifth element, the ether, where the separated forms that later were called angels might exist. He distinguished six kinds of motion: local motion, qualitative change, growth, decay, generation, and corruption; and these correspond to kinds of accidents inhering in the substances. There were precise definitions, rigorous methods of inference, and plenty of opportunity for empirical verification and technical application. The historical fact that many of the practitioners in these sciences did not fully avail themselves of these facilities is no refutation of their soundness. The historical fact that these sciences flourished and dominated the intellectual world for almost two thousand years, lending their rational light to two great religions, is perhaps too heavy a confirmation.

One other historical fact poses a problem for us. The period of Platonic and Aristotelian science corresponds with the period of the development of natural law. One should probably not identify natural law as exclusively Platonic or Aristotelian, but the negative evidence for this is overwhelming. Modern science, from the seventeenth century on, does not easily yield a natural-law doctrine. It is not yet time to conclude that it cannot do so. But at present we are faced with a hard choice. Either we re-instate Aristotelian science and show how it can assimilate and improve modern science, or we assume that it is dated and out-moded, abandon it, and trust our legal and moral future to the inherent regenerative powers of reason and observation. The latter alternative puts us back with the original problem of the Greeks.

One feature of the older science must be noted and emphasized again. It yielded not only rational science but also a rational method for identifying essences and ends, and these make most of the difference. Our sciences are silent or fatefully confused about value. But if we remove ourselves from the high level of pure science to technology, we find tremendous energy and courage put to the service of values. And the teleological theme in the form of utilitarianism not only informs the technological activity and theory, it projects itself back to the pure science itself. It is currently being said that the test of a hypothesis is partly, but essentially, nevertheless, the cost of its being wrong in practice. The phrase conceals a strong simplistic teleological or purposive bias. The similarly pragmatic scientific method has long used operational workability as a test for scientific validity. This may be a dialectical trope by which modern science temporarily devotes itself to the good in some technical form in order to return to a truth that can include ends and values. Perhaps we should not only be patient but view this turn of affairs with enthusiasm.

However predominant Aristotelian scientific influence was in the two thousand years in which it flourished, it was never the only style of scientific thought. It suffered from the erosions of time and habit, but it also gave ground to opposing thought. One of the resultants of the conflict is a break in its own speculative fabric. The break corresponds to a distinction that Aristotle himself made between nonrational and rational potencies. Inanimate elements, plants, and animals obey the imperatives of their natures implicitly. A stone falls and a plant grows without taking thought; it has no choice. It realizes its potency automatically, as it were. On the other hand, a man has rational potencies, and these involve thought, the entertainment of contradictions and contraries, choice between them, and the possibility of disobedience to the imperatives of his nature. The nonrational potencies therefore seem to come under the non-Aristotelian sciences of atomism and mathematical physics in which fate or determinism, but not ends, supplies the laws. It appears that man with his powers of rationality and choice escapes those kinds of necessary laws, but as the empirical and mathematical sciences progress, they bring more and more of a man's psyche under mechanical and mathematical laws. The result is that the rational potencies retreat and become isolated and imprisoned.

The defenders of the classical tradition of natural law, who should assert teleology as a parallel and coextensive interpretation with mathematical physics, actually defend teleology only in man. The reflective reason in man is clearly purposive, but the rest of nature sleeps in its mechanical and mathematical order. Technical man can impose purposes on natural objects by quasi-magical arts; he can even invent purposes and bend nature to his will. Even the Bible has authorized such control and exploitation, but in the modern style no inference is made about the implicit purposiveness in nonrational things that makes his mastery a success. The classical doctrine of human nature then exists in the modern world as a mere humanism. This, I believe, is what paralyzes the doctrine of natural law in the modern world, and prevents it from reviving its full force by penetrating the equations and the mechanisms that pervade both natural and social science. This is the reason that so-called secondary natural law seems arbitrary, dated, and dogmatic when it makes particular determinations. Science must be the mediator of natural-law thinking, and there is confusion in this area.

If I am right in finding the locus of the difficulty in the confusion of the sciences, or, to give it another name, the explosion of the notion of nature, we cannot put natural law together again without going to the center of several problems. One of these is the puzzles that modern algebra, or analysis, poses. This is very much unfinished business with both mathematicians and philosophers. Another problem comes with the great difficulty of validating the empirical scientific method. Both of these raise serious problems for natural-law theory because they are the present screen through which we think we acquire natural knowledge. They show no signs of delivering knowledge of values or ends. Natural-law theory avoids open conflict or criticism of the academic going concerns that are committed to these methods, and it seems unable to comprehend and transcend them. The writings of Lon Fuller show the frustration that results.

There are several working alternatives to the formidable task indicated above. F. S. C. Northrop boldly states the outlines of current natural knowledge based on mathematical physics, connecting it with the long mathematical tradition from the Pythagoreans to the present. Still more boldly, he allows such natural knowledge to extend itself to the human nervous system. He asserts that the latest neurology and the neurology immediately in prospect supply adequate physiological correlates of the rational human powers familiar in the humanistic tradition. At present, Northrop makes no claim that the natural law that he sees developing in his hypothetical construction yields anything but hypothetical values, and there is at present a presumption running through his thought that nothing more is needed. One must wait for developments. It is, of course, possible that such explorations will make discoveries.

As if to balance this effort, there is Jacques Ellul's description of the great technological phenomenon in *La Technique*. The technical phenomenon is the product of human art, the organization of means to human ends. From separate and isolated origins the arts as techniques have come together, have meshed and spread, and are now connected in one great system by machines, mathematical formulas, and massive organizations of men. The

REDISCOVERING NATURAL LAW

term *technical phenomenon* is not an accidental choice. The system as a whole is an appearance, perhaps an illusion as long as we fail to understand it, a moment in a historical dialectic that will presently negate itself. But as it stands at present, it is self-augmenting, universal in principle; increasingly interdependent in its parts, and autonomous in that its ends are intrinsic and not responsive to other ends. In these respects it is like the classical natural universe in its teleological phase. But it is obviously artificial, an imitation of the natural universe as this was understood by the Roman Stoics. It demands and get human acquiescence and for the most part enthusiastic obedience; in this it is like the living law of the legal realists. It has large contributions from science, but uses these for its own ends, and in turn to a great extent directs scientific investigations and sets the workable standards for scientific validity. It is as if Ellul had seen the aim of Plato's integration and criticism of the human arts and had transferred the survey to the modern situation; he also sees the sophistry and tyranny that lie potentially in technics, waiting for exploitation or for clarification. Ellul does not appeal to natural law for the latter purpose; he appeals rather to divine law, but is not very hopeful of an effective response.

Beside Fuller, Northrop, and Ellul we must put Messner's *Social Ethics: Natural Law in the Modern World*. In the first hundred pages this is a beautifully clear exposition of the classical and Catholic orthodox theory of natural law as it is derived from human nature. Then it goes on to show the presence of natural law in contemporary law, politics, and economics. In its frequent and often long passages in fine print it fights the battle of jurisprudence against its many confusers and detractors. The battle is justly and fairly fought so that clarities are exposed on both sides. But the final effect is to encapsulate a sublimity in the glass case of a museum. It does not grasp and help to reformulate the inarticulate problems of the contemporary world. When it reaches out to do so, it too often becomes an apologetic for a problematic status quo, not to say a status quo ante. Because of its restricted humanistic premises, it is not able to take on the needed critique of the natural sciences; it honors man, but it does not take into account the rest of nature and the technology in which he lives his life; it does not note the net of correlations, probabilities, and techniques in which man is already enmeshed. The following section of this paper is an attempt to state the problems that Messner leaves unresolved.

THE KINGDOM OF NATURE

I am persuaded at this stage that technology is the unclarified phenomenon that poses the most important problems in jurisprudence. The fates of both science and government are epitomized in its dark oracular operations. The best light I have on it comes from Kant, who thought and wrote about these matters just as the scientific and industrial revolutions were precipitating the political revolutions and innovations of the modern world. His categorical imperative is prophetic.

The categorical imperative in its first formulation provides the cardinal criterion of civil law: choose the maxims of your acts as if they were to serve as universal laws of nature. This is advice to legislators and judges. To the philosopher of law the second formulation puts it this way: all maxims ought by their own legislation to harmonize with a possible kingdom of ends as with a kingdom of nature. For the citizen the third formulation reads: treat all human beings as ends-in-themselves, not merely as means.

The habitual natural lawyer will find these formulations heavily impregnated with the terms of natural law, and this first impression will be literally accurate; but on second reading he will be disturbed by an air of the subjunctive or even optative mood. Kant seems to be saying: treat law, think about it and deal with it, *as if* the doctrine of natural law, its rational teleology, were true science. Natural law in the subjunctive or optative mood becomes then an idealistic, almost a romantic, teaching, perhaps touched with nostalgia. This also is an accurate impression, and the mood familiar in much of our contemporary jurisprudence.

In addition to Hume and Leibniz, Kant had another beloved teacher, Christian Wolff, through whom he learned an eighteenth-century version of scholastic doctrine. Much of the *Critique of Pure Reason* is a critique of Christian Wolff and his teaching, and the logic of the criticism is the logic of Newtonian mathematical physics. Kant had a great deal to do with making this logic "constitutive" of classical physics and the method of the natural sciences until fairly recently. The intellectual weight of the *Principia Mathematica* and the sharpness of Kant's critique and defense of it shifted the center of gravity away from Wolff's scholastic metaphysics and left the latter in a problematic realm that Kant called the "Ideals of Pure Reason." Kant's formulations of these ideals are unique, but they are not without context; they epitomize the scientific and philosophical thought from Nicholas of Cusa and Galileo to Newton and Leibniz. Kant might, as many of his successors did, have simply canceled out the realm of Pure Reason, but he did not do this. He emphatically and repeatedly said that the ideas of reason must be thought, they cannot be escaped; but on the other hand, they must not be allowed to invade the realm of empirical science.

But, although this separation of power is the emphatic conclusion of the critique of pure or speculative reason, it is not the final word by any means. In later works the great theme of the spontaneous legislative powers of the human mind gives a new dignity and power to the ideas of reason. These ideas are "regulative" of all the operations of the human mind; that is, they give rules for the deployment of all the constitutive concepts of science, morals, and jurisprudence. The best example of this regulative function of ideas is relevant to the theory of natural law. The idea of purpose in the universe is an idea of reason, one that should not be allowed to invade and displace the idea of mechanical cause, but it issues an imperative or rule to the investigating scientist in biology or physiology. He must conceive an organism as a system of reciprocal means and ends, and then because he has done this he must exhaustively trace the instrumental relations in the mechanisms of reciprocal efficient causes. Applied to jurisprudence, this would mean that the ideal of reason expressed in the categorical imperative demands that legislative enactments must have reasoned preambles and that judicial decisions must be reasoned opinions, both kinds of reasoning reaching to the common good and to the facts.

The notion that natural law is regulative in the Kantian sense perhaps clarifies one of the difficulties in understanding the traditional notion. It is often said that natural law is more gen--

eral and abstract than civil law and never should be identified with it; it is even said that natural law is unwritten, not reducible to formula or code. And yet it is found or discovered sometimes as the principle of common law or in difficult cases where conflict or ambiguity of positive law occurs. It is further said that positive law cannot be deduced from natural law; instead, it is said that positive law is a determination of natural law by way of specification rather than deduction. Kant's natural law as a regulative ideal of reason throws these puzzles into an intelligible pattern. In part, Kant's genius lay in his skill in translating abstract concepts into rules of operation; he was an early operationalist. When an idea becomes regulative, it becomes a rule for the strategic application of other concepts. Kant revised Aristotelian logic by treating the major premise of syllogism as a rule for inferring the conclusion from the minor premise.

If we conceive natural law as a body of rules for the making, administration, and adjudication of positive laws, we have something like a solution of the preceding puzzles. Regulation by natural law then becomes the rules for referring legislation, administration, and adjudication to the rule of reason and demanding due process of law for all citizens. Natural law does not dictate positive law, but it sets the processes of law in operation and directs their activity and influence through dialectic, analogy, and example, those nobler parts of the art of rhetoric. Natural law, as reason, sits within the mind of the magistrate, lawyer, and citizen as the internal teacher.

The first formulation of the categorical imperative, cold and empty as it seems, is a good example of this function. As a legal formula it derived from the classical definition of law: a law must be universal; that is, it is rule of reason. This means that it must have equal incidence upon persons and situations; it must not be discriminatory, "a respecter of persons," or tend to be a bill of attainder or in principle be limited to a locality. But its frequent comparison with the golden rule, Do unto others as you would be done by, or, Love thy neighbor as thyself, shows that it can invoke charity as well as justice and thus qualify the common good as the intention or end of law in general. It says not only to make law itself reasonable, but to exhaust all possible reasons in the use of law. It puts law in the rich context of practical reasoning about means and ends for the sake of human action, individual and collective.

I have always been puzzled by the tortuous reasoning by which Kant ostensibly arrives at the insight that the categorical imperative expresses; the reasoning is much less revealing and convincing than the bare insight. It is as if Kant in the field of morals were surrendering to his own skill in intellectual intuition, whose validity he so fiercely denied in the first *Critique*. In the formula above, by sheer thought he grasps the rational root of the mysterious *ought* in human affairs. By apparently similar intuitions, he reaches the related content of the other two formulations. Treat all human beings as ends-in-themselves, not merely as means. Conceive nature as a kingdom of ends. Put together, these separate formulas say that all good laws must be rules of reason within a kingdom of nature, or ends in which men are masters or the ends-in-themselves.

This is good natural-law doctrine, and I have purposely omitted the phrases that in the original give it the subjunctive and romantic mood. I should like to continue in the imperative and realistic mood in order to explore the intrinsic meaning of what for Kant seems to have been a utopian ideal or vision. The metaphysical teleology that I have expounded in an earlier part of this paper is the substance of Kant's vision, but for him it is like Plato's utopian construction in the *Republic*: "a pattern laid up in heaven, beholding which, a citizen or a ruler can set his house in order." In this sense it is a regulative idea of reason.

Whatever there may be of theological overtones or presuppositions in the vision, the key phrase is "a kingdom of nature." The regulative consequences of the vision ought to appear from an examination of the constitution of this kingdom. Part of the kingdom consists of persons as rational beings whose dignity and freedom are exercised in giving to themselves universal laws in the acts of their wills. By virtue of this power of self-government, they are ends-in-themselves. The constitution of the kingdom of nature is violated if any of the kingly persons are treated merely as means. This does not mean that they are never to be treated as means. The constitutional situation is rather that the persons act reciprocally as means and ends regarding one another, or as mutual means to their common end, as the organs in an organism or as members of a free community. They may serve each other, but the royalty in each servant must also be respected. This part of the kingdom, for the sake of concreteness, can be seen in Rousseau's republic of self-governing citizens, from which Kant's vision is partly derived.

For further illustration, consider the modern business corporation. It is a rudimentary community of persons. Part of its rude state is due to its radical oligarchic polity, which is said to be unavoidable if the organization is to carry out its purpose and obligations—the running of a business. On occasion it is necessary for one oligarch to use his fellow oligarchs, with or without their permission, or to issue orders that call for sacrifice for the sake of the firm. Even if this does not actually happen, the constitution is such that it can "correctly" take place. The lines of authority from senior to junior executives and managers is more oligarchic, and to the worker employees still more so. Business being what it is, the highest imperative of the firm is to use its manpower efficiently; that is, to manage so that each member can put his full efforts to the use of the company. The ends-in-themselves in these communities are understood in law and in practice to be the stockholders; all the others consent to put themselves to the service or use of these kings.

But even at the origin of these communities there is a token recognition of each man as an end-in-himself. When an employee takes a job, he is understood to have made a free contract, to have freely consented to the service for which he is hired, and in consideration of this he is given a salary or a wage. Even in a slave system the master recognizes his obligation to feed and clothe his servants. All these devices—wages, food, and clothing—can be understood as forms of coercion, but the residue of consent can never be quite eradicated; respect for consent, no matter how small or deceptive, is nevertheless respect for man as an end-in-himself.

Latterly, the corporation has been acquiring a conscience, it is said, and the sign of this is that it makes concessions to demands or anticipates them by offering to serve the employees by supplying the means of a decent life, giving longer contracts for jobs, installing safety devices on the job and medical care for employees and their families, and establishing insurance and pensions. These services are offered for all sorts of prudential and secondary reasons, but, whatever these may be, there still remains the inescapable respect for the person as an end-in-himself and the recognition that means and ends in the corporation must operate reciprocally. Thus, the categorical imperative regulates the corporation, and there is a rising demand throughout the world that human beings shall be associated in such kingdoms of ends. The wide gap between the demand and the realization in the world as well as in the microcosm of the corporation measures the wide gap between the utopian ideal and the actual associations under its regulation.

So much for the royal class in the kingdom or cosmopolis of nature, which is not to be confused with the kingdom of heaven, with which it has some similarities. The royal or citizen class is a true natural kingdom, the kingdom of rational human nature. In fact, it is the part of the kingdom of nature upon which the traditional natural lawyer concentrates his attention. The other part of the kingdom is the rest of nature, the nonrational part of nature, anciently divided into animals, plants, earth, air, fire, and water. In spite of the fact that Kant's world no longer trusted this division or knew the essences that identified the parts, his kingdom of nature as a kingdom of ends included all those things that come under law, the laws of mechanics as well as the regulative laws of teleology. The evidence for this subsumption ought still to appeal to the modern mind: natural things are preeminently those things that welcome the imposition of human purposes in technology and industry. The ancient testimony was that God had given man dominion over all these creatures.

Although Kant did not explicitly elaborate this point, I shall not be violating his ideal and vision if I amend the third formulation of the categorial imperative to read: each natural thing, whether rational or nonrational, must be treated as an end-in-itself, not merely as a means. This follows the metaphysical teleology that I

have expounded earlier. The essences and existences, the forms
and matters, the potencies and the actualities of all those things
that come under law, make them ends-in-themselves as well as
means, and the just knowledge of them as ends is as necessary to
the technician who puts them to use as his detection of their
connections as means. Furthermore, they all belong to a community of reciprocal means and ends in which the condition for
the human use of nature is always men's service to nature, as any
farmer, craftsman, or engineer knows. To quote Plato again, a
shepherd's essential business is tending sheep, let the butcher's
or merchant's be what it will, and the principle so illustrated
runs throughout the human arts.

Perhaps the point is worth further elucidation. We tend to understand causes, for instance, efficient causes, as falling into linear
series, with action passing through them in one direction, say,
from past to present and future in time. But we know on second
thought that there is always a feedback, as it is called at present.
There are causes that act through reaction as in Newton's third
law of mechanics, where every action entails an equal and opposite reaction. For this observable schema Kant set up a separate
category that he called community of causation, which is now
well recognized in electrical and other energetic fields. So it is
with final causes: every end that is served by means in turn serves
the means in some respect. The system of final causes that we call
a community is to be understood in this way.

But this lower part of the kingdom of nonrational nature, although it is made up of things that are ends-in-themselves as well
as means, does not show the equality of ends that prevails in the
upper rational part. Rational persons rule themselves, but they
also practice a justice with respect to their nonrational subjects
that takes due account of the inequality of goods that they embody. All nature is divided into species according to essential
differences. Rational human beings are equal because they belong
to one species by virtue of their rationality; the rest of nature is
divided according to the diversity of the other essences, and
among the many species there are essential inequalities, therefore
different goods that arrange themselves in a hierarchy.

But this hierarchy, still taken for granted in common sense, is inherited from the scholastic tradition of natural law. In that context, the order of intrinsic natural goods-in-themselves constitutionally governs the ordering of means to ends. Since a plant had more being than inanimate nature, it had, as it were, a natural right to use earth, water, and air for its subsistence; earth, water, and air fulfilled their own ends by serving plants in what we would call their biochemical roles. Similarly, plants served natural ends by becoming food for animals, and animals in turn reached a higher level of being and goodness by serving as food and beasts of burden for men. The order of intrinsic goods, or ends-in-themselves, indicated and regulated the order of means. By contrast, in the human arts there can be inversions of the order of means and ends that violate the hierarchy of intrinsic goods. Many of the rules developed by the craftsmen in their guilds were prohibitions of these inversions, and these rules would have been recognized as just by craftsmen anywhere, even in Plato's Athens.

But there is no possibility of recovering a teleological ordering of nature in the mathematical physics of Descartes and Newton and the sciences that follow their methods and styles. The essences and species that determine goods in the hierarchy are dissolved in the variables and numbers of mathematical formulas, and these seem to offer to men many new alternative orders of means that are not subject to any regulation except human ingenuity and advantage in technology, industry, and commerce. The nonhuman things in nature are no longer judged by their intrinsic goods, but only by their unmediated subordination as means to human ends. This is the revolution in the kingdom of nature that Kant is legitimizing. The new constitution of nature is given in Newton's mathematical physics, and it is to be protected from interference by the traditional hierarchical constitution that is relegated to the realm of the Ideals of Reason. But Kant's proposed new regulative function of the old constitution is a little like the working of the regulative agencies in Washington: the regulated usurps the authority of the regulator. The new science and technology often determine the rules, whose ends only occasionally coincide with the ends of the older rules. Regulation, therefore, results only in the confusion of the hierarchy with the paradoxical vagaries of means without ends.

✿   ✿   ✿

As a consequence of, and contributing to, the confusion there are several fashions of thought that have dominated the revolutions that have ushered in the modern world: the scientific revolution, the technical revolution, and the industrial revolution. Viewed in retrospect, this period has been marked by the unregulated exploitation of nature, both human and nonhuman. It opened with the factory system, where human beings were counted as labor power and even the pious master of the factory thought he had a vocation to recruit and direct as much human energy as possible for the manufacture of goods. Even the workers themselves at first found a new utility for their powers and consented to the conspiracy of exploitation. Later, when they realized that they were being not only used but also used up, they gradually withdrew consent. But by this time the factory and the business system were recognized as the master organizations of men for the exploitation of natural resources. As natural resources became the new name for the lower orders of the kingdom of nature, so "goods" became the name for the products of the factory as they poured into the market. The only limit on the spread of exploitation of this kind was the demand of the market and the ingenuity of the producers. Both of these were objects of scientific and managerial attention, the science of economics for demand and supply, the natural sciences for the methods of natural investigation. Both kinds of science became mechanistic, ready to serve any purpose, and public, ready to serve any agent of exploitation. The accompanying styles of thought were matter-of-fact and utilitarian. Law and morals followed the fashions at decent distances.

I wish here to use the word *exploitation* in an original technical meaning. It was first applied in the mid-nineteenth century to mining. Mines and quarries were exploited; that is, their contents, minerals and chemicals, were being reduced to means and materials for the manufacturing process. It was later applied to men who were being reduced to labor power. The ends were "goods," imitations of the products that had always been the ends of the human arts. I shall not generalize too much if I mean by exploitation the reduction of natural goods to means. If I am allowed this usage, I shall be able to penetrate the dark technical phenomenon that Ellul describes. The absorption of men, machines, and materials by technology blots out the intrinsic goods, the ends-in-themselves, of the kingdom of nature, and substitutes for them the quite incommensurable and wayward series of means.

The word *machine* has an instructive history. Originally it meant a tool or instrument in a human art. Separated from the agent and its purpose and attached to a prime mover, it could operate on its own and become an automaton. Abstracted and combined with others, and the ensemble studied for itself, it seemed to take on a macabre life of its own, the Newtonian mechanical universe. Ellul, without being too explicit about it, detects a technique in a human art, abstracts it from its context, combines it with other similarly abstracted techniques, and presents the ensemble as the technical phenomenon for our and his amazed contemplation. Ellul shows how this concatenation of means has grown, at first gradually by linkages of isolated units, latterly by an apparently built-in acceleration, until it is now unified, all but universal, self-generating, and inherently expansive over all human activity, individual and collective. His most telling observation is that in the system all ends are transformed into means; even the participating human beings are automated links, and their purposes are "values" of the variables in the technical formulas. This means that the technical phenomenon as a whole is a vast system of exploitation without a purpose. The technician who is enthusiastically building and serving the system says that society will eventually see the system and supply the purpose, but Ellul quickly answers that both the technician and society are already built into the system, and the voice of human freedom and responsibility is a programmed voice of the technical ideology.

The American humanistic critic sees this European account as an extrapolation of his own earlier warning of the gradual surrender of human affairs to the machine. He will say that we have justifiably put the nonrational parts of nature under the regime of exploitation for human welfare. This is what man's dominion or control of nature requires. But the realm of human nature must

retain its ends and purposes. This is the present position of the
traditional natural lawyer, also. The technician shall not pass.
But this split in our culture, between material and spiritual, between the materialist and the idealist, between the technical and
the cultural, has peculiar consequences. The immediate direct
judgment and enjoyment of natural things, both human and
nonhuman, are sharply inhibited and redirected. We all note and
some of us mourn the drainage of values from work and organization. Some of us used to accept the gray neutrality of means in
the lively hope that a better world was in the making. The making
of means was the building of the road to a better day; the
postponement and projection of ends was required by progress.
We had learned the right disciplines and sentiments from theology
and economics. But the better day has been coming into view,
and we now see that the deferred ends have themselves become
means.

In a kind of despair we have increasingly turned to the fine
arts, where the bare data of nature are separated off from their
sources in nature, are refined and transformed by artifice, combined and represented in theaters, museums, records, and cameras
for nothing but the immediate contemplation and enjoyment of
their artificial surfaces. The fine artists and the critics join, not
always happily, in cults and schools that imitate, sometimes
deliberately, the lower practices of pagan and orthodox religions.
They also identify the painting, the dance, or the symphony with
the beatific vision of an unknown god. The technicians combine
these cults and build them into a technical epiphenomenon, the
entertainment that eases the surrender of men to the technical
system itself. The sign that signifies the takeover of technics is
the appearance of massive exploitation in the entertainment or
show business, the exploitation of sentiment and frustration in
the audience as well as of talent and ambition in the performers.

But there are other cults that organize themselves around
isolated remnants of the kingdom of nature, the apostolic lines
that originated with naturalists who had literary and artistic gifts,
such as Goethe and Leonardo. These original deviants from the
dogmas of exploitation have more or less worthy successors, such
as Ruskin, Thoreau, Fabre, Kropotkin, and Schweitzer, or even

Whitman, Tagore, and Tolstoy. Schweitzer is an interesting case because he has deliberately made connection with those massive primitive and peasant cultures that survive like promontories from continents of tradition where the kingdom of nature has always been taken for granted without benefit of theoretical apology. Systems of medicine based on the Hindu, Chinese, and Malayan respect for life, which includes what we would call inanimate things, are extending our pharmacopeia as well as our psychiatric lore of images and symbols. These cultures are now passionately responding to the magnetism of the technics of exploitation, and it may be expected that a two-way osmosis between the old and the new kingdoms of nature will take place.

But I am not recommending the cults of the fine arts and the naturalists as methods of research in natural law; they are only occasions for reminding ourselves of lost insights. We presumably have learned the hard way that human beings should not be exploited even with their consent. We have learned that the farming that becomes the quarrying and exhaustion of the soil is not true farming; that the industries that pollute air and water and turn cities into slums are not true industries; that the cities that devastate the countryside and reduce it to desert are not true cities; that the nations that destroy forests to feed smelting furnaces, or a countryside to make roads, or even wildlife to make sport, are not true polities; that even mining, the original occupation that established exploitation, if it exhausts natural resources, is not true mining. Such frustrated human arts do not belong to the kingdom of nature, no matter how well they may serve apparent human goods. The appeal to merely human ends and values does not justify or rationalize them.

We have had a rough history of learning some of these things. As long as our natural resources, so-called, were open to unlimited exploitation by free enterprise, we gradually came to realize not only that beauty was disappearing but that we were using up resources. So there was the conservation movement. Gifford Pinchot and Theodore Roosevelt were able to isolate and establish national parks, and these have become monuments to the courage of their conviction that exploitation should be limited. But such conservation was relatively empty until it was discovered that the nursing care of national parks had high unintended uses, namely the increase in ground water and the building of soil. Following this discovery, there now exist tree farms where industrial lumbermen have learned to care for trees and therefore to increase the lumber supply as they pursue the lumber business. This and other similar lessons have now led to long-term planning for the allocation of resources in which the aim of the prudent saving of resources for future use is always combined with the increase and enhancement of nature. Such thinking is perhaps best epitomized in the original act that established the TVA. Its stated purpose was to serve the welfare of the valley, and the purpose was carried out by planning forests, fertilizer plants, soil analysis, and flood control as well as electric power. The welfare of the valley obviously and necessarily includes concern for natural ends, nonhuman as well as human.

Out of this dialectical learning there has developed a new and somewhat mysterious science, ecology. As I understand it, ecology was originally an attempt to collate various lines of linear exploitive planning, such as an industrial firm might practice, to make an integral pattern of the side effects and unintended consequences of procurement, employment, and production. Industrial production in a complex city would present the acute problem. The result of the attempt led to another definition and posing of the problem, namely to conceive the plant as an organism with the city as the environment. Soon it was necessary to conceive the city as an organism with its environment. And so one might go on to national economies and to the world community. This is surreptitious teleological thinking, which, made explicit, would mean that everything in the situation would be viewed reciprocally with the others as means and ends. Such a conception is the aim of Patrick Geddes and Lewis Mumford when they take the organic view of the neotechnic period in technology. The purpose of the city in the valley would be the enhancement of nature, including human nature, in the valley. Human beings would no longer be exploiting nature or themselves. They would be free citizens in a constitutional kingdom of nature.

CONCLUSION

The foregoing reconsideration of Kant's ideal of a kingdom of nature persuades me that Jacques Ellul's somewhat puzzling account of technology is the objective description of the pathological result of an epoch of unlimited exploitation in technical development. Under the guidance of a liberal humanism in which men were allowed a teleological understanding of themselves, but nonhuman nature was not so respected, the industrial technological system progressively destroyed its ends, even its minimal human ends, which are often identical with natural ends. This system reduced itself to an automaton that has all but devoured its creators. In the face of this fait accompli, Ellul is daring us to reassert human freedom and responsibility; in other words, to conceive the artificial phenomenon as a kingdom of natural ends.

In an earlier part of this paper, I was summoning courage to answer Ellul by a head-on attack on the methods of the natural and social sciences. This would involve a critical reconsideration of analytic mathematics and some attempt to see through its opaque formulas to essences and substances or some adequate theoretical alternatives. It would in addition require a validation of an objective knowledge of goods as means and ends, perhaps the subjection of the whole technological realm to rational teleological modes of thought. I confess that I am overwhelmed not only by the fact that the current sciences are strongly entrenched in habit and going concerns but also by the enormous intellectual energy and discipline that such a critique would require.

Ellul's descriptive mosaic of the technical phenomenon shows the human arts and human doings in a massive confusion, suffering the contagions and the inversions of means and ends that recall Plato's simpler critique of the arts in Athens. Ellul is saying that we are past the point when this confusion can be brought to terms. But our system is under the test of transplanting itself part by part to undeveloped regions. As this takes place, there will be occasions when it has to be dismantled and partially reassembled, and these occasions will allow the introduction of ecological teleologicial planning. On these occasions, as if by flashback, we can reassess our mistakes, preeminent among them the regulative idea of unlimited exploitation of nature, the progressive fragmentation of the kingdom of nature. Where the backward peoples have not already been corrupted, there will be opportunities to observe primitive and peasant models of the arts whose ends conform with nature's ends. With proper attention and control, these could become the elements or the building blocks for a true community of means and ends.

But, of course, the chances of rapid further contagion and corruptions of the old and new systems are very great. There must be determined attention and strong control of the process if it is to provide the precious insights that are only suggested by the ecologist and the planner. Americans are afraid that the Communists have the only doctrines and controls that are needed. I am persuaded that neither we nor the Russians at present have such disciplines, and our deficiencies remind me of the Romans and their reliance on law when they came upon similar problems. As I have described them, they were able to understand their laws well enough to extend them to distant and diverse cultures, but still to give the proper measures of support to both local autonomy and total order. They were guided in this by the Stoic distinction between levels and kinds of law—civil, common, and natural. Kant is borrowing heavily from them in his exposition of the kingdom of nature as the substance of the categorical imperative.

I infer from these problems and their archetypes in Hellenic civilization that we need to rise above the clichéd issues of the cold war, that we need to delve deep into the problems that both sides have uncovered, the ordering of a runaway automatic technology, by the discoveries of new liberties under law.

Perhaps the problems can be epitomized and at the same time analyzed in the question of what corporations ought to be chartered and constitutionalized for the development of backward nations. The corporation is the elementary instrument in which technology and law are put to human use in communities that want to be kingdoms of nature. Communities on the periphery of our civilization will not only allow, they will demand the required innovation. When we have done for them we may be able to learn for ourselves. There will then be the occasion to reconsider the state of the intellectual arts that can restore the sciences that minister to rational jurisprudence.

The rediscovery of the kingdom of nature might also make it possible to love as well as use the new world that is coming into being.